Volker Sellin
European Monarchies from 1814 to 1906

Volker Sellin

European Monarchies from 1814 to 1906

A Century of Restorations

DE GRUYTER
OLDENBOURG

Originally published as *Das Jahrhundert der Restaurationen, 1814 bis 1906*,
Munich: De Gruyter Oldenbourg, 2014.

Translated by Volker Sellin

ISBN 978-3-11-063448-8
e-ISBN (PDF) 978-3-11-052453-6
e-ISBN (EPUB) 978-3-11-052209-9

Library of Congress Cataloging-in-Publication Data
A CIP catalog record for this book has been applied for at the Library of Congress.

Bibliographic information published by the Deutsche Nationalbibliothek
The Deutsche Nationalbibliothek lists this publication in the Deutsche Nationalbibliografie;
detailed bibliographic data are available on the Internet at http://dnb.dnb.de.

© 2018 Walter de Gruyter GmbH, Berlin/Boston
This volume is text- and page-identical with the hardback published in 2017.
Cover Image: Louis-Philippe Crépin (1772–1851): Allégorie du retour des Bourbons le 24 avril 1814:
Louis XVIII relevant la France de ses ruines. Musée national du Château de
Versailles. bpk / RMN - Grand Palais / Christophe Fouin.
Printing and binding: CPI books GmbH, Leck

♾ Printed on acid-free paper
Printed in Germany

www.degruyter.com

Contents

Introduction

In 1989, the world commemorated the outbreak of the French Revolution two hundred years earlier. The event was celebrated as the breakthrough of popular sovereignty and modern constitutionalism. The names of Sieyès and Mirabeau recall the achievements of the first French National Assembly, the abolition of feudalism, the declaration of the rights of man, and the democratic constitution of 1791.

In 2014, another event of French history was commemorated as well, though it has been given much less significance in historical memory than the outbreak of the French Revolution: the fall of Napoleon and the restoration of the monarchy under the house of Bourbon. It is true that a whole era has been named after this event, but the term restoration does not bring to mind objectives which have remained valid till today. The concept rather denotes the questionable attempt to renew an obsolete reality in opposition to the spirit of the time. The history of the Bourbon restoration in France seems to confirm this judgment, since the restored dynasty remained in power for only sixteen years. Two hundred years after the accession of Louis XVIII, the time has come to subject the prevailing interpretation of the Restoration to a critical examination.

The term itself is equivocal. Contemporaries viewed the return of the Bourbons to the French throne as a restoration not so much because monarchy as such, but because divine right monarchy was reinstated and the principle of popular sovereignty which every regime in France since 1789 had been based on, was repudiated. If Louis XVIII had accepted the offer to become a democratically legitimized King of the French which the Napoleonic Senate had inserted in its draft constitution of 6 April 1814, the monarchy would likewise have been reinstated, but not in the sense of a restoration. Even though Louis was the descendant of the old French dynasty, he would not have become King by historic right, but King by the revolution, "un roi par la revolution," as Jacques-Claude Beugnot wrote in a letter to Louis on 2 June 1814, and instead of obtaining the recognition of his inherited right to rule and of having the revolution absorbed by the monarchy, he would have permitted the monarchy to be absorbed by the revolution.[1]

It was only the renewal of divine right legitimacy that imparted to the return of the monarchy the character of a restoration. The legitimacy of a government is

---

1 Jacques-Claude Beugnot, Rapport au Roi, 2 June 1814, Archives Nationales Paris 40 AP 7, fol. 114; cf. Volker Sellin, *Die geraubte Revolution. Der Sturz Napoleons und die Restauration in Europa* (Göttingen: Vandenhoeck & Ruprecht, 2001), 277.

the acknowledgement on the part of the subjects of its right to rule. Accordingly, in order to be successful the restoration had to bring back to life convictions which had been lost during the Revolution and the Empire. The operation succeeded thanks to the courage, the shrewdness, and the perseverance of Louis XVIII. He handled the draft constitution of the Senate with utmost circumspection and instead of repudiating it out of hand he only insisted on its revision. In the course of the revision in which members of the Senate and the *Corps législatif* participated, instead of the nation the monarch was declared the author of the constitution and its democratic basis was replaced by the monarchical principle. In this way the King remained in full possession of power, without however excluding the nation altogether from concurring in the determination of policy. When the revision was completed Louis XVIII imposed the constitution as a constitutional charter (*Charte constitutionnelle*).[2] In the Middle Ages a *charte* or *carta* was a document by which a ruler conferred privileges. A privilege was a voluntary gift to which the recipient did not possess any rightful claim. By imposing the Charte the King formally recovered the legitimacy which his brother Louis XVI had gambled away during the Revolution. Therefore the imposition of the Charte must be regarded as the essential act of the Restoration. It is true that by conceding the constitution Louis XVIII acknowledged substantial achievements of the Revolution, but at the same time he avoided basing on the Revolution his right to rule. Instead he transformed the Revolution from a menace to the monarchy into a pledge for its stability.

Louis dated the Charte from the 19th year of his reign as if the monarchy had remained in uninterrupted existence. As a matter of fact he had never acknowledged neither the usurpation of the constituent power by the nation in June 1789 nor the abolition of the monarchy in September 1792. If, however, the monarchy had not perished during the Revolution there was no need to restore it, and if it had perished nobody in the world could have brought it back to life in the plenitude of its historic right, not even the nation which could only have conferred democratic, not divine right legitimacy. Louis XVIII was convinced that only the monarch himself was in the position to restore the monarchy and that its restoration did not mean remaking it but only consolidating it again and procuring its general acceptance.

If Louis XVIII imposed the Charte in order to recover the recognition of divine right legitimacy, the imposition of 1814 did not essentially differ from the impositions of constitutions to which other monarchs in the course of the next one hundred years were to recur. Accordingly, these impositions should no

---

2 On the origins of the Charte constitutionnelle cf. ibid., 225–73.

less be interpreted as monarchical restorations and restoration turns out to be not a singular act, limited to a specific moment in history, but a method which the European rulers adopted between the French Revolution and the First World War if required, in order to render their imperiled thrones secure. Instead of an epoch of European history restoration thus turns out to be an epoch in the history of each particular monarchy, and the 19th century is revealed as a century not only of revolutions, but of restorations as well.

Nevertheless, the French restoration of 1814 occupies a special place within this series. By imposing the Charte constitutionnelle Louis XVIII transmitted constitutional government as created by the Revolution to the new century. One might even attribute a revolutionizing effect to the Restoration, since no less than the Revolution it served the progress of liberty. Therefore, next to the revolutionaries of 1789 Louis XVIII must be numbered among those who paved the way for constitutionalism in Europe. By imposing the Charte constitutionnelle he demonstrated to the 19th century how elementary demands of the Revolution could be rendered compatible with divine right legitimacy. The stronger the revolutionary menace grew, the more restoration on the French example became the strategy of survival in other monarchies as well. Not constitution making by constituent assemblies based on popular sovereignty, but the imposition of constitutions as in France in 1814 determined the constitutional development in the monarchies on the continent, and the breakthrough of modern constitutionalism in Europe is much less due to the Revolution itself than to the several restorations which have been staged in the intent of avoiding or overcoming revolutions. Whereas the Charte in its original form remained in force until 1830, and after its revision during the July Revolution for another 18 years, some of the constitutions which in other monarchies had been framed on its example enjoyed an even much longer lease of life.

Restoration is opposed to revolution. Without the revolutionary menace restorations would not have taken place. The appearance and the magnitude of the menace determined the moment of the recourse to restoration. Restorations always originated from a crisis of monarchical legitimacy. The chance durably to overcome the crisis was seen exclusively in the imposition of a constitution. By the imposition monarchs sought to control the development instead of succumbing to it. In 1814, a restoration took place in France only. Only in France the nation had abolished the monarchy and declared itself the source of sovereign power. Therefore after the collapse of the Napoleonic Empire only in France the renewal of divine right monarchy implied the renunciation of principles which had triumphed in the age of the Revolution. In the other countries which had come under the domination of Napoleon, monarchs had not been deposed by their respective nations, but by victorious France. By their expulsion alone, however, they could not lose the assent of their subjects. Therefore after the fall of the Empire they were not in need of a restoration of monarchical legitimacy, and the period should no longer be named the age of restoration in general, but of French restoration only.

The present essay aims at the rehabilitation of the concept and a reevaluation of the policies of restoration. With this in mind the breakthrough of monarchical constitutionalism will be studied in selected European monarchies of the 19th century. The discussion will start by analyzing the French restoration of 1814. The French restoration differs from the later restorations because the dynasty had effectively lost the throne whereas in other countries restorations were undertaken in time with the hope to prevent the fall of the monarchy. Both types of restorations resembled each other in that they sought to attain their end by the concession of a constitution. By granting fundamental rights and political participation the monarchs hoped to secure the consent of the citizens. The next chapter is devoted to the restoration of monarchy in that part of Poland which Russia had annexed in 1815, at the hands of Alexander I. By imposing a constitution he hoped to reconcile the Poles with their new sovereign. In Germany, the first constitutions were imposed after the liberation from Napoleonic domination. The examples of Baden, Bavaria and Württemberg will demonstrate that the constitutions were meant to facilitate the political integration of these states which had all been considerably enlarged since 1801. In December 1848 the King of Prussia imposed a constitution with the intention of checking the revolution which had broken out in March. In 1834 the *Estatuto Real* was imposed in Spain in the hope of overcoming the dual crisis which had broken out after the death of Ferdinand VII, the minority crisis and the succession crisis. In Italy immediately before the outbreak of the revolution of 1848 in every state except Lombardy and Venetia constitutions were rashly imposed in order to preserve the monarchical principle. After the failure of the revolution they were repealed everywhere except in the Kingdom of Sardinia. In the course of Italian unification the *Statuto albertino* became the constitution of the Kingdom of Italy. The transition of Russia to constitutionalism by the imposition of the fundamental laws in April 1906 was an attempt to overcome the state crisis which had, a year before, resulted in the outbreak of the revolution.

The investigation is centered on a number of typical examples. Austria, the Scandinavian countries, the Netherlands, Belgium, and Portugal are not taken into consideration. The comparison of different restoration processes in 19th century European history aims at the analysis of an identical phenomenon, the act of restoring, as embedded in a variety of changing circumstances. This objective will be obtained only if the crises of legitimacy which required the imposition of constitutions are studied along with their preconditions. The usefulness of comparisons depends to a large extent on the choice of the phenomena which are being compared. The exclusive application of the concept of restoration to the epoch which followed the deposition of Napoleon has led researchers to compare the policies of monarchs who had opposite objectives in mind. Under the heading of restoration regimes both the Spain of Ferdinand VII and the France of Louis XVIII have been analyzed. After the fall of Napoleon both monarchs returned home from their forced exiles, and both of them were expected to sanction a constitution which had been elaborated for them on behalf of their nations, in Spain by the *Cortes*, in France by the Napoleonic Senate. Unlike Louis XVIII, however, Ferdinand VII refused acceptance of the constitution and had their authors persecuted. In Italy no ruler was presented with a constitution on his return.

The present essay is based on a broad variety of primary and secondary sources related to the restorations taken into consideration. To be sure, studies in which restoration is analyzed as a general phenomenon and not confined to one particular country are rare. One of them is the book by the Austro-American historian Robert A. Kann of 1968, *The Problem of Restoration. A Study in Comparative Political History.*[3] Kann's approach differs in more than one respect from the present one. For Kann the term denotes the restoration of perished political or social systems and not primarily the recovery of monarchical legitimacy. Accordingly, he numbers the return of the Bourbons in 1814, but not the other impositions of constitutions during the century, among the restorations, because in France only the restoration of divine right monarchy had been preceded by a republican interlude. His broad understanding of the term is shown by the fact that he regards the foundation of the German Empire in 1871 as a restoration of the Holy Roman Empire which had ceased to exist in 1806.[4] Kann's interpretation follows a three step model where an original state is followed by an intermediary stage, brought about by revolution or political decay, and this in turn at last gives way to restoration. The model is applied to cases which go back to early Antiquity.

The history of the concept of restoration is discussed by Panajotis Kondylis in the article "Reaktion, Restauration" of 1984.[5] Based on a variety of sources

---

3 Robert A. Kann, *The Problem of Restoration. A Study in Comparative Political History* (Berkeley/Los Angeles: University of California Press, 1968).
4 Kann, "Restoration that came too late. From the Dissolution of the Holy Roman Empire in 1806 to the Proclamation of the Second German Empire in 1871," ibid., chap. 17, 349–383.
5 Panajotis Kondylis, "Reaktion, Restauration," in: Otto Brunner, Werner Conze, and Reinhart Koselleck, eds., *Geschichtliche Grundbegriffe. Historisches Lexikon zur politisch-sozialen Sprache in Deutschland*, vol. 5 (Stuttgart: Klett-Cotta, 1984), 179–230.

Kondylis shows that since the early nineteenth century the term has chiefly denoted the attempt to bring back to life outdated beliefs and institutions.⁶ At the same time, however, he cites a memorandum by the general and diplomat Joseph Maria von Radowitz for King Frederick William IV of Prussia of 4 February 1850, in which the term refers to the consolidation of an existing monarchy through reform. Kondylis does not further dwell on this variant. On 2 February Frederick William IV had signed the revised constitution for the State of Prussia. In his memorandum Radowitz traces the origins of this constitution from the revolution of March 1848. The imposition of the Prussian constitution of 5 December 1848 he calls the first step of a "process of restoration." He explains that during the following stages of the revolution "within the constitutional party the two elements" had been separated, namely "the constitutionals in the abstract sense of the term, the doctrinaires, who considered the constitution as the essential achievement and the monarch only as a requisite within the same," on the one hand, and "the conservative constitutionals who regarded a strong and dignified royalty as the main thing, the center, and the constitution only as a device designed to limit it by positive rights of the people," on the other. With these words Radowitz pointed at the distinction between democratic and monarchical principle, between democratic and monarchical constitutionalism. Of the revised constitution he wrote accordingly that it had "in the main preserved the conservative monarchical character"; "the doctrinaire party had been eliminated" and had "lost its final struggle against the crown." Radowitz called the triumph of the revised constitution an "organic restoration." For the future he recommended to eliminate "step by step and strictly legally" the elements of the "false constitutionalism," "both in the heads and in the institutions." The objective ought to be "an organically arranged monarchical government that was not limited except by the true rights of the subjects."⁷

The key concept in the memorandum is "organic restoration." Radowitz used the term restoration even though in Prussia the monarchy had not been abolished during the revolution. In the given context the term refers to the recovery of political vitality by the monarchy after its temporary paralysis in March 1848. In Radowitz' eyes the recovery succeeded because an alliance with the "monarchical-constitutional party" had enabled the government to push back the influence of the democrats. Radowitz called this restoration "organic," be-

6 Ibid., 179.
7 Joseph Maria von Radowitz, "Denkschrift, vorgelesen dem Könige am 4. Februar 1850," in: Josef von Radowitz, *Nachgelassene Briefe und Aufzeichnungen zur Geschichte der Jahre 1848–1853*, ed. Walter Möhring (Stuttgart and Berlin: Deutsche Verlagsanstalt, 1922), 159–160; see also Kondylis, "Reaktion, Restauration," 196.

cause the King had defended his monarchical point of view, without "departing altogether from the constitutional principle."[8] In this way Radowitz equates Frederick William's concession of a constitution with the concession of the Charte constitutionnelle in 1814. In a similar mode of reasoning the Austrian envoy to Naples, count Karl Ludwig von Ficquelmont, had used the term "restoration" on 1 April 1824, in a letter to state chancellor Metternich. Ficquelmont pointed out that after the introduction of consultative bodies in the Kingdom of the Two Sicilies "la véritable restauration de la monarchie" (the true restoration of the monarchy) could start.[9] The King of Naples had not been deposed either, and the monarchy had not been abolished. In the revolution of 1820 Ferdinand I had simply been forced to introduce the Spanish constitution of 1812. A year later the military intervention of Austria brought the constitutional interlude to an end.

For both Ficquelmont and Radowitz restoration of the monarchy does not mean its reinstatement after a republican period. Instead the term refers to the process of consolidating it through reform or through the imposition of a constitution. Radowitz' concept of an "organic restoration" is applicable to every restoration in 19th century Europe.

The present essay resumes the themes of earlier books of the author: a book of 2001 on the fall of Napoleon and the restoration of the French monarchy in 1814, and an analysis of the foundations of monarchical legitimacy in the age of revolution of 2011.[10] In the seventh chapter of that book the legitimizing capacity of constitutions is discussed. The present work reverts to and deepens these reflections.

---

8 Radowitz, *Denkschrift* (see note 7), 159.

9 Ficquelmont to Metternich, 1 April 1824, in: Ruggero Moscati, ed., *Il Regno delle Due Sicilie e l'Austria. Documenti dal marzo 1821 al novembre 1830* (Naples: Presso la R. Deputazione, 1937), vol. 2, 238 – 239. See below, p. 100.

10 Sellin, *Die geraubte Revolution* (see note 1); Sellin, *Gewalt und Legitimität. Die europäische Monarchie im Zeitalter der Revolutionen* (Munich: Oldenbourg, 2011).

France 1814

In the spring of 1814 France experienced a fundamental change of regime: the Napoleonic Empire broke down and the Bourbons returned on the throne.[1] The political overthrow resulted from the simultaneous actions of several independent agents. After the failure of Napoleon's Russian campaign of 1812 Russia, Prussia, Austria, and Great Britain had in the course of the year 1813 concluded a military alliance. In early January 1814 the coalition armies advanced into French territory. On 31 March 1814 they entered into Paris. In the first days of April Tsar Alexander I was the sovereign who exercised the greatest influence. The Austrian emperor Francis I and foreign secretary Metternich had remained in Dijon and Frederick William III of Prussia readily subordinated himself to the Tsar for fear of endangering the promises which Alexander had made in the treaty of Kalisz. The English Prince Regent had not repaired to the Continent. The British interests were taken care of by foreign secretary Lord Castlereagh, but he too arrived in Paris only after the city had surrendered. On the French side the most important agent was Talleyrand. After the entrance of the allies he persuaded the French Senate formally to depose Napoleon and to adopt a monarchical constitution which reserved the throne for the count of Provence, brother of Louis XVI, who lived on exile in England. The count who had ever since 1795 named himself Louis XVIII, accepted the invitation and returned to France, but was determined to rule on his own conditions. In view to restoring divine right he subjected the Senatorial constitution to a fundamental revision. It was only this revision that turned the change of regime into the Restoration.

The restoration could only succeed if Napoleon was deprived of his power. Originally the taking of Paris and the overthrow of the Empire had not been the aims of the coalition. Only Alexander I had, after the burning of Moscow in 1812, resolved to march into the French capital and to take revenge on Napoleon. He considered it his mission to liberate Europe from the yoke of Bonaparte. The Austrian foreign secretary Metternich, on the contrary, had hoped well into March 1814, to conclude a negotiated peace with the Emperor. Under the lead of Napoleon, he believed, France would continue to form a strong counterpoise to the power of Russia and in this way contribute to the independence of Central Europe. As late as December 1813 Metternich was ready to concede to Napoleon the border of the Rhine in exchange for a peace treaty. To this proposal the British Foreign Secretary Castlereagh had objected from the outset. Great Britain wanted to secure the independence of the Netherlands

---

[1] For the change of regime in France see Volker Sellin, *Die geraubte Revolution. Der Sturz Napoleons und die Restauration in Europa* (Göttingen: Vandenhoeck & Ruprecht, 2001).

DOI 10.1515/9783110524536-001

against the French menace by means of a broad territorial barrier which would include at least Antwerp and the estuary of the Scheldt. The advance of the coalition forces on French soil superseded the controversy. From now on the coalition aimed at the restoration of France within the borders of 1792, the year when the first revolutionary war had broken out.

On 5 February 1814 at Châtillon-sur-Seine a congress was opened at which Russian, Austrian, Prussian and British plenipotentiaries set out to negotiate the end of hostilities with the French foreign secretary Caulaincourt. During negotiations the war continued. Napoleon had never made any concessions before, since he had always felt sure to defeat his enemies. Therefore it was a great surprise when at the meeting of 7 February Caulaincourt came up with the inquiry whether the allies would consent to an immediate cease-fire if France accepted their conditions of peace.[2] The unexpected volte-face is explained by the defeat Blücher and the Prince of Württemberg had inflicted upon Napoleon at La Rothière on 1 February. The Emperor was afraid that the armies of the coalition would take advantage of the situation and proceed to the capital.[3] Obviously, Napoleon understood that the loss of Paris would terminate his reign.

Caulaincourt's inquiry thrust the coalition into a crisis. On the very same day the Russian plenipotentiary count Razumovsky obtained consent from his allies that an answer to the French foreign secretary was postponed until new instructions had been secured from the various governments. The Tsar tried to protract negotiations, because he still hoped to make true his long-cherished aim and march into Paris. These tactics, however, could not be pursued indefinitely, since the French government had signaled readiness to accept the conditions of the coalition. To resolve the crisis Metternich invited the allied governments to the allied headquarters at Troyes. Since Caulaincourt had already assented to the territorial demands of the coalition, at Troyes the governments sought to reach an agreement on their further course of action and their ultimate war aims. Whereas Austria and Great Britain were ready to conclude an immediate armistice with Napoleon, Tsar Alexander preferred to continue the war and effect a change of dynasty in France. In order to facilitate the deliberations, Metternich presented the governments with a questionnaire on the war aims to be pursued.

---

2 Floret's Journal, in: August Fournier, *Der Congress von Châtillon. Die Politik im Kriege von 1814. Eine historische Studie* (Vienna: Tempsky, 1900), Appendix VII, 374; cf. Stadion to Metternich, 8 February 1814, ibid., Appendix V, 310; Sellin, *Revolution*, 93–94.
3 Bassano to Caulaincourt, 5 February 1814, in: Charles-Tristan, comte de Montholon, *Mémoires pour servir à l'histoire de France sous Napoléon. Notes et Mélanges*, vol. 2 (Paris: Didot; Bossange, 1823), 323; also in: Napoléon Ier, *Correspondance*, vol. 27 (Paris: Imprimerie Impériale, 1869), no. 21285, 185, n. 1.

Castlereagh and Metternich had already in January tried to reach an agreement on the dynastic question before the opening of the congress at Châtillon. The only alternative to Napoleon they took into consideration was the return of the Bourbons. They thus excluded both an Austrian regency for Napoleon's three year old son and the appointment of the Swedish crown prince Bernadotte favoured by the Tsar. During the ensuing debates at Langres the allies agreed that a change of dynasty in France should not originate with them, but that they would not impede the return of the Bourbons if such was the wish of the French people.[4] For the time being the conflict with the Tsar was adjourned. Since the military operations were to continue, Alexander hoped to arrive in Paris before the congress would have produced results, whereas Metternich sought by all means to reach an understanding with Napoleon before Paris was taken.

Caulaincourt's intervention of 7 February seemed to indicate that Napoleon was at last ready to sign an agreement. The British and the Prussian representatives concurred with Metternich in the conviction that the opportunity should be seized, all the more so since they did not doubt the legitimacy of Napoleon's rule. In a paper he had prepared for state chancellor Hardenberg the Prussian state councilor Friedrich Ancillon argued that the French Emperor had in fact made a "bloody and deplorable use" of his power, but that he had not in the ordinary sense of the word "usurped" it.[5] Metternich as a matter of principle denied the monarchs the right to interfere in the form of government of an independent state. If they ventured to meddle in the lawful succession in another state they "endangered the existence of every throne."[6] Neither Castlereagh nor Hardenberg perceived symptoms indicating that the citizens of France were tired of Napoleon's government.[7] The Tsar, however, insisted on his original plan. He kept ready to conform to the wishes of the French nation, yet he maintained that these could not be ascertained before the allies had marched into Paris. Upon arrival they should summon the members of the leading constitutional bodies and other dignitaries and have them decide who should henceforth govern France.[8] It was in vain that Castlereagh pointed out to the Tsar the risks of this plan

---

4 Sellin, *Revolution*, 99.

5 Denkschrift Ancillon, Geheimes Staatsarchiv Preussischer Kulturbesistz, I. HA Rep. 92, Nachlass Albrecht, no. 56, fol. 95–96.

6 Vote autrichien, in: Fournier, *Congress*, Appendix III, 287.

7 Castlereagh to Liverpool, 16 February 1814, in: Charles K. Webster, ed., *British Diplomacy 1813–1815. Select Documents Dealing with the Reconstruction of Europe* (London: Bell, 1921), 150; Viscount Castlereagh's Answer to the Austrian Queries, 13 February 1814, ibid., 155; Hardenberg's response, in: Geheimes Staatsarchiv Preußischer Kulturbesitz, I. HA Rep. 92, Nachlass Albrecht, no. 56, fol. 117[r].

8 Conférence tenue à Troyes le 13 février 1814. Questions posées par l'Autriche. Réponse du Cabinet de Russie, in F. M. Brunov, *Aperçu des principales transactions du cabinet de Russie sous les*

and warned him that this course of action might oblige the allies to support Louis XVIII with their forces in a civil war against Napoleon. Such a constellation, however, would burden a serious liability on the restoration of the Bourbon monarchy.[9] The King would be blamed that he had recovered the throne with foreign support only. The breach of the coalition seemed imminent.[10] It was averted only because from 10 to 14 February at Champaubert, Montmirail, Château-Thierry, and Vauchamps Napoleon scored several successes in battle and immediately withdrew the powers he had given to Caulaincourt under the impression of the defeat at La Rothière. Once more the end of the war moved far off and the chances of a return of the Bourbons on the French throne anew became uncertain.

In a letter to Metternich dated 15 February the journalist Friedrich Gentz expressed his surprise at the fact that to all appearances the four governments had, in marked contrast to their monarchical character, acquiesced in the principle of popular sovereignty in that they had conceded to the French nation the right to determine their form of government by themselves.[11] If the French were permitted to depose Napoleon it had to be explained in which way such a step might be warranted. Gentz recognized only two ways of justifying a deposition. Napoleon had either illegally usurped the throne or he had made an unjust use of his powers. Even if Napoleon had usurped the throne, this deficiency had long ago been remedied by the tacit consent of the nation and the recognition of his imperial dignity by his European fellow monarchs. A deposition of the Emperor for the abuse of the powers conferred upon him presupposed the existence of someone who was entitled to state the abuse. Such a contingency, however, was not provided for by the constitution, quite apart from the fact that one could not concede to the French nation "the initiative of a revolution of throne and dynasty" without at the same time conceding the same right to all other nations as well. In this way, however, one would proclaim a universal "right of rebellion."[12] If Napoleon was a legitimate ruler who could be deposed through a rebellion only, then the ensuing restoration of the Bourbons would likewise be an "arbitrary

---

règnes de Cathérine II, Paul I et Alexandre I, in Gody učenija ego imperatorskago naslednika cesareviča Aleksandra Nikolaeviča, vol. 2 (St. Petersburg 1880) (Sbornik Imperatorskago Russkago Istoričeskago Obščestva 31), 377.

9 Castlereagh to Liverpool, 16 February 1814, in: Webster, Diplomacy, 151.

10 Hardenberg to Frederick William III, 14 February 1814, in: Fournier, Congress, Appendix III, 291.

11 Gentz to Metternich, 15 February 1814, in: [Friedrich von Gentz], Briefe von und an Friedrich von Gentz, ed. Friedrich Carl Wittichen and Ernst Salzer, vol. 3, part 1 (Munich: Oldenbourg, 1913), no. 145, 243–255; also in: Clemens von Klinkowström, ed., Aus der alten Registratur der Staatskanzlei. Briefe politischen Inhalts von und an Friedrich von Gentz aus den Jahren 1799–1827 (Vienna: Braumüller, 1870), 58–75; cf. Sellin, Revolution, 107–110.

12 Gentz to Metternich, 15 February 1814, in: idem, Briefe, vol. 3, part 1, no. 145, 247–249.

and violent act."[13] Gentz' commentary revealed the embarrassment the revenge-fulness of the Tsar had brought down upon the allies. He wished that the "break-neck question of the dynasty" had not been posed at all.[14] Gentz believed that the allies were not allowed to depose Napoleon and didn't even have the right to support a revolt of the French nation if it occurred without their interference. In his view the monarchs of Europe were not even allowed to promote the rees-tablishment of Bourbon rule in France.

At about the same time a staunch advocate of monarchical legitimacy ar-rived at an entirely different conclusion. On 10 February Baron vom Stein, former imperial knight and outstanding Prussian reformer, reminded Tsar Alexander that within a few days he would get the opportunity "to depose the tyrant, to se-cure a durable peace, and to return to France her legitimate sovereign." If, how-ever, the allied sovereigns should consider making the form of government in France "dependent on the formation of the national will," they would attribute to the French a right that these did not possess. The house of Bourbon had "not committed any act by which it had forfeited its right to the throne."[15] Stein agreed with Gentz that a legitimate ruler could be deposed on the condition only that he had abused his powers. Other than Gentz, however, he regarded Na-poleon as a ruler who had never enjoyed legitimacy.

On 17 February the congress reassembled at Châtillon under most adverse circumstances. The allies presented the draught of a peace treaty in which France was conceded the territorial extension it had possessed in 1792. Napoleon how-ever kept insisting on the border of the Rhine. Not even during the following weeks did a compromise materialize. On 19 March the congress was broken off without any result. Caulaincourt had again and again pressed in on the Emperor to make him consent to the terms the coalition had offered. No later than 18 Jan-uary he had pointed to the danger of a revolution.[16] On 3 March he wrote the "tocsin" was ringing.[17] He reported the visit of Prince Paul Esterházy whom Met-ternich had sent to transmit a last warning. By this move the Austrian foreign secretary once more revealed how eagerly he wanted to preserve Napoleon's throne. Esterházy had added that the allies were under the impression that Na-poleon risked everything for the sole reason that he expected to regain every-

---

13 Ibid., 250.

14 Ibid., 245.

15 Stein to Alexander I, 10 February 1814, in: Karl Freiherr vom Stein, *Briefe und amtliche Schrif-ten*, ed. Walther Hubatsch, vol. 4 (Stuttgart: Kohlhammer, 1963), no. 767, 515–517.

16 Caulaincourt to Napoleon, 18 January 1814, Archives du Ministère des Affaires Étrangères Paris (MAE), Mémoires et Documents (MD) France, vol. 668, fol. 119ʳ.

17 Caulaincourt to Napoleon, 3 March 1814, ibid., fol. 346ʳ.

thing. This impression was fatal because it undermined the position of those who hoped to end the war through negotiations.

By refusing to depart from his exaggerated war aims and to enter into negotiations Napoleon irrevocably played into the hands of his fiercest opponent, Tsar Alexander of Russia. Trusting on his superior military abilities he obviously was losing his sense of reality. But time was working for Alexander. On 24 March the allies decided to march on Paris. Before departure, on 25 March, they turned to the French public with a declaration in which they put the blame for the failure of the congress of Châtillon on Napoleon and defended their insistence on the borders of 1792 by the incessant menace to the peace which had for many years originated with Napoleon. The declaration ended with an appeal to the French nation to stand up against their Emperor: "Where should the guarantee for the future come from unless such a destructive system is terminated by the general will of the nation?"[18] In their helplessness the representatives of monarchical Europe appealed to the revolution to make Napoleon cede. Gentz' warnings had been of no avail.

On 29 March the allied armies appeared before Paris. On the next day French units engaged them in heavy fights. Within the capital the political responsibility rested with Napoleon's brother Joseph. In January, before he left for the front, the Emperor had appointed him his plenipotentiary and president of a regency council. The fighting in front of the city walls caused Joseph to lose all of his courage. He followed the Empress and her son to Rambouillet and gave full power to marshals Marmont and Mortier to conclude a capitulation at their discretion. Marmont used this power that night. The French troops were given free conduct to Fontainebleau. On the morning of 31 March Alexander of Russia and Frederick William III of Prussia entered Paris at the head of the allied armies without fighting. Napoleon had taken precautions for this eventuality and given order that every dignitary of the regime abandon the city before it would be taken. The enemy should not meet anybody in Paris with whom he could conclude political agreements. Napoleon had expressed a particular warning of Talleyrand who until 1807 had served as foreign secretary under him. "That is surely the greatest enemy of our house," he had enjoined to his brother.[19] Talleyrand at this time performed the scarcely more than ceremonial duties of vice-president of the Senate, by the title of *Vice-Grand-Électeur*. Like all the other dignitaries of the regime he had on 30 March made for Rambouillet, but be-

---

18 Déclaration des Puissances Alliées lors de la rupture des négociations de Châtillon, portant confirmation solennelle de leurs Traités, 25 March 1814, in: Comte d'Angeberg (L. J. B. Chod'zko), ed., *Le congrès de Vienne et les traités de 1815, précédé et suivi des actes diplomatiques qui s'y rattachent*, vol. 1 (Paris: Amyot, 1863), 146.

19 Napoleon to Joseph Bonaparte, 8 February 1814, in: *idem*, Correspondance, vol. 27, no. 21210, 132.

fore his departure taken care that at the Barrière des Bonshommes he would be refused passage by the commander of the National Guard on duty and thus compelled
to remain in the city.

When the allied armies marched into the capital the Russian foreign secretary
Nesselrode visited Talleyrand at his residence in the rue Saint-Florentin. In the afternoon the Tsar, the King of Prussia, and the commander-in-chief of the coalition
army, Prince Schwarzenberg, joined the company. Alexander accepted the invitation
to stay in Talleyrand's house along with his foreign secretary.[20] As the decision to
march on Paris had already shown the allies had abandoned all hope to arrive at
a negotiated peace with Napoleon. But how could the Emperor be removed from office? Who should succeed him? And how could the consent of the French nation to
a change of regime been secured? These were the questions the Tsar discussed with
Talleyrand. In a country the governments of which had since a quarter of a century
been based on the principle of popular sovereignty, in the given situation the next
step to take would normally have been the call of a constitutional assembly. However, the holding of elections alone would have implied the usurpation of an authority which was still in exclusive possession of the Emperor. Holding elections would
have been difficult due to the fact that vast areas of territory were still occupied by
the coalition armies and the remainder under the control of Napoleon. Furthermore,
they would have taken weeks to carry out, thus creating a dangerous power vacuum
for an indefinite period of time.

But history presented more than one instance where constitutional bodies
without formal legitimacy in times of necessity had adopted the role of advocates of the national interest and brought about a change of regime. A suitable
model for the solution of the actual problems of France appeared to be the Glorious Revolution of 1688. Whereas in England, Parliament had changed the dynasty by decree, Talleyrand, in his discussions with Tsar Alexander, brought into
play the Napoleonic Senate. Once more an intensive debate unfolded about who
should follow Napoleon on the throne. More than one solution was discussed,
including those which the coalition had already rejected. Talleyrand would
have preferred that Napoleon had been killed in battle. In this case a Regency
government could have been set up for his son, as he explained to the Duchess
of Courland in a letter of 21 March.[21] This alone proves that he cannot, as he as-
serts in his memoirs, have won over the Tsar for the case of the Bourbons by ar-

20 Sellin, *Revolution*, 131, 195–196.
21 Talleyrand to the Duchess of Courland, 21 March 1814, in: [Charles Maurice de Talleyrand-
Périgord, duc de Bénévent], "Correspondance du prince de Talleyrand avec la duchesse de Courlande," *L'Amateur d'autographes. Revue historique et biographique* 1 (Paris 1862/63), 45.

guing that Louis XVIII was "the legitimate King of France."[22] If at all, Talleyrand had used this argument not so much in order to propose the removal of the house of Bonaparte, but to dissuade the Tsar from supporting candidates other than the count of Provence. In any case to claim legitimacy for the house of Bourbon did not mean that the monarchy of the Ancien Régime should be restored. Talleyrand himself reports to have assured the Tsar that both the adherents of the old monarchy and the advocates of "a new monarchy under a liberal constitution" strove at the return of the Bourbons. For this reason alone the Bourbons should, if they were invited to return, "not be placed on the throne of Louis XIV."[23] This would certainly have contradicted the revolutionary role that the Senate was forced to play with a view to bringing about the change of regime under the appearance of a legal procedure. The Senators would scarcely have agreed to depose the Emperor invoking the national will and then to entrust a member of the Bourbon dynasty with unlimited authority.

After the meeting in the rue Saint-Florentin Tsar Alexander ordered a proclamation to be published on behalf of the allied sovereigns announcing that there would be no more negotiations with Napoleon or a member of his family.[24] In this way he put pressure on the formation of the French national will since the proclamation left to the French only one choice: Napoleon or peace. If Napoleon was prohibited from negotiating the bloodshed could only be brought to an end if the nation created a new government. With his proclamation the Tsar offered Talleyrand and the Senate his support in their attempt to depose the Emperor.

Talleyrand convened the Senate for the afternoon of 1 April. Actually the constitution of the Empire had reserved this right to Napoleon himself, but the office of vice-president gave Talleyrand at least the appearance of a justification for the move. The most important result of the meeting of the Senate was the creation of a provisional government under the presidency of Talleyrand. It is true that in this way the second step preceded the first, since a provisional government was needed only after the deposition of Napoleon. It is obvious however that Talleyrand wanted to make sure that no power vacuum would occur. Only on the following day the Senate decided to declare Napoleon and his family deposed and to absolve the French people and the army from their oaths of allegiance. Senator Lambrechts was charged to provide the decree of deposition before its final deliberation on 3 April with a catalogue of legal justifications. The

---

22 Charles Maurice de Talleyrand-Périgord, duc de Bénévent, *Mémoires*, ed. duc de Broglie, vol. 2 (Paris: Lévy, 1891), 165.
23 Ibid., 163–164.
24 *Le Moniteur universel*, 2 April 1814.

Senate thus placed the act in the tradition of depositions of rulers by their subjects. In the same manner the revolting Dutch had deposed Philipp II of Spain in 1581, the British Parliament had deposed James II in 1688, and the American colonists had deposed George III in 1776 and thereby declared themselves independent from the mother country.[25]

In all these cases the charges against the ruler were meant to prove that he had abused his power and broken the law and thus turned into a tyrant. As a tyrant, however, he had forfeited his right to rule. The argument was based on the idea of a contract which obliged the subjects to obedience only as long as the ruler lent his protection to them. In this sense the deposition served to defend the long-established law against an unjust ruler and appears thus as an essentially conservative measure. The line of reasoning is made explicit in the decree of the Senate. It is said that Napoleon had at first governed firmly and prudently and had thus given reason to expect further "acts of wisdom and justice" from him in the future. Instead he had broken "the contract" which had united him "to the French people."[26] The charges against the Emperor include the collection of taxes without authorization, waging war without permission of the legislative bodies and suppressing the freedom of the press. As a violation of his oath of office was construed the fact that "instead of governing exclusively in the interest of the benefit, the well-being, and the glory of the French people," he had "accomplished the misfortune of the country by his refusal to accept terms of peace which were in accord with the national interest and did not offend French honour."[27] From these offences the inference is drawn that the imperial government had "ceased to exist." The wording indicates that as a consequence of his unjust dealings Napoleon had already forfeited his government and did therefore not have to be formally deposed.

The second chamber of the Empire, the *Corps législatif*, sanctioned the Senatorial decree of deposition on the same 3 April. The decree was justified by the consideration that Napoleon had "broken the constitutional contract."[28] Obviously, the charge that the Emperor had disregarded the institutions of the Empire

---

25 Cf. Erich Angermann, "Ständische Rechtstraditionen in der amerikanischen Unabhängigkeitserklärung," *Historische Zeitschrift* 200 (1965), 61–91.

26 Sénatus-consulte portant que Napoléon Bonaparte est déchu du trône, et que le droit d'hérédité établi dans sa famille est aboli, 3 April 1814, *Bulletin des lois du Royaume de France*, 5th series, vol. 1, no. 1, 7–9; also in *Le Moniteur universel*, 4 April 1814.

27 Ibid.

28 Acte par lequel le Corps législatif, adhérant à l'acte du Sénat, reconnaît et déclare la déchéance de Napoléon Bonaparte et des membres de sa famille, 3 April 1814, *Bulletin des lois*, 5th series, vol. 1, no. 1, 9–11.

and thereby forfeited his right to rule only confirmed the validity of these institutions. In this way the Senate's justification of the deposition made it imperative that the institutional continuity was preserved beyond Napoleon's fall from power. The distinction between Napoleon and the institutions which had been created during the Revolution and further developed in the Empire made it easier for the nation to agree with the deposition of the Emperor, but at the same time it obliged the Senate to institute new government in conformity with the principles of the Revolution. The institutions of the new regime would therefore, inevitably, resemble much more the Empire than the ancient monarchy. In this way, the restoration was only left with limited room to manoeuvre.

On 6 April the Senate approved a new constitution. On the following day the corps législatif gave its assent. The constitution contained 29 articles. The first article provided for a constitutional monarchy hereditary by right of primogeniture. The second article confirmed the sovereignty of the people. According to its wording "the French people freely called" on the throne of France Louis-Stanislas-Xavier de France, "brother of the last King" and after him the other members of the house of Bourbon "according to the ancient order of succession." Article 29 determined that the constitution was to be submitted to a referendum and that Louis-Stanislas-Xavier would be proclaimed "King of the French," as soon as he had sworn an oath on the constitution and signed it. Louis-Stanislas-Xavier de France was the real name of the count of Provence. By using this name it was made clear that it was the constitution alone that would confer royal dignity upon the candidate and that he did not possess any historical or dynastic claim to the throne. For this reason emphasis was laid on the fact that the appointment of the count was a voluntary act and had not been decided upon in recognition of an inherent right of the dynasty to rule. In agreement with the democratic character of the constitution article 29 conferred on the ruler the title of a "King of the French" instead of King of France. The denial of all dynastic claims is also expressed by calling the count of Provence "brother of the last King." From a strictly monarchical point of view the last King had not been Louis XVI but his son who had died in prison in 1795. The count of Provence was his uncle and since the royalists counted the dauphin who had never been on the throne as Louis XVII he styled himself Louis XVIII.

By inserting articles 2 and 29 the Senate aimed at preventing the King from retracting the achievements of the Revolution and the Empire. Other articles point in the same direction. Article 24 confirmed the sale of the national domains, article 15 proclaimed equality of taxation, and article 27 proclaimed equality of admission to the public service. Article 28 confirmed that the existing legal system and in particular Napoleon's Code civil would remain in force. A number of basic rights were guaranteed, but were not assembled in a separate catalogue: freedom of religion and of conscience (article 22), freedom of the press (article 23), the right of petition (article 26) and the guarantee of the public debt (article 24). Article 25 excluded political purges. It ruled that nobody would have to answer for his political conduct under any of the preceding regimes. The constitution accorded parliament great weight. The legislative power was to be exercised by the King and parliament jointly, and both Houses were to have the right to initiate legislation (article 5).

Owing to its liberal character the Senatorial constitution was unable to pave the way for a restoration of the monarchy of the Ancien Régime. If it resurrected a regime of the past it was the constitutional monarchy under the constitution of 1791. Insofar the Senate aimed at a democratic restoration, the only kind of restoration compatible with the principles of the Revolution. However, the Senatorial constitution differed considerably from the constitution of 1791. It was much shorter and omitted details, did not include a catalogue of basic rights, provided for a two chamber legislature, permitted membership of ministers in one of the two houses, and contained a good deal of articles aiming directly at preserving the institutions of the Napoleonic Empire for the new regime. In this way it created an entirely new monarchy which shared with the constitutional monarchy of 1791, apart from its democratic character, the dynasty.

The constitution did not provide for the case that the count of Provence refused his nomination. Obviously, a restoration of the monarchy was considered feasible only with the Bourbons. This conviction stands in marked contrast to the principle that the King could claim those rights only which the constitution reserved for him. It is true that the Bourbons were denied the right to restore the monarchy on their own. This right was claimed by the nation alone. But if the nation decided to return to the monarchy, then obviously the Bourbons alone were considered the rightful candidates for kingship. His invocation of the national will notwithstanding the Senate could not have chosen any other dynasty or simply leave the question open. This strengthened the position of the candidate which as was soon to be revealed, he would be able to turn to his advantage. In her memoirs the duchess of Fleury reports a conversation which she pretends to have had about the future government of France with Talleyrand before Napoleon was deposed. When Talleyrand proposed the duke of Orléans for the throne she affirms to have replied that even though the duke would be "a usurper of a better family than any other," he would nonetheless remain "a usurper."[29]

---

29 Aimée de Coigny, duchesse de Fleury, *Mémoires*, ed. Étienne Lamy (Paris: Calmann-Lévy, 1906), 241.

Years later Talleyrand used the same argument in his memoirs.[30] From this it follows that not even a referendum on the Senatorial constitution might have absolved a candidate other than the count of Provence from the verdict of being a usurper. Therefore the choice of the count was after all less arbitrary than the second article pretended it to be.

It was only under the protection of the coalition armies that the Senate was safe to proceed to the formation of a provisional government, to the deposition of the Emperor, and to the elaboration of a new constitution. In the meantime Napoleon stayed not far from the capital at Fontainebleau. Though he would have preferred to prevent the allies from taking Paris, he refused to admit defeat. Instead, he made plans for the reconquest of the city. When on the morning of 4 April he revealed this project to his marshals, they refused allegiance. The revolt of the marshals determined Napoleon to abdicate. At first he tried to preserve the throne for his son, but after the unintended passage of Marshall Marmont's corps to the enemy the Tsar saw no more reason to accommodate him. The only concession Napoleon was able to obtain was a formal treaty of abdication in which the Isle of Elba was adjudged to him, Parma and Piacenza to Empress Marie-Louise, and to both of them substantial pensions at the State's expense.[31]

Talleyrand demonstrated all his political skill when he chose the procedure of Parliament during the Glorious Revolution of 1688 as a model for the change of regime in France. However, the concessions the count of Provence was obliged to make extended far beyond the reforms which Mary Stuart and William of Orange had to confirm before ascending the throne. The count of Provence had never acknowledged neither the sovereignty of the people which the National Assembly had for the first time proclaimed in 1789, nor the constitution of 1791. A short time before it was completed he had, unlike his brother, on 21 June 1791 managed to leave the country and seek refuge abroad.[32] Therefore it was entirely unforeseeable whether he would follow the example of Henry IV and, departing from his convictions for the crown's sake, adopt the constitution that had been created for him.

Owing to a gout attack the count's departure from his exile at Hartwell in England was delayed. Instead his brother, count Artois, soon announced his arrival in Paris. Following the custom of the Ancien Régime the count of Provence had appointed him Lieutenant General of the Kingdom and his representative during his absence. As was to be expected, on his arrival Artois demanded

---

30 Talleyrand, *Mémoires*, vol. 2, 155.
31 Traité dit de Fontainebleau, 11 april 1814, artt. 3 and 5, Angeberg, *Congrès*, vol. 1, 148 – 149; for the history of Napoleon's abdication see Sellin, *Revolution*, 173 – 194.
32 Philip Mansel, *Louis XVIII* (London: Blond & Briggs, 1981), 53 – 55.

that the government be formally handed over to him. This demand greatly embarrassed the Senate. Before the count of Provence had taken an oath on the constitution, the Senate was not ready to recognize the appointment of his brother. For the time being they regarded Artois merely as a private gentleman and refused to welcome him solemnly at his entrance into the city on 12 April 1814 at the barrier of Bondy. But when he arrived there amid the cheers of the population, riding on horseback and wearing the white cockade of the monarchy, he was met by the provisional government, the city council and the leading authorities. Artois expected the Senate formally to hand over to him the government. But the Senate hesitated since up to this moment the count of Provence had not yet declared that he accepted the constitution which had been worked out for him. Fouché, the former minister of the police, found a way out of the difficulty and proposed that if the Senate could not recognize the powers the count of Provence had given to his brother, as long as he had not formally accepted the constitution, the Senate itself should confer authority on Artois. To this proposal the Senate consented on 14 April.[33] Thus Artois could continue to regard himself as authorized by his brother, whereas the Senate regarded him as authorized by themselves. By this compromise the actual conflict was resolved, but the apprehension persisted that with a view to the increasing approval of the return of the Bourbons the authority of the Senate would not be sufficient to extract from the count of Provence the prescribed oath on the constitution from which the accession to the throne should depend. A deep conflict was on the verge of breaking out which at the return of the candidate might easily have degenerated into a civil war. Tsar Alexander got uneasy to the point that on 17 April he sent a letter to England to the count of Provence admonishing him to pay respect to the "national will," if he wished to spare the country new convulsions. He explained to the King that he would win every heart if he made room for "liberal ideas" aiming "at the maintenance and confirmation of the specific historical traditions of France."[34] When talking of the specific traditions of France he at this point naturally alluded to the achievements of the Revolution and the Empire. That of all people the Tsar demanded the preservation of these achievements is easily explained. Over the restoration of the ancient constitution the great powers gave priority to the recovery of political stability. The quest for stability set limits to every literal desire for restoration.

---

33 Minutes des procès-verbaux du Sénat conservateur, 14 April 1814, Archives nationales Paris, CC 986.

34 Alexander to Louis, 5/17 April 1814, in: A. Polovtsoff, ed., *Correspondance diplomatique des ambassadeurs et ministres de Russie en France et de France en Russie avec leurs gouvernements de 1814 à 1830*, vol. 1, St. Petersburg 1902, 2; also in: Brunov, *Aperçu*, 411–412.

On 20 April, the day when Napoleon took leave of his guard and departed for the Isle of Elba, the count of Provence abandoned his English exile at Hartwell. On 24 April he disembarked at Calais. Five days later he arrived at Compiègne. To Compiègne he had invited Napoleon's marshals with a view to securing the support of the army. To this day he had not wasted any word about the Senatorial constitution he was expected to confirm. But since he conquered the hearts of his subjects wherever he passed it had become entirely unthinkable that he should be sent back into exile if he refused the oath on the constitution. His long expected comment was at last drawn up on 2 Mai at Saint-Ouen on the outskirts of Paris and published in the capital on the following morning.[35]

About the Senatorial constitution it was said in the Declaration that "its foundations were good" but since a great many "of articles displayed the hurry" with which they had been worded "it could not, in its actual shape, become the fundamental law of the state." Since, however, he was determined to create "a liberal constitution," the King would invite members of the Senate and the legislative body to form a committee and entrust the necessary revision of the text to them.[36] The wording of the order of revision gave the impression as if the count of Provence confirmed the constituent power as claimed by the two chambers. If the revision should be limited to the rectification of defects due to the hurry in which Talleyrand hat forced the text through the Senate, one could ignore the fact that the candidate for the throne was not ready to accept the constitution as it had been presented to him, all the more so since he promised with few exceptions to guarantee the preservation of essential achievements of the Revolution and the Empire as listed in the constitution. By its wording the Declaration of Saint-Ouen skillfully obscured the fact that the count of Provence in reality rejected precisely the "foundations" of the Senatorial constitution. This is already shown by the very first line of the Declaration. Not the count of Provence had issued it but "Louis, by the grace of God King of France and of Navarre." This was a resounding slap in the face of the Senate and a square rejection of their claim to commit the King to the recognition of the national will and to make his elevation on the throne conditional on this recognition. In his own eyes Louis had been King for 19 years already, that is to say King of France by the grace of God and not King of the French by the will of the people.

The ideas of legitimacy to which the King on the one hand and the Senate on the other adhered were entirely incompatible with each other. The Senate had acted in accordance with the principle contained in the Declaration of the Rights

---

35 On the origins of the Declaration of Saint-Ouen see Sellin, *Revolution*, 222–223.
36 Déclaration du Roi, Saint-Ouen, 2 May 1814, *Bulletin des lois*, 5th series, vol. 1, no. 8, 75–76.

of Man and the Citizen of 1789 and since respected by every regime in France, the principle that no assembly and no individual could claim political authority unless expressly empowered by the nation.[37] In keeping with this rule the Senate had deposed Napoleon and voted the restoration of the monarchy under the Bourbons on behalf of the nation. Another road to the restoration of the monarchy was not compatible with the sovereignty of the people. Louis, however, considered himself superior to the Revolution. In his eyes the monarchy had never been abolished. He believed that the National Convention of 1792 had not possessed the right to such a measure. If, however, the monarchy had never ceased to exist, there was no need for the Senate to restore it, quite apart from the fact that the very idea of a restoration of kingship was incompatible with monarchical legitimacy. If the monarchy by divine right had in fact succumbed during the Revolution, no power on Earth could have restored it, since such a restoration presupposed a power the legitimacy of which was superior to the legitimacy of the King. The idea of such a power, however, was incompatible with the concept of divine right monarchy. Therefore, from a monarchical point view what happened in 1814 was not a restoration of the monarchy, but only the removal of the impediments which had for more than two decades prevented the King from effectively taking up his government. In this sense restoration did not mean the recovery of a right which had been forfeited, but rather the assertion, by the ancient dynasty, of a claim which had never ceased to remain valid. This assertion, however, demanded more than the simple return of the King from exile. Its success depended on the fulfillment of the expectations which had developed during the Revolution, and on the King's promise of a liberal government. The Declaration of Saint-Ouen shows that Louis XVIII had understood. His promise "to adopt a liberal constitution" was soon followed, as he had also announced, by the formation of a committee for the revision of the Senatorial constitution. The committee numbered 22 members and on 22 May initiated their deliberations under the presidency of chancellor Dambray. Following the King's instructions they transformed the Senatorial constitution within a week into the Charte constitutionnelle. The very name of the new constitution demonstrates that it was not based on the sovereignty of the nation but on the power of the monarch. The term *constitution* reminded of the Revolution, whereas *charte* was the traditional expression for a document by which under the Ancien Régime privileges had been accorded by the kings.[38]

---

37 Déclaration des droits de l'homme et du citoyen, 26 August 1789, art. 3, in: Jacques Godechot, ed., *Les constitutions de la France depuis 1789* (Paris: Garnier-Flammarion, 1970), 33–34.
38 On the origin of the Charte constitutionnelle see Sellin, *Revolution*, chap. 7, 225–273; Pierre Simon, *L'élaboration de la Charte constitutionnelle de 1814*, Paris 1906.

The proclamation of the Charte constitutionnelle was scheduled on 4 June 1814 at a *séance royale,* a solemn session of both chambers in the presence of the King. During the preceding night Jacques-Claude Beugnot, a public servant who had made his career under Napoleon and meanwhile acted as General Director of the Police, composed a preamble to the document.[39] The historical significance of this text derives from the fact that here for the first time the so-called monarchical principle was enunciated according to which even under a constitution the monarch retained full power, whereas the chambers merely participated in its exercise. The monarchical principle defined monarchical in contrast to democratic constitutionalism which was based on the sovereignty of the people and which had marked both the French constitution of 1791 and the Senatorial constitution of 1814. The Charte constitutionnelle introduced into history an entirely new type of constitution. The Charte was imposed by the monarch who claimed to be and remain in full possession of political power. Therefore it obtained force of law without confirmation by the nation or their representatives. Prior to Louis XVIII only Napoleon had reverted to a similar procedure of constitution-giving, not in France, where every constitution and every revision of a constitution was confirmed by plebiscite, but in satellite kingdoms such as the Kingdom of Westphalia in 1807 or of Spain in 1808. By imposing the Charte a century-old monarchy made concessions to the revolutionary spirit of the times in order to preserve his traditional monarchical legitimacy. Napoleon, by contrast, imposed constitutions in the hope of consolidating monarchies of revolutionary origin. The essential mark of distinction of the Charte constitutionnelle and of all other constitutions which were modeled after it was the association of traditional monarchical legitimacy and liberal reforms. The reforms were carried just far enough to meet the basic expectations of the citizens. Louis XVIII was determined to preserve as much as possible of his royal prerogative. This is demonstrated by the dispute within the constitutional committee on the right to initiate legislation. In the beginning the King had wanted to retain this right, an "ornament of his crown," without limits. Since the majority of the committee opposed this desire a compromise was sought and the chambers were accorded a right of petition. Articles 19 and 20 of the Charte gave both Chambers the right to petition the King for the introduction of a bill and article 21 demanded that the petition be transmitted to the King only after both Chambers had endorsed it.[40]

---

39 Volker Sellin, "Die Erfindung des monarchischen Prinzips. Jacques-Claude Beugnots Präambel zur Charte constitutionnelle," in *Tour de France. Eine historische Rundreise. Festschrift für Rainer Hudemann,* ed. Armin Heinen and Dietmar Hüser (Stuttgart: Steiner, 2008), 493–497.
40 Sellin, *Revolution,* 254–257.

Thanks to the imposition of the Charte constitutionnelle Louis XVIII succeeded in restoring the monarchy in France, not in the sense of a literal restoration of the ancient monarchy, but of a renewal which took into account the spirit
of the times. Not the Senate but the King himself had restored the monarchy. In
this way the achievement of Louis XVIII remained during the whole century the
authoritative model for the renewal of monarchies threatened by revolution. Everywhere the method followed the same pattern. By imposing constitutions and
thus meeting essential demands of the Revolution without infringing upon the
traditional monarchical legitimacy the greater part of the monarchies could be
preserved until the end of the First World War and beyond.[41] Whereas the constitutions of the Revolution in France had all been abolished again after a few
years only, the Charte constitutionnelle of 1814 remained in force until the July
Revolution of 1830 and after its revision for another eighteen years. It was to a
great extent by the Charte of 1814 that the heritage of the French Revolution
was transmitted to the 19th century. The same is true of the constitutions
which in other monarchies were modeled on the example of the Charte. The liberal principles which had developed since 1789 were transformed into durable
institutions not so much directly by the numerous revolutions but rather indirectly by means of restoration.

Even though the French were not invited formally to confirm the restoration of
1814 by a referendum, they nevertheless consented tacitly and thus informally to the
Charte and to the return of the monarchy. In this way they retracted the abolition of
the monarchy of 1792. This step was made possible by the guarantees contained in
the Charte. Insofar the French restoration of 1814 was based on a contract between
monarchy and nation. Ferdinand VII of Spain and the numerous Italian princes who
returned on their thrones after the fall of Napoleon, did not need a similar contract,
because they had not been expelled by their subjects but by the foreign conqueror.
Therefore they saw no reason to concede constitutions, but resumed government almost everywhere in the form of the harshest absolutism.

The monarchy of Louis XVIII was the first French regime since 1789 that was
not based on the national will but on divine right in the style of the Ancien Régime. The restoration of divine right monarchy rested on the fiction that the ancient monarchy had never ceased to exist and that consequently there was no
need to bring her back to life. To this conviction the demeanor of Louis XVIII
after his return from his English exile at the end of April 1814 corresponded perfectly. He did not await a formal act of recognition but from the very beginning

---

41 Sellin, *Gewalt und Legitimität. Die europäische Monarchie im Zeitalter der Revolutionen* (Munich: Oldenbourg, 2011), in particular chap. 7 ("Verfassung"), 171–216.

acted as sovereign. Accordingly he did not attribute his return to the invitation by the Senate. The main reason why he was far from considering the situation in this light was the fact that he deeply despised the Senate and denied him every right to deliberate on the future of France. His real opinion is to be found in a commentary on the Senatorial constitution which he had put down in writing article by article. On the last article which stated that he could become King only after having taken an oath on the constitution, he remarked: "Louis XVIII, by the grace of God King of France and of Navarre, deposes the present Senate for its complicity in the crimes of Bonaparte and appeals against them to the French people."[42] The remark shows that in his desire to restore divine right monarchy the King believed to act in accordance with the wishes of the French people. He regarded the Senatorial constitution simply as a proposal and not as a condition he was bound to accept. In the last resort, then, to him it was the royal will alone from which could emanate the new monarchy.

The view of the King differed from the views of the citizens. The majority of the French seems to have regarded the government of Louis XVIII as a new regime the legitimacy of which did not rest on the dynasty but on the institutions it had promised to preserve. It was on purpose that in their constitution of 6 April the Senate had meticulously avoided to construe their scheme of a democratic monarchy as a restoration of the historical monarchy of France. This strategy reveals the prevailing interpretation. To Louis XVIII the restoration was the return to the ancient monarchy, to the nation it was the renewal of the liberties gained in 1789. The French restoration of 1814 obviously meant two different things at the same time: the renewal and consolidation of the monarchy by divine right, and the reconciliation of that monarchy with fundamental achievements of the Revolution. It was chiefly this compromise that gave reason to hope for the durability of the new regime.

---

42 Archives du Ministère des Affaires Étrangères, Paris, MD France, vol. 646 (Fonds Bourbon), fol. 41^v; of Louis' commentary only fragments have been preserved: Sellin, *Revolution*, 218–219.

Poland 1815

From 1772 to 1795 Russia, Prussia, and Austria partitioned the aristocratic republic of Poland (*Rzeczpospolita Polska*) between them. For twelve years the Polish nation remained without its own polity. It was only the Prussian defeat in the war of the fourth coalition that paved the way for the formation of a new, albeit reduced, Polish state. Through the peace of Tilsit of 1807 King Frederick William III of Prussia ceded to Napoleon the greater part of the territories his country had acquired in the course of the second and third partition of Poland. The ceded territories were transformed into the Duchy of Warsaw (*Księstwo Warszawskie*). Napoleon gave it a constitution and made King Frederick August I of Saxony King of Poland, thus binding together Saxony and Poland in a personal union. By the peace of Schönbrunn of 1809 Emperor Francis I ceded to the King of Saxony and Poland Western Galicia and other pieces of territory Austria had gained at the partitions. These acquisitions were annexed to the Duchy of Warsaw which was simultaneously promoted to the rank of Grand-Duchy. Even though the Grand-Duchy comprised but a small part of the former Polish Republic, its formation generated among the Poles hopes of recovering unity and independence. When Napoleon in 1812 opened the war against Russia many Poles joined him. They sought to take advantage of the opportunity and recover the territories which the Tsar had annexed during the partitions: Vil'njus, Grodno, Minsk, Mogilev, Vitebsk, Volyn', Podol'e, and Kiev, the so-called Western governments of Russia. But the Grande Armée failed. In the wake of Napoleon's retreat Russian troops occupied the Grand-Duchy of Warsaw. On 13 March 1813 Tsar Alexander I installed a military government, the Provisional Supreme Council (*Rada Najwyższa Tymczasowa*) under General Governor Vasilij S. Lanskoj. Nikolaj N. Novosil'cev was appointed Vice-Governor.[1] Notwithstanding staunch British and Austrian opposition at the congress of Vienna Tsar Alexander transformed the Grand-Duchy into a Kingdom, gave it a constitution, and tied it to the Russian Empire by means of a personal union. Most of the territories of the new Kingdom consisted of former Prussian gains from the partitions of Poland. Prussia contented itself with Danzig and a strip of territory at the Northwestern edge of the new Polish Kingdom which permitted it to straighten the frontier between Silesia and Eastern Prussia. This territory then became the Grand-Duchy of Poznan. For the loss of its former Polish possessions Prussia was indemnified in Saxony and on the Rhine.

---

1 Józef Bojasiński, *Rządi tymczasowe w królestwie polskiem. Maj-grudzień 1815* (Warsaw: Laskauer, 1902), 9.

DOI 10.1515/9783110524536-002

The foundation of the Kingdom of Poland by Alexander I is an astonishing occurrence. Of all sovereigns the Russian Tsar was the first to imitate Louis XVIII by imposing a constitution on Poland. The chief purpose of the imposition was without doubt the hope of securing the allegiance of his new Polish subjects. This policy might have been even more successful if the Tsar had transferred to the new Kingdom those territories as well which Russia had annexed between 1772 and 1795 in the course of the partitions of Poland. One is tempted to suppose that by founding the Kingdom of Poland Alexander more than anything else hoped to increase Russian influence in central and Western Europe. If the liberal institutions of the new state worked it was in fact to be expected that they would exert a considerable attraction on the Polish subjects of the neighbouring great powers Prussia and Austria and render more difficult the efforts of these two countries to integrate their recently acquired Polish territories. The prospect would increase that at the cost of the two German partitioning powers additional parts of the former Rzeczpospolita were united with the new Kingdom. The Poles would hail the Tsar as their liberator and from his position as King of Poland Alexander could easily extend his influence way into Central Europe. This effect could not come to pass if the Tsar accepted the proposal of the British Foreign Secretary Lord Castlereagh to partition the Grand-Duchy of Warsaw among the three neighbouring great powers as it had already been agreed upon at the congress of Vienna. A formal annexation of the Grand-Duchy by Russia, however, would in no case have been tolerated by Great Britain and Austria. It was only on condition that the Grand-Duchy become a separate constitutional state, albeit in personal union with the Russian Empire, that the great powers finally assented to Russian dominion over it.

The antecedents of Alexander's Polish policy go back to 1791. On 3 May of that year the Polish Diet adopted a modern liberal constitution.[2] Simultaneously the ancient elective monarchy was transformed into a hereditary monarchy. This unexpected consolidation of the instable and weak Polish state induced King Frederick William II of Prussia and Tsarina Catherine II two years later to proceed to a second partition of the country. The new act of violence committed against Poland provoked a rebellion under the lead of Tadeusz Kościuszko in March 1794. The rebellion was suppressed and the Tsarina had the estates of those members of the Polish aristocracy confiscated who had taken part in it. To the magnates concerned belonged Prince Kazimierz Czartoryski who was descended from one of the most eminent noble families of the country. Czartoryski

---

2 Ustawa rządowa z dnia 3-go maja 1791 roku, in: Marceli Handelsman, ed., *Konstytucje polskie 1791–1921* (Warsaw 1922), 1–20.

was not ready to reconcile himself with the expropriation and strove for the recovery of his estates. The Tsarina consented on condition that as pledges for his future good conduct the prince send his sons Adam and Constantine as hostages to the court of St. Petersburg where they were to enter Russian services.[3] Adam, the elder of the two, was 25 years of age; Constantine was younger by four years. On 24 May 1795 the brothers arrived in the Russian capital.[4] The tasks that would be assigned to them had not yet been determined. As Adam reports in his memoirs, the two brothers did not care at all about the rank that would be accorded to them in the services of the Tsarina: "Can a traveler who by mere chance gets to Japan, to Borneo or to the territories of Central Africa, attribute to the forms, the distinctions, and the honours which are of use among those barbarians, the least significance?"[5] Later on the brothers were appointed officers of the Imperial Guard. Of historical consequence was the acquaintance with the eighteen-year-old grand-duke Alexander, the future Tsar Alexander I. Adam Czartoryski and Alexander became friends. Soon Alexander revealed his repugnance toward the policies of his grandmother, Tsarina Catherine II. As Czartoryski later wrote, Alexander "passionately loved justice and freedom, deplored the fate of Poland and wished to see that country happy!"[6] An immediate source of the political opinions of the young Alexander is a letter he directed to his Swiss instructor La Harpe on 27 September 1797 where he reveals his intention to give to Russia a "liberal constitution" in order to save it forever from "despotism" and "tyranny." This would be, so he judged, "the best kind of revolution, carried through by a legal government."[7] The letter reflects the convictions which the heir to the throne and Czartoryski shared. As an example of the arbitrary government of an unlimited ruler Alexander had before the eyes his father, Tsar Paul I, whose assassination in March 1801 cleared the way for his accession to the throne.

At the beginning of his reign the new Tsar drew the friend of his youth into the innermost circle of his councilors. Together with Viktor Kočubej, Nikolaj Novosil'cev, and Pavel Stroganov Czartoryski became a member of Alexander's Se-

---

3 Marian Kukiel, *Czartoryski and European Unity 1770–1861* (Princeton: Princeton University Press, 1955), 15.

4 W. H. Zawadzki, *A Man of Honour. Adam Czartoryski as a Statesman of Russia and Poland 1795–1831* (Oxford: Clarendon Press, 1993), 7; Adam Czartoryski, *Mémoires et correspondance avec l'empereur Alexandre Ier*, vol. 1 (Paris: Plon, 1887), 37.

5 Ibid., 76.

6 Ibid., 98.

7 The letter is printed in: Nikolaj Karlovič Šil'der, *Imperator Aleksandr Pervyj. Ego žizn' i carstvovanie*, vol. 1 (St. Petersburg: Suvorin, 1897), 280–282.

cret Committee (*neglasnyj komitet*).[8] In the fall of 1802 he was appointed deputy of the aged foreign minister Voroncov and two years later was himself promoted to be foreign minister. From 1803 he also served as curator of the University of Vil'njus. In this capacity he was responsible for education in the eight Western governments Russia had annexed in the course of the partitions of Poland. Even in the Russian service Czartoryski remained an ardent Polish patriot. Since Alexander had more than once confessed his repugnance against the Polish policies of his grandmother, Czartoryski saw reason to hope that as Alexander's foreign minister he would sooner or later get the opportunity to reverse the fate of his home country.

An opportunity seemed to arise in the fall of 1804. After Napoleons's breach of the peace of Amiens which had been concluded two years before, the British government was in search for allies on the continent in the renewed war against Napoleonic France. Foreign minister Czartoryski took advantage of the situation and advised the Tsar to send the minister of Justice Novosil'cev as a special envoy to London to negotiate a long-term British-Russian alliance. The instructions which Czartoryski drew up on behalf of the Tsar contained nothing less than the project of a fundamental reform of the political system of Europe. Great Britain and Russia were assigned the roles of "saviours of Europe" (*sauveurs de l'Europe*).[9] The proposals were justified with the persisting French menace. In the first paragraphs of the instructions it was pointed out that "the strongest weapon which the French had used so far and with which they continued to threaten every country," was their ability to spread the erroneous conviction everywhere that they fought for the freedom and the welfare of nations. Therefore "the welfare of mankind and the true interest of the legitimate governments" demanded that this powerful weapon be taken from the French and instead turned against France itself.[10] The precondition of such a step, the instructions continued, was the universal advocacy of constitutions by every government which fought against France. By the imposition of constitutions the nations would be "reconciled to their governments" and make sure that these were striving at nothing else but "the greatest welfare possible of the peoples subjected to them."[11] In this way the promise of a liberal constitution should be turned into an ideological weapon in the war against France. For the post-war period

---

8 Marc Raeff, *Michael Speransky, Statesman of Imperial Russia*, 1772–1839 (The Hague: Nijhoff, 1957), 34, n. 1.

9 Instructions secrètes à M. de Novosiltzow allant en Angleterre, le 11 septembre 1804, in: Czartoryski, *Mémoires*, vol. 2, 34.

10 Ibid., 28–29.

11 Ibid., 33.

the Tsar proposed the creation of a system of collective security, of a confederation which "would grant to the states the highest possible degree of quiet and safety."[12] The stability and durability of such a confederation demanded that the frontiers of the states be drawn in keeping with geography, along mountain ranges or rivers. To all countries was to be granted access to the international markets where their citizens could sell their products, and the countries themselves ought to be composed of "homogeneous peoples able to communicate with each other and to adjust to the governments which direct them."[13]

This was a revolutionary and as well a utopian program. By the argument of ethnic homogeneity one could easily justify the demand to restore an independent Polish state. It was doubtful, however, if the Tsar would really be ready to renounce the Russian acquisitions of Polish territory and agree that the Western governments of his country be included in the territorial revision. The two other partitioning powers – Austria and Prussia – were to be indemnified elsewhere for their losses. The prerequisite of putting into practice these projects was the defeat of Napoleon. Alexander hoped for victory in the war which was expected to break out in 1805.

In this war Napoleon suffered a devastating defeat at sea. On 21 October 1805 near Trafalgar off the Southern coast of the Iberian Peninsula not far from Cádiz the British admiral Nelson destroyed the combined Spanish and French fleets. As a consequence the Emperor was forced to renounce his plans of an invasion of the British Isles. By land, however, he achieved the most brilliant victory of his career. On 2 December he defeated the allied Russian and Austrian armies near Austerlitz in Moravia. This catastrophe prevented Alexander and Czartoryski from going straight ahead with their plans of a fundamental reordering of Europe, quite apart from the fact that the defeat affected the relationship between the Tsar and his foreign minister. On 1 July 1806 Czartoryski was dismissed, but remained a member of the Senate and the State Council and Curator of the University of Vil'njus.[14] His personal relations to Alexander were not interrupted either. So in December 1806 he could venture to transmit to the Tsar a new memorandum and a plan for the restoration of Poland.[15]

The Prussian defeat at Jena and Auerstedt on 14 October had opened up new opportunities. The battle had not ended the war, since Russia, Prussia's ally, did not admit defeat. As Czartoryski asserted in his memorandum, the victory would

---

12 Ibid., 35.
13 Ibid., 36.
14 Kukiel, *Czartoryski*, 76, 79; Zawadzki, *Man*, 159.
15 Adam Czartoryski, "Mémoire sur la nécessité de rétablir la Pologne pour prévenir Bonaparte (5 décembre 1806)," in: id., *Mémoires*, vol. 2, 148–158.

enable Napoleon to transform the Polish provinces of Prussia into a separate state. The Poles would enthusiastically support such a project and place their resources and their fighting power at the disposition of France, motivated by the hope that with the help of the victorious Emperor they would soon be able to liberate those parts of their country as well which had still remained under Russian domination. Whereas Napoleon would have no difficulty to find comrades-in-arms among the Poles in his war against Russia, the Russian government would avoid recruiting soldiers among the Polish population under its domination because it was afraid they would, once in arms, turn against Russia instead of France. Therefore Russia would stand passively by and watch the enemy taking advantage of these human resources.[16] In order to forestall the creation of a Polish state at the hands of Napoleon, Czartoryski pressed upon Alexander to proclaim a Polish state with the frontiers of the ancient aristocratic republic and declare himself hereditary King. In this way the Tsar, not Napoleon, would obtain the Polish resources and gain the allegiance of the Poles.[17] To be sure, the Tsar would attain this end only if he gave to the Poles a government "according to their wishes and in consonance with their former laws." Everything else would remain a "half-measure" and could "not secure any of the advantages hoped for."[18]

Czartoryski entered one by one into the objections he expected would be raised against his proposal. If Poland were restored within its ancient limits all partitioning powers would have to renounce their acquisitions, and Russia would have to cede its Western governments to the new Polish monarchy. This would certainly meet strong resistance in Russia. In point of fact, however, the Tsar would not incur any loss, because the Polish crown should indissolubly be tied to the Russian throne. "Far from suffering losses Russia would gain the entire remainder of Poland." Another objection Czartoryski foresaw was that the Tsar would be obliged to break his alliance with Prussia if he wanted to restore to the future Kingdom of Poland the Polish provinces that Prussia had acquired at the partitions. To this Czartoryski remarked that it was no longer Frederick William III who governed in Berlin but Napoleon Bonaparte who by his victory at Jena and Auerstedt had become the real master of Prussia. Therefore the Tsar would not seize the possessions of an ally if he contributed to the formation of a greater Poland, but simply snatch the spoils from the enemy. As to Austrian Galicia Czartoryski recommended that before the proclamation of the

---

16 Ibid., 149.
17 Ibid., 150.
18 Ibid., 154.

Kingdom of Poland Alexander enter into contact with Vienna and settle the future of Austrian Poland through negotiations. Czartoryski was not afraid that the proclamation of the restoration of Poland would protract the present war. Instead he believed that Napoleon would more readily assent to peace negotiations if the prospect of obtaining the Polish resources had vanished. For this reason alone the advocated step should not be delayed any further.[19]

Alexander did not heed Czartoryski's advice. Napoleon brought the war to a victorious end and in July 1807 dictated the peace terms to Prussia and Russia at Tilsit. Of the provinces Prussia had acquired in 1793 and 1795, he disposed exactly as Czartoryski had foreseen. Whereas he made Danzig a free city, he united the remaining provinces to become the Duchy of Warsaw and elevated King Frederick August I of Saxony to the dignity of King in the new Napoleonic satellite Kingdom, thus creating a personal union of Poland and Saxony. At the same time he gave it a constitution, the *Statut constitutionnel du duché de Varsovie*.[20] Russia obtained the district of Białystok. Through the peace of Schönbrunn concluded by France and Austria two years later, the duchy of Warsaw was enlarged by Western Galicia, the city of Cracow and the district of Zamość.[21] Simultaneously the Duchy was promoted to Grand-Duchy. The partitioning powers did not permit that the name of the new Kingdom contained the word Poland, for fear that from the Polish name would be deduced the right to have the old Commonwealth restored. A short time after the conclusion of the peace of Tilsit Tsar Alexander had written to his mistress Maria Naryškina: "At least there will be no Poland but a ridiculous Duchy of Warsaw."[22] Nevertheless, the Poles regarded the Grand-Duchy as germ-cell of a new all-Polish state.[23]

Napoleon presented the agreements of Tilsit to the Tsar as a division of Europe into a French and a Russian sphere of influence and therefore as an achievement that would endure. In reality the Tsar felt threatened by the crea-

---

19 Ibid., 153–157.

20 Comte d'Angeberg, ed., *Recueil des Traités, Conventions et Actes Diplomatiques concernant la Pologne 1762–1862* (Paris: Amyot, 1862), 470–481; the Polish text of the statute in: Handelsman, *Konstytucje*, 27–39. Owen Connelly, *Napoleon's Satellite Kingdoms* (New York and London: Free Press, 1965), did not reserve a chapter for the Grand-Duchy of Warsaw on the ground that it was not governed by a member of the House of Bonaparte; ibid., ix.

21 George Frédéric de Martens, ed., *Nouveau recueil de traités*, vol. 1 (1808–1814) (Göttingen: Dieterich, 1817), Traité etc., 15 October 1809, Art. 3, paragraph 4, 212.

22 Quoted from Emanuel Halicz, "La question polonaise à Tilsitt," *Acta Poloniae Historica* 12 (1965), 62.

23 Marian Kallas, *Konstytucja Księstwa Warszawskiego. Jej powstanie, systematyka i główne instytucje w związku z normami szczegółowymi i praktyka* (Toruń: Zakłady Graf. W Toruniu, 1970), 20.

tion of a Polish satellite state of France right on his borders. The reason of this was not only the geographical and strategic position of the new state but also the apprehension that it might develop into a focus of unrest and destabilize the former Polish territories in the Western part of the Russian Empire. The Duchy of Warsaw made up only a small part of the former Rzeczpospolita that before the first partition in 1772 had comprehended over 730.000 square kilometers. The population had numbered about 11 million. By contrast, in 1807 the Duchy of Warsaw comprised 102.744 square kilometers and a population of less than 2.6 million. As a consequence of the Austrian cessions of territory in Galicia in 1809 the surface was to increase to 155.430 square kilometers and the population to 4.3 million.[24] The surface of the Grand-Duchy thus attained a little more than one fifth of the surface of the ancient Polish elective Kingdom. As the partitioning powers had apprehended the Poles regarded its foundation as the beginning of their national revival and, allied to the apparently invincible Emperor of the French, made strong efforts to liberate and reunite to the Grand-Duchy also those parts of their country that had been annexed by the neighbouring great powers. The Polish patriots had placed their hopes on Napoleon already at the period of the Directory, when Polish exiles, organized in legions, fought in Italy against Austria, one of the three partitioning powers, under the leadership of the young general Bonaparte in the hope of earning French support for the liberation of their country. On 20 January 1797 the leader of the Polish legions, General Jan Henrik Dąbrowski, appealed to his compatriots to join him with a view "to fighting for freedom under the valiant Bonaparte." The appeal goes on stating: "The triumph of the French Republic is our only hope left."[25] When Napoleon after his victory at Jena and Auerstedt in November 1806 was about to invade Prussia's Polish provinces, the same Dąbrowski together with Józef Wybicki appealed again to his compatriots and invited them to fight for their freedom side by side with Napoleon: "Poles! It is in your hand to live and to possess a fatherland. Your avenger, your creator has arrived."[26]

In order to counter the menace at the Western border of his Empire Tsar Alexander towards the end of the year 1810 considered waging a new war against France. For such an undertaking he needed the support of the Poles. Napoleon had in the meantime strengthened the Grand-Duchy. In May 1811 the Pol-

---

24 Piotr S. Wandycz, *The Lands of Partitioned Poland, 1795–1918* (Seattle and London: University of Washington Press, 1974), 3, 43.

25 Proclamation aux Polonais, pour leur annoncer la formation des légions d'Italie, 20 January 1797, in: Angeberg, *Recueil Pologne*, 423.

26 Proclamation de Jean-Henri Dombrowski et Joseph Wybicki aux Polonais, 3 November 1806, ibid., 441.

ish army numbered no less than 60.000 men. With such an enemy in the rear Alexander could not dare to send his army on the road to France. Therefore he had no choice but to try to release the Poles from their alliance with Napoleon and to lure them into the Russian camp. The plan had a chance of success only if he convinced them that it was him rather than Napoleon who was able to meet their national aspirations. On 25 December he disclosed his plans to Czartoryski. The moment had arrived, wrote Alexander, "to prove to the Poles that Russia was not their enemy," but "their real and natural friend." They should realize that it was from Russia that they could expect the restoration of their Kingdom. Alexander thought of opening the campaign with a public proclamation of this war aim.[27] In his reply Czartoryski confirmed to the Tsar that all Poles desired the reunification of their country, "the unification of all their parts into a single nation, under a national and constitutional government."[28] However, it would not be easy to convince them that this objective was easier to attain with Russian help than in alliance with Napoleon. The Poles regarded the French as their friends and the Russians as their inveterate foes, "both for political reasons and from personal aversion."[29] Since Russia had gained the greatest area increase at the Polish partitions it would not be sufficient for the Tsar to promise to them the preservation of the Grand-Duchy of Warsaw. If he wanted to secure the support of the Poles in the war against Napoleon, he had to grant the fulfillment of three conditions: The reintroduction of the Polish constitution of 1791, the unification of all Poles under one government and sufficient opportunities for the Poles to sell their products on the international market.[30] In principle, the Tsar assented to these demands and agreed that in the future the rivers Duna, Beresina, and Dnjepr form the Eastern borders of Poland, but posed two conditions. On the one hand the Kingdom of Poland was for all times to remain tied to Russia in a personal union, on the other hand he requested an unequivocal declaration by the Polish nation, presented in writing by the leading representatives of the country, to the effect that the Poles were ready to join the Tsar.[31] This promise Alexander could not obtain. Instead the Polish elite continued to place their hopes on the Emperor of the French.[32]

---

27 L'empereur au prince Adam Czartoryski, 25 December 1810, in: Czartoryski, *Mémoires*, vol. 2, 250 – 51.
28 Le prince Adam Czartoryski à l'empereur, 18/30 January 1811, ibid., 256.
29 Ibid., 258.
30 Ibid., 260 – 61.
31 L'empereur au prince Czartoryski, 31 January 1811, ibid., 272.
32 Zawadzki, *Man*, 201.

In May 1811 the Lithuanian prince Michał Ogiński proposed to the Tsar to unite the eight provinces of the former Rzeczpospolita which Russia had acquired at the Polish partitions, under the historic name of Lithuania and transform them into an autonomous political entity. The head of this state should be appointed by the Tsar. Lithuania should get its own court and a parliament. The ancient Lithuanian laws should remain in force. By such a substantial concession to the patriotic hopes of the Poles Alexander would, so Ogiński believed, exert greater attraction on this nation than Napoleon.[33] The proposal was presented at this moment, because Ogiński was convinced that a war between Russia and France was impending. As long as the Poles believed, Ogiński continued, that Napoleon was determined to restore the ancient Polish commonwealth he would win the sympathy even of those members of that nation who lived under the Tsar. In case of war this would endanger the Russian cause. Napoleon had already sent several times delegates into the Russian parts of ancient Poland ordering them to incite the inhabitants to sedition and to assure them that he would extend the borders of Poland to the Volga.[34] To a powerful Empire it was easy to conquer new provinces, but it took many years in the conquered territories "to win the inhabitants over to its side, to accustom them to the change and to make them forget their former existence."[35] In this respect Napoleon was a model. As soon as he had conquered a piece of territory he imposed a constitution and carried through reforms in order to obtain the assent of the population. By instituting the Grand-Duchy of Warsaw he had won over not only the citizens of this state but also the inhabitants of the eight Western governments of Russia who from now on placed their hope of restoration of an independent Polish state on Napoleon. Therefore Ogiński recommended to the Tsar to steal a march upon Napoleon and to employ the Napoleonic method in these governments. As soon as the war broke out Alexander should declare himself King of Poland. By the foundation of an autonomous Lithuanian state within the Russian empire the Tsar would tie "the almost eight million inhabitants of these territories to himself" and at the same time secure "the support of the Poles in the Duchy of Warsaw." Napoleon on the other hand would lose his partisans in the Russian part of

---

33 Michał Ogiński, "Mémoire du prince Michel-Cléophas Ogiński, ancien grand-trésorier de Lithuanie, adressé à l'empereur Alexandre Ier, sur les intentions de l'empereur Napoléon Ier à l'égard de la Pologne, et sur ce que devrait faire Alexandre Ier à l'égard de la Pologne en général, et de la Lithuanie en particulier, dans le cas d'une guerre entre la Russie et la France, 3/15 May 1811," in: Angeberg, *Recueil Pologne*, 521–529.
34 Ibid., 523.
35 Ibid., 525.

Poland and the inhabitants of the Grand-Duchy of Warsaw would share the admiration and gratitude of the Lithuanians towards the Tsar.[36]

Alexander was impressed by Ogiński's memorandum and asked him to define the steps to be taken one after the other for putting into practice his proposals. Thereupon in October 1811 Ogiński presented the Tsar with the draught of an ordinance about the organization of Lithuania. The first article announced the transformation of the Western governments into a single province by the name of Grand-Duchy of Lithuania. The capital of the province was to be Vil'njus, its official language Polish.[37]

On 1 December 1811 Ogiński transmitted a further memorandum to the Tsar in which he went beyond the recommendations of May and suggested that the Tsar immediately adopt the title of King of Poland for the Grand-Duchy of Lithuania. This would assure the citizens of the Grand-Duchy of Warsaw that the Tsar was determined to restore the Kingdom of Poland. Ogiński expected that sooner or later the Grand-Duchy of Warsaw would be united with Lithuania. In detail he proposed that the Tsar issue a "proclamation to the Polish nation in which he promised a constitution" which "comes close to" the constitution of 3 May 1791.[38]

In an oral comment of 15 December 1811 Tsar Alexander disclosed sympathy towards Ogiński's new considerations. The restoration of Poland would not in the least contradict Russian interests and would not lead to the "alienation of the conquered provinces" the inhabitants of which would surely be "happy and satisfied if they received a constitution." He would be ready to adopt the name of King of Poland if by this act he "could please all Poles."[39]

Less than a year later Napoleon's Russian campaign ended in failure. When Russian troops were about to occupy the Grand-Duchy of Warsaw, Czartoryski asked the Tsar if he now intended to return to his former projects concerning Poland.[40] Alexander replied that he had not departed from his former convictions but added that a number of difficulties had to be overcome before his ideas could be put into practice. Since the Poles had invaded Russia in Napoleon's company the readiness to restore former Polish territory had declined in his country. In addition, if he announced the restoration of Poland he would drive Austria and Prussia into the French camp at the very moment when after the fail-

36 Ibid., 526–528.

37 Ogiński, "Projet d'oukase sur l'organisation du grand-duché de Lithuanie, 10/12 October 1811," ibid., 531–532.

38 Id., Mémoire, 19 November/1 December 1811, ibid., 538–540.

39 Réponse verbale de l'empereur Alexandre Ier, 15 December 1811, ibid., 540–541.

40 Le prince Adam Czartoryski à l'empereur, 6 December 1812, in: Czartoryski, *Mémoires*, vol. 2, 297.

ure of the Grande Armée he could hope to persuade them to leave the Napoleon-ic alliance.[41] Since Alexander was determined to pursue Napoleon all the way to Paris he was obliged to win over on his side the two German great powers and to offer them something in exchange. Since Napoleon had not been defeated yet a change of alliances was not without risks for the two powers. In this situation the interests of the Polish patriots had to be set aside. Through the treaty of alliance of Kalisz and Breslau he concluded with King Frederick William III of Prussia at the end of February 1813, the Tsar promised to the Prussian King the restoration of part of the former Polish territories he had ceded in the peace of Tilsit. In the second of the secret articles he inserted an express guarantee of the preservation of East Prussia including an area that would connect this province with Silesia.[42] Since 1807 this area belonged to the Duchy of Warsaw. By these promises the Tsar succeeded in winning the Prussian King from the French alliance over on his side in the war against Napoleon. It follows that a complete restoration of the ancient Polish Rzeczpospolita conflicted even in the eyes of the Tsar with overall European interests. Notwithstanding the Russian concessions to Prussia Czartoryski did not abandon his hopes that Alexander would abide by his plans of giving birth to a greater Polish state including at least the remaining parts of Polish territory and the Western governments of Russia.[43]

But even against this project resistance was growing among the elites of the Empire, even in the very entourage of the Tsar. One of his closest confidants, Karl Robert von Nesselrode, in early 1813 opposed Czartoryski's proposals in a mem-orandum for Alexander.[44] He reminded the Tsar that ever since 1805 the Russian government had always offered to the Poles its help for the recovery of the lost provinces when in exchange it could expect Polish support in the war against France. The last offer of this kind had been made towards the end of 1810. If Po-land had consented Russia could have enlarged her forces by 40.000 men and secured her routes of communication with Germany and France. However, the restoration of Poland had always been looked upon from the angle of Russian interests, not as an objective in itself. Today there was nothing left to gain for Russia in Poland. The army of the Duchy of Warsaw had been reduced to 8.000 men, the treasury was heavily indebted. The restoration of ancient Poland would drive Austria on Napoleon's side and Russia would lose valuable provin-

---

41 L'empereur au prince Adam Czartoryski, 13 January 1813, ibid., 303–304.
42 Traité de paix, d'amitié et d'alliance conclu entre la Russie et la Prusse, à Kalisch, le 16/28 février, et à Breslau le 27 février 1813, in: Martens, *Nouveau Recueil*, vol. 3, 237–238.
43 Le prince Adam Czartoryski à l'empereur, 23 April/4 May 1813, in: Czartoryski, *Mémoires*, vol. 2, 309–315; id. to id., 27 April 1813, ibid., 315–325.
44 For the date see Zawadzki, *Man*, 214, n. 20.

ces. Even if at first they lived under the same monarch, Poland would make every effort to obtain complete independence. The tsar could not be expected to reconcile the roles of an autocrat in Russia and a constitutional king in Poland. Nesselrode's last argument against the restoration of Poland was the "extreme repugnance" every Russian would feel. The nation had "declared itself strongly opposed to the restoration of Poland." Its sacrifices had decisively contributed to the defeat of Napoleon by the Tsar. Therefore it would be "neither just nor wise" to disregard its opinions. The nation would consider the restoration of Poland as "a reward" precisely of those provinces of the Empire "that deserved it the least," and an award for those among Napoleons auxiliaries who "during the invasion had committed worse acts of cruelty and barbarism than the French themselves."[45]

In a memorandum of 20 October 1814 another advisor of the Tsar, the Corsican count Carlo Andrea Pozzo di Borgo, argued similarly.[46] He warned against renouncing the Western governments the acquisition of which had been recognized by all countries. Pozzo di Borgo also thought that the title of constitutional King of Poland was incompatible with the title of Emperor and autocrat of all the Russians. The Russians who were conscious of their force and power would be condemned "to an existence without freedom"; the "weak and humiliated" Poles, however, would be permitted "to govern themselves in liberty."[47] In a memorandum of 6 October 1814 Freiherr vom Stein also warned of the unavoidable conflicts between despotic Russia and constitutional Poland. The Poles under Russian dominion would try to attain full independence and the Poles in Austria and Prussia would strive towards union with the remaining parts of their nation.[48]

The opposition to Alexander's plans of Polish restoration referred in the first place to the separation from Russia of the eight "Western governments," annexed by Catherine II, whereas the future of the Grand-Duchy of Warsaw aroused much less criticism at court. This part of Poland had never belonged to Russia. Therefore the Empire would not suffer a loss if it was transformed into a separate

---

45 Copie du mémoire remis à l'empereur Alexandre Ier par le comte Ch. de Nesselrode en 1812 à la suite d'une communication du prince Czartoryski, envoyée de Galicie, et demandant le rétablissement de la Pologne, in: A. de Nesselrode, ed., *Lettres et papiers du chancelier comte de Nesselrode 1760–1850. Extrait de ses archives*, vol. 4: 1812 (Paris: Lahure, 1905), 313–20, 319.
46 Zapiska predstavlennaja imperatoru g-nom Pocco di Borgo, in: Nikolaj Turgenev, *Rossija i russkie*, translated from the French by S. V. Žitomirskij (Moscow 2001), 493–500.
47 Ibid., 496.
48 Denkschrift Steins, 6 October 1814, in: Karl vom Stein, *Briefe und amtliche Schriften*, vol. 5, new ed. by Manfred Botzenhart (Stuttgart: Kohlhammer 1964), 158–159.

Kingdom. Though his advisers prevailed on him seriously to envisage this restricted solution of the Polish question it appears that Alexander at first did not take it into consideration. When in October 1814 he arrived at the great congress of the powers at Vienna which was supposed to reorder Europe, he persistently pursued his original plans to unite the Grand-Duchy of Warsaw with the Western governments of the Russian Empire to form a Polish Kingdom under his rule. On 2 October 1814 the British Foreign Secretary Castlereagh reported to Prime Minister Liverpool from Vienna a conversation of two and a half hours with Alexander and his futile attempts to dissuade the Tsar from these plans.[49] In a detailed memorandum to Alexander he after the meeting explained once more the reasons of his opposition to the Russian ideas. Before all he pointed to the menace the new expansion of Russia towards the West would involve for Central Europe and especially for the two German great powers. The proposed frontier was militarily untenable and would for this reason alone undermine the hopes of a durable peace settlement on the continent.[50] At last the Tsar gave in. The final act of the congress provided only for the restricted solution of the Polish question. With the exception of a number of enumerated border provinces and of the district of Cracow the Grand-Duchy of Warsaw was for all times "united to the Russian Empire." The Tsar added to his other titles the dignity of a "King of Poland." The opposition the Tsar had a long time put up against this solution is reflected in the regulation that the Tsar "reserved to himself the right to give to this state which possessed an administration of its own, the interior extension he deemed appropriate."[51] The wording left room to expect that the Tsar would in due course revert to his plans for the restoration of Poland in its original extension.

The constitution of the Kingdom of Poland was proclaimed on 27 November 1815.[52] It was an imposed constitution and resembled in many respects the French Charte constitutionnelle of 4 June 1814. As in France the ruler's possession of undivided sovereignty is not prescribed by the constitution but implied. Accordingly article 4 states that the purpose of the constitution is the definition

---

49 Castlereagh to Liverpool, 2 October 1814, in: Charles K. Webster, ed., *British Diplomacy 1813 – 1815* (London: Bell, 1921), 197– 99.
50 Memorandum de Lord Castlereagh, au sujet des traités entre les alliés relatifs au duché de Varsovie, 4 October 1814, in: Comte d'Angeberg, ed., *Le congrès de Vienne et les traités de 1815, précédé et suivi des actes diplomatiques qui s'y rattachent*, vol. 1 (Paris: Amyot, 1863), 265 – 270.
51 Acte final du Congrès de Vienne, Art. 1, in: Angeberg, *Congrès*, vol. 2, 1389: "S. M. Impériale se réserve de donner à cet État, jouissant d'une administration distincte, l'extension intérieure qu'elle jugera convenable."
52 Charte constitutionnelle du royaume de Pologne de 1815, Varsovie, le 15/27 novembre 1815, in: Angeberg, *Recueil Pologne*, 707– 24.

of "the kind" and "the principle" of the "exercise of sovereignty." The article thus reflects the distinction between possession and exercise of the supreme power, characteristic of the monarchical principle. Article 31 provides for the formation of a national representation (*reprezentacja narodowa*) in a *Sejm* which was to consist of the King and two chambers, the chamber of deputies (*Izba poselska*) and the Senate (*Senat*). The lower chamber is composed of 77 deputies to be delegated by the provincial assemblies of the aristocracy, and of 51 delegates of the towns (Article 118). The number of Senators must not exceed one half of the number of deputies (Article 109). The right to vote depends on the payment of 100 *złoty* of taxes per year. The minimum age of a deputy is fixed at 30 years (Article 121). By these provisions approximately 100.000 citizens were given the right to vote, a remarkable number if one takes into consideration that in contemporary France with a population of ten times the size, only 80.000 citizens were enfranchised.[53] Article 86 attributes the legislative power to the King and the two chambers. The right to initiate law is reserved to the monarch alone (Articles 90, 94). There is no mention of a right of the chambers to petition the King for the introduction of a bill as in articles 19 to 21 of the French Charte. The *Sejm* assembles every two years in Warsaw (Article 87). In addition the King is empowered to summon extraordinary diets (Article 88). Under the heading of general guarantees (*zaręczenia ogólne*) in the articles 11 to 34 the constitution contained a catalogue of fundamental rights, among them the freedom of religion (Article 11), the liberty of the press (Article 16), the equality before the law (Article 17), the principle of *habeas corpus* (Articles 20 and 21), the right of property (Article 26), and the use of the Polish language in the public administration, at court, and in the army (Article 28). Article 29 states that only Poles were admitted in the public service.

A unique provision of the constitution of Congress Poland in comparison to other constitutions of the period is the connection of the Kingdom with Russia. The first article stated: "The Kingdom of Poland is forever connected with the Russian Empire" (*Królestwo Polskie jest na zawsze połączone z Cesarstwem Rosyjskiem*).[54] Conferring the dignities of Emperor of Russia and of King of Poland upon the same person made it imperative to appoint a viceroy in the Kingdom

---

53 Angela T. Pienkos, *The Imperfect Autocrat. Grand Duke Constantine Pavlovich and the Polish Congress Kingdom* (New York: Columbia University Press, 1987), 30.

54 Charte constitutionnelle du royaume de Pologne, Art. 1, 707: "Le royaume de Pologne est à jamais réuni à l'empire de Russie"; see also Acte final du Congrès de Vienne, Art. 1: "Le duché de Varsovie [...] est réuni à l'Empire de Russie. Il y sera lié irrévocablement par sa constitution, pour être possédé par S. M. l'empereur de toutes les Russies, ses héritiers et ses successeurs à perpétuité."

of Poland. The right of appointment belonged to the King. The viceroy was obliged to take residence in the Kingdom and possess Polish citizenship, unless he was a member of the imperial family (Articles 5 and 6). Tsar Alexander appointed viceroy general Zajączek, not, as many had expected, prince Czartoryski. The Russian Empire itself remained without constitution. Unlike Louis XVIII and Charles X, his successor on the French throne, Alexander's political existence did not depend on the consensus of the population of the Kingdom of Poland. As long as his position as autocrat of the Russian Empire remained undisputed, the Tsar remained at any time in the position to suppress eventual Polish resistance with the overwhelming military power of Russia, as in the course of the century was to be demonstrated by the suppression of the November uprising of 1830 and the January revolt of 1863. For this reason Congress Poland was placed under special conditions, different from other constitutional states of the period. In fact constitutional practice soon demonstrated that the foreign King did not make great efforts to meet the aspirations of the citizens.[55]

At the very beginning of his reign the King and Tsar provoked the citizens by two appointments. At first he appointed his brutal and undisciplined brother, Grand-Duke Constantine, supreme commander of the Polish army. In numerous letters to the Tsar Czartoryski lamented Constantine's repeated illegal conduct. In the spring of 1816 he reported an incident when the Grand-Duke illegally acted as judge of a citizen, and added that acts of this kind destroyed "public security" and "annihilated" all benefits of the Tsar. He appealed to the Tsar to remove Constantine.[56] A few weeks later Czartoryski wrote that Constantine's conduct obstructed the beneficial policies of the Tsar in Poland and prevented them from bearing fruit as he had hoped.[57] This was a devastating assessment of Alexander's constitutional policies in Poland. His second provocation was the appointment of Nikolaj N. Novosil'cev as his "delegate and plenipotentiary" in Poland.[58] During the following 15 years Novosil'cev intervened at liberty in all sections of the interior administration of the Kingdom and thereby gained considerable influence. His position had not been provided for in the constitution and clearly contradicted its article 29 which stated that the public service was reserved to Poles alone.

---

55 Frank W. Thackeray, *Antecedents of Revolution: Alexander I and the Polish Kingdom, 1815– 1825* (New York: Columbia University Press, 1980), 21: "In fact, the constitution was breached in substance and spirit even before its promulgation."

56 Czartoryski to Tsar Alexander, 24 March/5 April 1816, in: id., *Mémoires*, vol.2, 358.

57 Czartoryski to Tsar Alexander, 1/13 May 1816, ibid., 366.

58 Thackeray, *Antecedents*, 26

Formally, the imposition of the Charte constitutionnelle for Poland resembled the impositions in other monarchies of the continent in the course of the century. It was different, however, in that the imposing monarch was a foreign conqueror. The purpose of the imposition was, as everywhere, restoration in the sense of an enduring consolidation of monarchical rule. However, in the Polish case the restoration did not concern an ancient monarchy that had become fragile. Instead it aimed at the acquisition of consent on the part of the citizens to a recent military conquest which at the congress of Vienna had obtained the sanction of the law of nations. Alexander believed that the government of a new ruler could be stabilized by a constitution and that in this way peace would be secured as well.[59] By the same method Napoleon had already tried everywhere in Europe to render his conquests permanent. In Poland he had, as has been shown, in 1807 and 1809 founded the Grand-Duchy of Warsaw and provided it with a constitution. An essential difference between the restorations in France and in Poland is to be seen in the fact that in Poland the Tsar not only restored the monarchy, but accorded the nation a new Polish state with a Polish name, after an interruption of twenty years. He was a foreign sovereign belonging to a foreign dynasty, to be sure, but this disadvantage was doubly offset by constitutional law and through national policy, and the citizens of Poland had twofold reason to put their trust in the new ruler. Admittedly the national legitimacy of the new Kingdom depended, for the time being, more on the vague hopes of the citizens than on the actual fulfillment of their aspirations which extended far beyond the borders of the Kingdom.

The correspondence between Tsar Alexander and prince Czartoryski that followed Napoleon's debacle in Russia reveals how between Napoleon and Alexander a downright competition had arisen for the most efficient concept of restoration and for the consent of the citizens of the Kingdom. From the beginning a twofold objective was at the center of all considerations: the creation of a separate state and the concession of a constitution. At the bottom of this competition was the struggle for power on the continent. If, however, restoration is tied so narrowly to actual requirements of power politics, the sincerity of a concession may appear doubtful. Louis XVIII had in 1814 acted from the insight that if the Bourbon monarchy wanted once more to take root in France, he had to meet the expectations of the nation as they had developed during the Revolution and under Napoleon. His brother and successor Charles X did not respect this

---

59 Janet M. Hartley, "The 'Constitutions' of Finland and Poland in the Reign of Alexander I: Blueprints for Reform in Russia?", in: Michael Branch, Janet Hartley, and Antoni Mączak, eds., *Finland and Poland in the Russian Empire. A Comparative Study* (London: School of Slavonic and East European Studies, University of London, 1995), 49.

requirement. The consequence was the fall of the regime only six years after his accession to the throne. If the Tsar had given to the Poles a liberal constitution only because he had to outmatch Napoleon in order to win over the Poles, his generosity would certainly have declined as soon as Napoleon was overthrown.

From a constitutional point of view Alexander's persistent search for a greater Polish solution was consistent. If the imposition of a liberal constitution should permanently reconcile the subjects of the Kingdom with their foreign ruler the whole nation had to partake of its benefits as in France in 1814 and in Spain in 1834 and not only a segment of the nation which had been carved out of the whole more or less arbitrarily by the vicissitudes of European power politics. The connection of the new Polish state with the Russian Empire by personal union was a source of distrust on all sides. Whereas Metternich and Castlereagh saw in the creation of the Kingdom of Poland nothing but the veiling of the factual Western expansion of the Russian Empire, the Russian opponents of a greater Polish solution were afraid that the unification of the Western governments with the new Kingdom of Poland would only be the first step towards their separation from Russia.

At first sight it may have appeared strange to place the imposition of the Polish constitution on the same level as the imposition of the Charte constitutionnelle in France, since the Kingdom of Poland of 1815 was a new creation and the Houses Romanov had never before occupied the Polish throne. Nevertheless, the Polish constitution was imposed no less than the French one with a view to stabilizing a monarchy the future of which appeared uncertain in the face of the revolutionary menace. In this sense here as elsewhere an attempt was made to restore monarchical legitimacy.

In 1825 Alexander I unexpectedly died in Taganrog on the Sea of Azov. His brother and successor Nicholas I at first retained the Polish constitution but was unable to gain the confidence of the citizens of the Kingdom. The revolutions of 1830 in France and in Belgium extended to East-Central Europe. On 29 November an uprising occurred in Warsaw, and on 25 January 1831 the Sejm deposed King Nicholas. On 30 January Adam Czartoryski was elected president of a national government. By law of 8 February Poland was again defined as a constitutional monarchy and the Sejm was obliged soon to elect a new King.[60] But the Russian government refused to release the Kingdom of Poland into independence. In September 1831 Warsaw surrendered. The constitution of 1815 was abolished and former Congress Poland became part of the Russian Empire.

---

60 Wandycz, *Lands*, 105–109; Zawadzki, *Man*, 300–307.

Germany 1818 – 1848

In the person of Louis XVIII the dynasty returned to France which had governed the country since the 16th century. Through the peace of Paris of May 1814 the great powers confirmed the territorial extension the monarchy had possessed at its fall in 1792. The King himself emphasized the uninterrupted existence of the monarchy since Saint-Louis, and Jacques-Claude Beugnot equated the imposition of the *Charte constitutionnelle* with the bestowal of privileges by the French Kings of the Middle Ages. As to the restoration in Germany the contemporaries could scarcely have found adequate parallels in history and only in a small number of cases was there a question of reinstatement of dynasties. There had been no revolution and if monarchies had disappeared, it was due to the influence of Napoleon and was carried through by way of international treaties and Imperial legislation. The imposition of constitutions since 1814 served to consolidate monarchies which in many cases had greatly expanded at the Napoleonic period. To the majority of the citizens of Baden, for example, Grand Duke Charles Frederick was a new monarch. The same is true for a great many citizens of Bavaria and Württemberg and their rulers. The inhabitants of the former ecclesiastical territories on the Rhine were, in one blow, transformed into subjects of the protestant house of Hohenzollern. In the German states restoration aimed less at a return to the past than at the consolidation of divine right monarchy in the present. Notwithstanding the undeniable attempts at ceremonial and ideological revival of historical memories the policy of restoration sought in the first place to meet the requirements of the future. After the fall of Napoleon, Europe was in need of political stability and of securities against a continuation of war and revolution. A policy of restoration in this sense was pursued not only by ancient dynasties, but in new monarchies and under new dynasties as well.

Germany resembled France in that the age of Napoleon was followed by an era of monarchical constitutionalism. Whereas during the early modern period France had developed into a centralized monarchy with the royal court at its summit, the German Empire at the outbreak of the French Revolution was fragmented into a great number of single territories.[1] On the European stage the German Emperor's standing was based exclusively on the power he derived from the lands of his crown. Within the Empire itself his influence was limited. At the hands of Napoleon between 1801 and 1806 the territorial fragmentation of the Empire was reduced to approximately forty units, both by the secularization of

---

[1] Ingo Knecht, *Der Reichsdeputationshauptschluß vom 25. Februar 1803. Rechtmäßigkeit, Rechtswirksamkeit und verfassungsgeschichtliche Bedeutung* (Berlin: Duncker & Humblot, 2007), 29.

DOI 10.1515/9783110524536-003

the ecclesiastical and by the mediatization of many small and medium-sized secular estates. The ecclesiastical estates, the knighthoods and almost the totality of the numerous Imperial cities, not mentioning a great number of principalities and counties, were annexed by their more powerful neighbours. This far-reaching transformation of Germany had originated from the cession in 1801 of the left bank of the Rhine to France through the peace treaty of Lunéville. Under article seven of this treaty the Empire was obliged to indemnify those hereditary princes on the right bank of the Rhine whose territories had been located in part or as a whole to the left of the Rhine. In preparation of the indemnification process the Imperial Diet of Regensburg formed a *Reichsdeputation*, a committee composed of plenipotentiaries of several Imperial estates. The committee based its deliberations on a comprehensive outline which France and Russia had agreed upon beforehand. On 25 February 1803 the committee voted a draught resolution for the Diet. This draught resolution (*Reichsdeputationshauptschluß*) was adopted by the Diet as a fundamental law of the Empire (*Reichsgrundgesetz*) on 24 March.[2] The territorial shifts provided for by the law went far beyond the necessities of indemnifying. The secular territories located west of the Rhine the cession of which to France entitled to indemnities, comprised 463 square miles. The ecclesiastical territories east of the Rhine which were subject to secularization with only one exception, comprised as many as 1.131 square miles.[3] Even if only ecclesiastical territories had been used for indemnification, the greater part of them could have been preserved. The mediatization of the 41 imperial cities east of the Rhine, as prescribed by paragraph 27 of the Reichsdeputationshauptschluß, could well have been left undone. This shows that the principle of indemnification was only a pretext for a general restructuring of Central Europe. Similarly, the arbitrary annexation of the Imperial knights' territories by their neighbors in the following years and the mediatization of numerous principalities and counties by the peace treaty of Preßburg of 1805 and the Act of the Confederation of the Rhine (*Rheinbundakte*) of 1806 exclusively sprang from the political interests of the French Empire and the expansionist tendencies of many German princes. In the course of the territorial reorganization of Germany a great many of them not only were accorded considerable territorial accretions but also an upgrading of ranks. In Southern Germany the Elector of Bavaria and the Duke of Württemberg were promoted to the rank of Kings and the Margrave of Baden was made a Grand Duke. In the course of these developments the

---

2 Ibid., 50, 109; the text in: Ernst Rudolf Huber, ed., *Dokumente zur deutschen Verfassungsgeschichte*, vol. 1, 3rd ed. (Stuttgart: Kohlhammer, 1978), 1– 28.

3 Knecht, *Reichsdeputationshauptschluß*, 190.

German princes became partisans of Napoleon because it was to him that they owed the unprecedented growth of power and status. Napoleon alone could guarantee their new dignities and the permanent possession of their territorial acquisitions in the face of the great powers. The Empire itself succumbed in this process. On 6 August 1806 Emperor Francis II deposed the Imperial crown and thereby formally dissolved the Empire, after he had already in 1804, contrary to Imperial law, arbitrarily adopted the dignity of Emperor of Austria. For two years he had simultaneously possessed two Imperial crowns – the ancient German and the new Austrian one. By the dissolution of the Empire the former Imperial estates were turned into sovereign states.

After the fall of Napoleon in April 1814 the German Empire was not restored. The German princes clung to their only recently acquired sovereignty and refused to renounce their territorial acquisitions. In the interest of their external security and of the general peace in Europe the German states were bound together in the German Confederation (*Deutscher Bund*). Between the congress of Vienna and the outbreak of the revolution of 1848 in all German states with the exception of Austria and Prussia constitutions were imposed. Only in Württemberg the constitution of 1819 was the result of a convention between King and diet. Nevertheless, here as well, the King claimed unlimited sovereignty for the crown. According to § 4 of the constitution of Württemberg the King "united in himself full public power" and "exercised it in accordance with the constitution."[4] Prussia and Austria received constitutions only in the revolution of 1848 and 1849. The Austrian emperor Francis Joseph, however, repealed the constitution he had imposed under the pressure of revolution, as early as 1851.

As in France in 1814 constitutions were imposed in Germany with a view to consolidating divine right monarchy. But the circumstances were different. The German states had never before possessed modern representative constitutions and unlike the Bourbons of France no German dynasty had been deposed in a revolution. Nevertheless, in the German states as well the imposition of constitutions was a compromise between monarch and subject. In the course of the territorial restructuring of Germany and the far-reaching reforms of the Napoleonic period many ancient rights had been violated and almost all those institutions had disappeared upon which in the Holy Roman Empire security and liberty of the subjects had depended. The intermediate powers which to Montesquieu had been the safe-guards of liberty in a monarchy had largely been abolished. By the recent reforms the German princes had gained a degree

---

4 Verfassungsurkunde für das Königreich Württemberg vom 25. September 1819, in: Huber, *Dokumente*, vol. 1, 188.

of power without precedent, all the more so since with the Imperial Privy Council (*Reichshofrat*), the Imperial Chamber Court (*Reichskammergericht*), and the Emperor himself all those institutions had disappeared to which in the Ancien Régime citizens and estates could appeal against their superiors. The most vehement criticism of the despotism of the member princes of the Confederation of the Rhine was pronounced by Karl Freiherr vom Stein who in 1812 had entered the service of Tsar Alexander. He demanded that after the banishment of Napoleon in the German states be restored a state of things which granted to the single citizen "the safety of his person and his property."[5] The guarantors were to be the territorial estates (*Landstände*). Stein demanded that in the course of the reorganization of Germany estates should be introduced in every state.[6] From the experience of 1789 Stein had learned the lesson that political suppression sooner or later ends up in revolution. Therefore Bernd Wunder identified his call for a state under the rule of law (*Rechtsstaat*) to protect the subjects from arbitrary power, as "part of an antirevolutionary policy of restoration."[7] Stein was not alone in arguing along these lines. The envoy of Hesse-Darmstadt, Türckheim, reported on 21 September from Vienna, "the general tendency" at the congress was the conviction "that it was imperative to provide for the liberty of the German citizen and for security against arbitrary power and in this way effectively to prevent future revolutions."[8] Accordingly into the German Federal Act (*Deutsche Bundesakte*) was inserted article 13 which obliged every member state to introduce a constitution providing for "territorial estates" (*landständische Verfassungen*).[9]

Estates had existed in most territories of the ancient Empire. But Stein did not propose the restoration of the historical bodies. Such an attempt would have met with a number of difficulties. In states which at the time of Napoleon had expanded through annexation of neighboring territories the estates would have to be created anew with a competence for the enlarged state as a whole. In territories that had never possessed estates, they would have to be introduced for the first time. Unlike the estates of the Old Regime all estates should from now on be given not an imperative but a free mandate. It follows that for a vari-

---

5 Karl vom Stein, "Verfassungsdenkschrift," Prague, end of August 1813, in: idem, *Briefe und amtliche Schriften*, vol. 4, new edition by Walther Hubatsch (Stuttgart: Kohlhammer, 1963), 239.
6 Bernd Wunder, "Landstände und Rechtsstaat. Zur Entstehung und Verwirklichung des Art. 13 DBA," *Zeitschrift für Historische Forschung* 5 (1978), 144–150.
7 Ibid., 153.
8 Quoted from ibid., 161.
9 "Deutsche Bundesakte," 8 June 1815, art. 13, in: Huber, *Dokumente*, vol. 1, 88: "In every federal state a territorial constitution will take place."

ety of reasons article 13 of the German Federal Act of 1815 did not aim at the return to the institutions of the ancient Empire. Not in this sense it was meant to promote restoration, but by stabilizing the German monarchies and in this way rendering them secure from future revolutions. If by restoration something had to be confirmed, it was divine right monarchy regardless whether a monarch had governed his present territory already before the Revolution or not.

By inserting article 13 in the Federal Act and the Federal Act in the Final Act of the congress of Vienna the policy of restoration was made a concern of Europe as a whole. The same objective is already visible in the second peace treaty of Paris of 1815 in which the great powers obliged Louis XVIII to stabilize "the happily restored political order in France" by preserving royal authority" and by "restoring the Charte constitutionnelle."[10] After his return from the island of Elba, Napoleon had replaced the charte by the *Acte additionnel aux constitutions de l'Empire.*

The constitutional history of Germany between the fall of Napoleon and the revolution of 1848 may be studied by way of example in Bavaria, Württemberg, and Baden. In these three South German states constitutions were introduced only a few years after the congress of Vienna. As far as the two German great powers are concerned special attention is due to Prussia, since the constitution which had been imposed in the revolution of 1848 was afterwards revised, it is true, but not abrogated again as in Austria.

Unlike many other estates of the former German Empire the Electorate of Bavaria, the Duchy of Württemberg, and the Margraviate of Baden were preserved from annihilation in the age of Napoleon. They formed part of the so-called Third Germany, that is to say, of Germany other than the great powers Austria and Prussia. However, they were transformed to a degree that to all intents and purposes they were founded anew. The annexation of neighboring ecclesiastical and secular dominions, Imperial knighthoods, and Imperial cities bestowed upon them enormous accretions of territory. The reforms of the Napoleonic period aimed essentially at integrating the new provinces and subjects into the enlarged states. In July 1806 the new Kingdoms of Württemberg and Bavaria, the Grand Duchy of Baden, and the remaining small and medium-sized states the existence of which had been preserved by Napoleon, were bound together to form the Confederation of the Rhine (*Rheinbund*). Simultaneously they resigned membership in the German Empire.

---

10 Second Peace of Paris, 20 November 1815, in: Comte d'Angeberg (Leonard Jakob Borejko Chod'zko), ed., *Le congrès de Vienne et les traités de 1815,* vol. 2 (Paris: Amyot, 1863), 1596; Volker Sellin, *Die geraubte Revolution. Der Sturz Napoleons und die Restauration in Europa* (Göttingen: Vandenhoeck & Ruprecht, 2001), 285–286.

Government in the member states of the Confederation of the Rhine was centralized, modern, efficient, and practically unlimited. Doubtful was its legitimacy. Both the destruction of the German Empire and the expansion and restructuring of the single states were the result of violent and unlawful usurpations. For the time being Napoleon watched over the maintenance of the new political system. When his power began to decline the member princes of the Confederation became afraid that they would have to return at least part of their acquisitions. In order to avoid this eventuality they entered into negotiations with the powers of the anti-Napoleonic coalition asking for a guarantee of their possessions. King Maximilian of Bavaria took the lead. On 8 October 1813 he concluded the treaty of Ried with Austria. Other treaties between Austria and the medium-sized German states followed. As long as France had not been defeated the Austrian foreign minister Clemens Metternich deemed it more important to win over Napoleon's German allies than to contest their acquisitions. This did not prevent the victims of the political reorganization of Germany from fighting for the recovery of their former rights as before. As late as the congress of Vienna the princes who had once been directly subject to the Empire and had since by force been subjected to a more powerful neighbor, tried to recover at least a certain measure of independence. Conflicts arose also when territories subject to mediatization were claimed by more than one neighboring prince. Long after the congress of Vienna the King of Bavaria continued to claim the territories of the former Electorate Palatine located east of the Rhine including Heidelberg and Mannheim. In 1802 they had been accorded to the Grand Duke of Baden. The vast and to a great extent arbitrary territorial reorganization of the period impaired, in the eyes of many contemporary observers, the binding force of existing sovereign rights. In several territories of the Empire the governing personnel had changed more than once during the period. A telling example is the prince-bishopric of Salzburg. In 1803 it was secularized and became a principality. In 1805 it was handed over to Austria. In 1810 it became part of Bavaria and in 1816 it was again accorded to Austria. The bishopric of Würzburg was likewise secularized in 1803 and handed over to the Elector of Bavaria. In 1806 it gained independence under the government of Grand Duke Ferdinand of Tuscany of the house of Habsburg-Lorraine. In 1814 it was again handed over to Bavaria. The Breisgau and Freiburg were in 1803 accorded to the Duke of Modena. Two years later the territory was given to the Grand Duke of Baden. There were many more cases of this kind. It is easy to figure out the consequences that these repeated changes of government must have had on the legitimacy of power. The largest coherent territory to be distributed anew after the fall of Napoleon was the left bank of the Rhine. By the first peace of Paris of 30 May 1814 Louis XVIII had returned it to Germany after 20 years. Since the secular princes who had resided there before the revolutionary wars, had been indemnified by the Reichsdeputationshaupt-schluß, and since the ecclesiastical states had been secularized in the whole of the Empire, there was nobody left who could of right have put in a claim on these territories. The impression that the abandonment of such a vast territory made on the contemporaries, is revealed by a private letter of the former Jacobin and actual judge at the court of appeal at Kaiserslautern Andreas Georg Friedrich Rebmann of 4 September 1815:

> "The gods know if and when our souls in this country will be transferred to Baden, to Darmstadt, to Prussia, or to Austria. If only we remain together and are not subjected to a miniature prince, we might tolerate everything, but unfortunately it is all too probable, that on the Donnersberg not eagles, but crows and magpies make their nests, and that our souls will be used as tokens for balancing and filling up."[11]

In order to restore and strengthen the bonds between sovereigns and subjects, adequate strategies of legitimation had to be implemented. In the course of French imperial expansion Napoleon himself had been confronted with the task of gaining assent among the new subjects and of winning political legitimacy on foreign soil. He put his trust on constitution-making and on the Code civil. In Germany he employed this method for the first time in 1807 after the peace of Tilsit in the Kingdom of Westphalia which he had artificially composed of Prussian and other territories such as the Landgraviate of Hessen-Kassel and the Principality of Braunschweig-Wolfenbüttel. Appointed King of Westphalia was his younger brother Jérôme. Napoleon's methods of winning legitimacy are revealed in a letter of 15 November 1807 by which he transmitted to Jérôme a constitution for the new Kingdom. He reminded his brother that there was no safety for his throne but "the trust and the love of the population." Trust and love, however, he would only obtain by securing freedom and the rule of law as promised in the constitution. Once the former Prussian subjects in the Kingdom of Westphalia enjoyed the benefits of a wise and liberal government, they would never want to return under the arbitrary regime they had abandoned.[12] One

---

11 Rebmann to Hermes, Kaiserslautern, 4 September 1815, in: Günther Volz (ed.), "Briefe Andreas Georg Friedrich Rebmanns an Johann Peter Job Hermes aus den Jahren 1815 und 1816," *Mitteilungen des Historischen Vereins der Pfalz* 57 (1959), 178; Volker Sellin, "'Heute ist die Revolution monarchisch'. Legitimität und Legitimierungspolitik im Zeitalter des Wiener Kongresses," *Quellen und Forschungen aus italienischen Archiven und Bibliotheken* 76 (1996), 348; idem, *Gewalt und Legitimität. Die europäische Monarchie im Zeitalter der Revolutionen* (Munich: Oldenbourg 2011), 210 – 211.
12 Napoléon Bonaparte to Jérôme Bonaparte, 15 November 1807, in: Napoléon Ier, *Correspondance*, vol. 16, Paris 1864, no. 13361, 166; a survey of the history of the Kingdom of Westphalia

year later, under the pressure of Napoleon, Bavaria also received a constitution which, however, was never put into practice.

Among the most important addressees of Napoleon's policy of legitimization were the *Standesherren*. By the Act of the Confederation of the Rhine of 1806 the former imperial princes and counts who under the Ancien Régime had known no superior but the Emperor, were subjected to the middle-sized states which had been enlarged in 1803. They only reluctantly resigned themselves to the subjection to other princes who were their equals in rank. In a petition directed to King Frederick I in the spring of 1816 the Standesherren of Württemberg argued that they had never assented to the Act of the Confederation of the Rhine. Therefore they had been incorporated into the Kingdom of Württemberg only in fact, not of right. After the dissolution of the Confederation in 1813 they had *ipso facto* returned to their previous legal situation. Since, however, the German Empire had ceased to exist they had by now attained full sovereignty.[13] The King of Württemberg did not agree. But like the other German princes he sought to compensate the Standesherren for the loss of their legal position under the ancient Empire by granting special privileges to them. These privileges were inserted in the constitutions that were imposed one after the other during the period following the congress of Vienna. The policy of satisfying the Standesherren shows that one of the purposes of the early German constitutions was compensating for the loss of ancient political rights. The most important concession by the recently created sovereigns was the paragraph, as may be exemplified by the constitution of Bavaria (title VI, § 2, no. 4), that to "the heads of families of former Imperial princes and counts was granted" a seat and a vote in the First Chamber. In Baden as well the heads of the families of the Standesherren were made hereditary members of the Upper Chamber (§ 27, no. 2). In Württemberg the First Chamber was precisely named "Chamber of the Standesherren" (§ 129). At least some of the Standesherren acknowledged these privileges as a compensation for the loss of former political rights. This is demonstrated by Leo von Klenze's constitution column (*Konstitutionssäule*) that Franz Erwein count of Schönborn-Wiesentheid who had been forced by the Act of the Confederation of the Rhine to cede his sovereign rights to the King of Bavaria, had erected between 1821 and

---

is offered in Owen Connelly, *Napoleon's Satellite Kingdoms* (New York: The Free Press/London: Macmillan, 1965), 176 – 222.

13 Joachim Gerner, *Vorgeschichte und Entstehung der württembergischen Verfassung im Spiegel der Quellen (1815 – 1819)* (Stuttgart: Kohlhammer, 1989), 336.

1828 near Gaibach in the lower Main district for the glory of the Bavarian constitution.[14]

Accumulation and division of territories had occurred in Germany already under the Ancien Régime. The latest transfers of territory, however, differed in more than one respect from this tradition. The dimension of the process was without precedent and added to the impression of arbitrary violence. At the same time it rendered difficult the integration of the subjects who had in great numbers been assigned to rulers foreign to them. In the Grand Duchy of Baden, every second citizen was a new citizen. Therefore great efforts were required to help create among the newcomers the conviction that they from now on belonged to the new state and to its head. Under the Ancien Régime a ruler who acquired a foreign territory had as a rule left untouched its institutions as they had developed in history. Where there were estates he was obliged to swear an oath that he would respect their privileges and preserve the constitution and the customs of the country. New provinces were simply added to the previous possessions of the acquiring monarch and thus permitted to preserve their identity. The princes of the Confederation of the Rhine, however, adopted the principles that had triumphed in the French Revolution, and subjected their new provinces to a rational and centralized administration with no regard for their historical traditions and borders. The territories which were received into the new states lost their historical identity. At the same time all local instances that had possessed political functions of their own right, were deprived of their powers. Whereas changes of rule or dynasty had in the past occurred in secular territories only, it now happened that ecclesiastical elective monarchies and free cities were subjected to hereditary monarchies and in this way to a form of rule they had not experienced for centuries. Taken together these massive interventions in traditional social relations and rights of possession jeopardized the legitimacy of sovereignty as such and thereby endangered the political stability of the new states.

A solution to the crisis was expected from the imposition of constitutions on the French model. In the Kingdom of Westphalia Napoleon had demonstrated, at least on the programmatic level, how a group of heterogeneous subjects of various origin could by the introduction of a constitution be transformed into a political nation, and after the fall of Napoleon Louis XVIII had shown that a monarch could adopt a constitution without being obliged to let others partake of his

---

14 Sellin, *Gewalt*, 212–215; ibid. a photograph of the constitution column and a reproduction of the painting by Peter von Heß of the laying of the foundation stone of the column on 26 May 1821.

political power. The congress of Vienna had imposed upon the German princes to introduce representative constitutions. Several of them complied with this obligation, among others for the simple reason that they wanted to avoid intervention of the great powers in their interior relations. In the three South German states the elaboration of constitutions began immediately after the breakdown of the French Empire, in obvious continuity to the period of the Confederation of the Rhine. In Bavaria the elaboration of a draught constitution was entrusted to a special committee. Its commission was the "revision of the constitution of 1808."[15] Similarly in Baden the plans of creating a constitution went back to the elevation of the Margraviates to Grand Duchy in 1806.[16] There is another reason why the transition to constitutionalism must be understood as a consequence of confederation politics. The territorial expansion, the implementation of reforms and the never ending wars had in all member states caused a staggering increase of the public debt.[17] In this situation the introduction of representative assemblies was welcome for the simple reason that in this way public finance was subjected to control and the public credit was based on the guarantee of the country.[18]

The first constitution was proclaimed on 26 May 1818 by Maximilian Joseph of Bavaria.[19] Like Louis XVIII at the imposition of the charte the King of Bavaria emphasized two times in the preamble of the document that he had bestowed the constitution of his free will. In this way he underscored his claim to full possession of political power. The claim is repeated elsewhere in the constitution. In the first paragraph of the second title it says that the King is "Head of State" and "assembles in him the totality of public power." Obviously Maximilian sought to counter the impression as if he imposed the constitution for the sole reason to

---

15 Eberhard Weis, "Die Begründung des modernen bayerischen Staates unter König Max I. (1799 – 1825)," in: Max Spindler and Alois Schmid, eds., *Handbuch der bayerischen Geschichte*, vol. 4: *Das neue Bayern. Von 1800 bis zur Gegenwart*, part 1: *Staat und Politik* (Munich: Beck, 2003), 113.

16 Hans-Peter Ullmann, "Baden 1800 – 1830," in: Hansmartin Schwarzmaier, ed., *Handbuch der baden-württembergischen Geschichte*, vol. 3: *Vom Ende des Alten Reiches bis zum Ende der Monarchien* (Stuttgart: Klett-Cotta, 1992), 59 – 61.

17 Hans-Peter Ullmann, "Die öffentlichen Schulden in Bayern und Baden 1780 – 1820," *Historische Zeitschrift* 242 (1986), 34.

18 Hans-Peter Ullmann, *Staatsschulden und Reformpolitik. Die Entstehung moderner öffentlicher Schulden in Bayern und Baden 170 – 1820*, part 1 (Göttingen: Vandenhoeck & Ruprecht, 1986), 230.

19 For a comparative analysis of the constitutions of Bavaria and Baden of 1818 on the background of the *Charte constitutionnelle* see Markus J. Prutsch, *Making Sense of Constitutional Monarchism in Post-Napoleonic France and Germany* (Houndmills: Palgrave Macmillan, 2013).

comply with article 13 of the Federal Act. Accordingly the first article of the constitution states that the Kingdom of Bavaria was a sovereign monarchy. An essential function of a monarchical constitution is the determination of the succession. This was of primary importance in the Grand Duchy of Baden where the succession in the Hochberg line of the House of Zähringen was contested. The King of Bavaria claimed the territories of the former Electorate Palatine on the right bank of the Rhine, including Heidelberg and Mannheim. He based these claims on the doubtful legitimacy of the Hochberg line. Therefore the Baden constitution of 1818 expressly stated its right of succession. In defense of territorial claims of the neighbors § 3 of the constitution confirmed that the Grand Duchy was "indivisible and inalienable in all its parts." Similar regulations are to be found in the constitutions of Bavaria and Württemberg. The significance of these norms must be seen against the background of the territorial revolutions of the preceding years. It was only through the constitutions that the three monarchs obtained a durable guarantee of their possessions. All the South German constitutions were imposed on the citizens. In the preamble to the Bavarian constitution King Maximilian addresses the citizens as "his people," and he alludes to "the happiness of the fatherland" which he intended to promote by the constitution.[20] Grand Duke Charles of Baden hoped by means of the constitution to render closer and closer "the ties of trust that existed between Us and Our people."[21] The constitutions were indeed expected to increase the devotion of every single citizen towards the monarch. At the same time they were meant to melt the great number of citizens of vastly different origin into one nation with a common political conscience. Insofar the talk of a Bavarian or Baden nation went ahead of the actual development. The one nation was imagined as an effect of the constitution. Political and civil liberty were to bring about the political integration of the respective country into a universally accepted community under the monarchy.

Contemporaries emphasized the integrationist effect of the constitutions. Anselm Feuerbach, First President of the court of appeal in formerly Prussian Ansbach, in March 1819 wrote about the Bavarian constitution: "It is hard to believe what a great royal pronouncement such as our constitution can achieve within a short period of time. It was only through this constitution that our King has acquired Ansbach and Bayreuth, Würzburg, Bamberg, and so forth. It has become unthinkable by now that somebody should stand up and suggest

---

20 Verfassungsurkunde für das Königreich Bayern vom 26. Mai 1818, in: Huber, *Dokumente*, vol. 1, 156.

21 Verfassungsurkunde für das Großherzogtum Baden vom 22. August 1818, ibid., 172.

that we adopt other colours than blue and white"![22] Since the proclamation of the constitution only ten months had passed. If Feuerbach expressly emphasizes the shortness of this space of time, the conclusion is permitted that he was already aware of the changing political consciousness, and if he points out that from now on no subject of the King of Bavaria wants to be anything but a Bavarian, regardless under which sovereigns he had lived before, he underlines the integrating and stabilizing effect of this change of consciousness. In the same sense the professor of public law at Freiburg university, Carl von Rotteck, had already in 1818 given his opinion on the constitution of Baden, writing: "We have received a corporate constitution, a political life as a people [...]. We were subjects of Baden-Baden, Baden-Durlach, the Breisgau, the Palatinate, the Landgraviate of Nellenburg, and the Principality of Fürstenberg; we were citizens of Freiburg, of Konstanz, of Mannheim; a people of Baden we were not. But from now on we are a people possessing a common will, an acknowledged common interest, in other words, a common life and a common law. Only now we enter into history and play our own part."[23] There is no doubt: With these words Rotteck described the birth of a new nation. To a monarch who achieved this, a new source of legitimacy was inevitably disclosed. In this sense the constitutional policies of the German medium-sized states served the renewal and consolidation, in short, the restoration of monarchy, restoration not to be understood as a new creation after some kind of disappearance, because it had never been abrogated, but as a process of recovering strength and solidity.

After the crushing defeat at Jena and Auerstedt in October 1806 and the conclusion of the humiliating peace treaty of Tilsit in June 1807 Prussia also initiated a period of social and political reforms to be crowned by a constitution, as King Frederick William III had publicly announced several times. However, it was only during the revolution of 1848 under entirely different circumstances that the promise was fulfilled. There were various reasons for the delay. An essential aim of the Prussian reforms had been the desire to strengthen the state from within and enable it to liberate itself from Napoleonic domination and recover the lost provinces. With the fall of Napoleon and the victory of the coalition over France the objective was accomplished. Another reason for the delay in imposing a constitution was the heterogeneity of Prussian social structure. Whereas the east was agrarian and dominated by the landed aristocracy, in Berlin, on the Rhine and in Westphalia there was already a developed bourgeoisie, active in commerce and industry. Owing to the strong position of the landed aristocracy

---

22 Quoted from Sellin, *Gewalt*, 228.
23 Quoted ibid., 228 – 229.

east of the Elbe, in a chamber elected by census the conservative forces would easily have obtained the majority. On the other hand, even without a modern constitution, the state of Prussia was solid and powerful enough not to fear, like Baden and Württemberg, disintegration of its enlarged territory. As a consequence the country preserved the system of bureaucratic absolutism until the revolution of 1848.

Whereas the King of Naples, the Pope in his capacity as head of the States of the Church, the Grand-Duke of Tuscany, and the King of Sardinia after the outbreak of the revolution in Palermo had imposed constitutions in due time and thereby formally preserved full power, Frederick William IV of Prussia missed the chance to counter the revolutionary movement before it seriously endangered his position. When the revolution reached Berlin in March 1848, he had no choice but to call the meeting of an "assembly for the agreement of the Prussian constitution." In a series of proclamations the King simultaneously promised to fulfill essential demands of the revolution such as the guarantee of the elementary rights of man, ministerial responsibility and the oath of the standing army on the constitution.[24] The Prussian National Assembly met on 22 May 1848 in Berlin. The government presented a draft constitution which a committee of the department of the Prime Minister had elaborated on the model of the Belgian constitution of 1831.[25] By agreement in practice was understood a procedure by which the Crown reserved to itself adoption or rejection of the constitution which the assembly had worked out. In addition it meant that the assembly was expected to avoid resolutions the Crown could not ratify. On 17 June 1848 the constitutional committee of the national assembly initiated the debate on the draft constitution of the government. On 26 July the committee laid its own draft before the assembly.[26] In the following months the decisions of the assembly became more and more radical. A motion of the Left to renounce the principle of agreement and to claim undivided constituent power for the national assembly in its place, was rejected on 16 October, however. On 12 October after a prolonged debate the reference to divine right was removed from the royal title.[27] The deputy Borchardt reminded the assembly that in the March revolution it had depended

---

24 Proklamation des Königs über die Einführung einer konstitutionellen Verfassung, 22 March 1848, in: Huber (ed.), *Dokumente*, vol. 1, 449–450.

25 Gerhard Anschütz, *Die Verfassungs-Urkunde für den Preußischen Staat vom 31. Januar 1850. Ein Kommentar für Wissenschaft und Praxis*, vol. 1 (Berlin: Häring, 1912), 36–37; the text of the draft ibid., 608–614; Sellin, *Revolution*, 314–320.

26 Anschütz, *Verfassungs-Urkunde*, 42; text of the draft ibid., 614–623.

27 Verhandlungen der constituirenden Versammlung für Preußen 1848, vol. 6 (Leipzig: Thomas, 1848), session 73, 12 October 1848, 3920–3953; Sellin, *Gewalt*, 85–86.

"on the will of the people," whether or not "it wanted further to be governed by a King." Therefore the Prussians no longer possessed a "King by divine right," but "a King by the free will of the sovereign nation."[28] Hermann Schulze from Delitzsch asserted that "when a commercial enterprise had run bankrupt," it was not customary to take its name "over to the new business." Since absolutism had run completely bankrupt under the old firm "by divine right," he warned from its continuation.[29] On 31 October the National Assembly abolished the aristocracy.[30]

In anticipation of the development Frederick William IV had already during the summer excogitated scenarios in which he would send the assembly packing. As early as 21 May on the eve of the first session of the assembly he had written to Joseph von Radowitz that one of three cases he was not prepared to tolerate, was the proclamation of national sovereignty by the National Assembly.[31] The question of how to react if the assembly adopted inacceptable resolutions continued to trouble him. On 19 June he again wrote to Radowitz that if the assembly denied him the right to dissolve it and arrogated to themselves the right to present him with "a constitution of their own making" and "vote" it, he would be forced to dissolve it.[32] The King's anxiety for the maintenance of the throne and his claim to monarchical sovereignty was steadily growing. On 15 September a memorandum of his began by the remark that this was "the last chance for saving the throne, Prussia, Germany, and the concept of divine right in Europe."[33] His surroundings partook of his apprehensions. The general adjutant Leopold von Gerlach wrote on 21 October to count Friedrich Wilhelm von Brandenburg who six days later was to be charged with the formation of a new government as successor of Ernst von Pfuel:

> "The King, our sovereign, is in a morass, he feels that he is sinking, he calls for help, but nobody tears him out. Some people shout to him that he was making such inappropriate movements that he would sink even deeper, others that his body was too heavy, one couldn't lift this burden, others affirm they had not placed him there (which is not entirely true as far as the ministers are concerned), still others he should just wait, perhaps he

---

28 Verhandlungen, vol. 6, 3930.
29 Ibid., 946.
30 Ibid., vol. 8, Berlin 1848, session 90, 31 October 1848, 5023.
31 Frederick William IV to Radowitz 21 May 1848, in: Joseph von Radowitz, *Nachgelassene Briefe und Aufzeichnungen zur Geschichte der Jahre 1848 – 1853*, ed. Walter Möring (Stuttgart and Berlin: Deutsche Verlagsanstalt, 1922), 47.
32 Frederick William IV to Radowitz, 19 June 1848, ibid., 56.
33 Promemoria of King Frederick William IV concerning the constitution, 15 September 1848, in: Huber, *Dokumente*, vol. 1, 460.

could find solid ground before the water would close over his head. But nobody wants to act."[34]

The growing radicalization of the National Assembly at last drove the King to action. Under the pretext of liberating it from the pressures from the streets of Berlin, by decree of 8 November 1848 the assembly was transferred to Brandenburg and simultaneously adjourned till 27 November. The deputies reacted by voting a tax boycott. The government regarded this move as proof that with the assembly an agreement about the constitution was unattainable. Since public opinion also distanced itself more and more from the assembly the government proceeded to a coup d'état. On 5 December the King dissolved the assembly and imposed a constitution which left the royal prerogative unimpaired. By the imposition the government preserved the monarchical principle and prevented the national assembly from usurping the constituent power. But the King broke his promise of March to agree the constitution with the representatives of the nation. The entourage of Frederick William was divided in its judgment on the wisdom of this action. Joseph von Radowitz wrote to him from Frankfurt on 21 November:

> "Independently of its material contents the imposed constitution will always be regarded as a breach of all legal foundations and promises, place the Crown in the air and perpetuate the revolution."[35]

Obviously the government knew perfectly well that the dissolution of the chamber and the imposition of the constitution were unconstitutional. It tried to balance this deficiency by rendering the imposed constitution as liberal as possible. In this way it acceded to a demand the fulfillment of which had been judged unavoidable by many observers. Count Bülow, under-secretary of state in the foreign department of Prussia, for example, had admonished as early as 15 November that a dissolution of the National Assembly "would have to be combined with the imposition of a provisional charte, and that this charte would have to be of the most liberal kind."[36] In keeping with this advice the government did not revert to its original draft of 20 May, but to the version which on 26 July had been adopted by the constitutional committee of the National Assembly. However, it made a number of by no means insignificant changes in the committee draft. Among the changes were the replacement of the suspensive veto of the

---

34 Leopold von Gerlach, *Denkwürdigkeiten*, ed. by his daughter, vol. 1 (Berlin: Hertz, 1891), 224.
35 Joseph von Radowitz to Frederick William IV, 21 November 1848, in: Radowitz, *Briefe*, 65.
36 Graf Bülow to Ludolf Camphausen, 15 November 1848, in: Erich Brandenburg, *Untersuchungen und Aktenstücke zur Geschichte der Reichsgründung* (Leipzig: Quelle & Meyer, 1916), 277.

King by the absolute veto and a provision for emergency decrees. The opposition was to be assuaged by article 112 in connection with article 106. Article 106 permitted constitutional amendments by normal legislation. Article 112 stated that the "present constitution" should "be subjected to a revision by way of ordinary legislation immediately after the first meeting of the chambers."[37] By this article the constitution was from the outset declared provisional. From a political point of view the imposition of the constitution must indeed be understood as a device to overcome the stalemate in the relationship between Crown and assembly. It was an expedient by which the government of count Brandenburg sought for the time being to relieve the monarchy from the pressing dangers into which it had fallen. The King would have preferred to do without the imposition of the constitution and not to combine it with the dissolution of the National Assembly. On 23 November he wrote to Otto von Manteuffel:

> "The proclamation of the constitution immediately after the unavoidable dissolution looks, I would like to pronounce it with a voice of thunder, like a studied piece (of comedy) and smells, as wide and as broad as the State of Prussia is, of *mauvaise foi*."[38]

The solution that was chosen, clarifies why count Bülow had spoken of the imposition of a "provisional" charte. Obviously the illegality of the imposition should be smoothed over after the event by the application of article 112 that permitted revision. In other words: Unlike the Charte constitutionnelle in France the Prussian constitution was imposed pending the consent of the Chambers. The revision was prescribed because Frederick William IV saw himself bound by the promise to concert the constitution with the elected representatives of the nation, a promise Louis XVIII had never given.

Articles 106 and 112 should render the imposition acceptable to the public by providing space for the inclusion of demands that had not been taken into account. As Günther Grünthal rightly observes, if the reservation of revision could "not legalize the King's actions in public law, it could – so it was calculated – justify it from a political point of view."[39] On the other hand, the Crown had also reserved for itself a loophole in case of unwelcome developments in the fu-

---

37 Verfassungs-Urkunde für den preußischen Staat vom 5. Dezember 1848, in: Anschütz, *Verfassungs-Urkunde*, 632.

38 Frederick William IV to Otto von Manteuffel, 23 November 1848, in: Otto von Manteuffel, *Unter Friedrich Wilhelm IV. Denkwürdigkeiten*, ed. Heinrich von Poschinger, vol. 1: 1848–1851 (Berlin: Mittler, 1901), 47.

39 Günther Grünthal, *Parlamentarismus in Preußen 1848/49 – 1857/58. Preußischer Konstitutionalismus – Parlament und Regierung in der Reaktionsära* (Düsseldorf: Droste, 1982), 57.

ture. According to article 105, 2, the government could, "if the Chambers were not assembled," "in cases of urgency, under the responsibility of the entire department of the prime minister, issue decrees with force of law" which, however, had to be presented to the Chambers "for approval immediately at their next meeting."[40] It is obvious that this article accorded to the executive an almost unlimited power to legislate by decree. Urgency was not defined. The prerequisite of the application of the article, namely that the Chambers were not assembled, could be brought about by the King himself since article 49 conferred upon him the right to dissolve the Chambers.[41]

After the Chambers had in March 1849 confirmed the legality of the imposition they initiated a comprehensive revision of the constitution.[42] Every article was separately examined and put to the vote. In this way the principle of negotiating the constitution was after all applied, even if subject to negotiation were at this stage only eventual changes and amendments. Wherever there was no agreement between Crown and Chambers the imposed version was maintained. A conflict over the revision arose in fact between the King and the democratically elected Second Chamber. Thereupon the King dissolved the Chamber on 27 April 1849 and on 30 May he imposed a new electoral law having recourse to the emergency article 105. The government introduced a universal but unequal and not secret electoral law of men by which the electorate was divided into three classes, with the consequence that at the next elections the radical democrats would remain in a hopeless minority position (*Dreiklassenwahlrecht*). By the new electoral law the totality of electors was divided top-down into three classes in such a way that the amount of direct taxes paid was equal in every class. The three classes sent the same number of representatives to the Second Chamber. As compared to the modestly taxed citizens in the third class the highly taxed members of the first class thus disposed of many times the political weight. The Prussian Dreiklassenwahlrecht remained in force until the fall of the monarchy in November 1918.

The dissolution and reelection of the Second Chamber had interrupted the revision of the imposed constitution. The First Chamber had been adjourned. Only on 7 August 1849 the Chambers were opened again. One of their first decisions was the approval of the royal ordinance of 30 May by which the new electoral law had been introduced. Afterwards the examination of the revised constitution was continued and concluded in December 1849. Since both Chambers

---

40 Anschütz, *Verfassungs-Urkunde*, 632.
41 Grünthal, *Parlamentarismus*, 54.
42 Anschütz, *Verfassungs-Urkunde*, 54.

had incessantly been in contact with each other, they could present to the King a text in common. But the King hesitated to sanction it and to take the oath prescribed by article 52. Instead he ordered the government to present to the Chambers on 7 January 1850 15 propositions for revision of the constitution. The Chambers gave their assent to the greater part of the proposals. Frederick William IV sanctioned the constitution on 31 January and on 6 February he took the oath on it.[43]

The policy of Frederick William IV towards the Prussian National Assembly calls to mind the policy of Louis XVIII towards the Napoleonic Senate. Both monarchs had on behalf of the nation been presented with draft constitutions that infringed seriously upon their sovereign rights. Frederick William's situation was even more delicate than Louis XVIII's since the Prussian National Assembly had been called by the King himself and democratically elected by the nation. The French Senate, by contrast, had not been elected, and nobody had charged them to elaborate a constitution. It is true that the Senatorial constitution should in due course be subjected to a referendum. Thus far a democratic legitimation was envisaged. The Senate had referred to the same legitimacy when he formally deposed Emperor Napoleon who had himself based his rule on the national will. The two impositions of 1814 and 1848 resembled each other also in that they were carried through by coups d'état and aimed at replacing the democratic by the monarchical principle. Even the contemporaries had pointed to the similarities of the impositions of 1814 in France and in Prussia. Karl August Varnhagen von Ense commented the Prussian imposition of 5 December 1848 in his diary by writing: "The thing reminds me of the Charte of Louis the Eighteenth, but will scarcely play that long."[44] The prognosis was wrong. The Charte remained in force, if one includes its revision in the July Revolution, for a duration of altogether 34 years. The Prussian constitution, however, held its own, after the revision of 1850, to the end of the monarchy in 1918.

The resolves of the Prussian National Assembly of October 1848 by which the aristocracy and divine right were to be abolished, provoked a crisis of the monarchy. It was short of being transformed from a monarchy by divine right into a democratically legitimized monarchy on the model of the French constitution of 1791. Since the public continued to expect that the Crown would fulfill its promises of the spring, a return to bureaucratic absolutism of the pre-March era was out of the question. If the government did not want to cede to the demands of the National Assembly it had no choice but to recover the initiative. By the

---

43 Ibid., 58–60.
44 Karl August Varnhagen von Ense, *Tagebücher*, vol. 5 (Leipzig: Brockhaus, 1862), 327.

coup d'état of 5 December Frederick William IV restored the monarchical principle and consolidated monarchical legitimacy by imposing a constitution which highly corresponded to the aspirations of the country. Thus the Prussian constitution of 1850 belongs to the great number of constitutions of the 19th century in monarchies that were not elaborated by democratically elected constituent assemblies but imposed from above. The imposition consolidated the monarchy because it fulfilled essential demands of the revolution without infringing upon monarchical sovereignty. Therefore in Prussia as well, the transition to constitutionalism ended up in a long-term restoration of a monarchy shattered by revolution. It was only the crisis of the First World War to which it finally succumbed.

Spain 1834

The urgency of constitutional restorations depended on the magnitude of the menace to which the legitimacy of a monarchy was exposed. Since the French Revolution, monarchy was threatened everywhere. The breakthrough of popular sovereignty in the summer of 1789 and Napoleon's interferences in the structure of the European states system had shattered the safety of every monarchy. Monarchs did not always recognize the gravity of the menace and some of them delayed the necessary restorations. After the overthrow of Napoleon a constitutional or "organic" restoration took place in France only. In other countries similar measures were inaugurated only years later. However, a restoration remains no less a restoration, if it is carried through only gradually or a long time after the event that had rendered it necessary. On the other hand by repeated refusals of constitutional restoration it could also happen that the moment was missed at which consolidation of monarchical legitimacy was still feasible.

The best example of such neglect is Spain. Even before Napoleon's intervention the undignified conduct of King Charles IV had jeopardized the authority of the monarchy. In 1788 Charles had succeeded his father on the throne. The new King loved hunting but neglected his office and subjected himself unconditionally to his wife, Luisa of Bourbon-Parma. It was due to Luisa's influence that for almost two decades the government was in the hands of her favourite Manuel de Godoy. Godoy had been a member of the royal body-guard and was 21 when the Queen happened to make his acquaintance in 1788.[1] Before long the royal couple regarded him as their common friend. In 1792 he was appointed prime minister. The conclusion of the peace treaty that ended the Spanish-French war in 1795, earned him the title of "Prince of the peace" (*Principe de la Paz*). Three years later he lost the position of first minister but his decisive influence on the royal couple persisted until his inglorious fall in 1808. Contemporaries agreed that Godoy was hated in all classes of the population, albeit a little less than the Queen herself.[2] Spain had since 1796 been an ally of France and remained such under the Consulate and the Empire. But Napoleon did not trust the government in Madrid and in the course of the year 1807 he decided to dethrone the house of Bourbon and appoint a Bonaparte King of Spain. A pretext for sending troops into Spain was offered by the conflict of France with Portugal. Since the government of Portugal refused to participate in the continental blockade

---

1 Gabriel H. Lovett, *Napoleon and the Birth of Modern Spain*, vol. 1: *The Challenge to the Old Order* (New York: University Press, 1965), 8.
2 Ibid., 16.

DOI 10.1515/9783110524536-004

and to banish British ships from its ports, Napoleon by the treaty of Fontainebleau secured from the government in Madrid the permission to march to Lisbon
through Spanish territory. A French army under general Junot had already invaded Spain by that time. Further armies followed, and by March 1808 more than
100.000 French soldiers had assembled on the Iberian Peninsula. The French
took one fortress after the other and treated Spain as if it were an occupied country.[3] As early as 20 February 1808 Napoleon had appointed his brother-in-law
Joachim Murat as his lieutenant in Spain. While Charles IV made preparations
for the flight into the Southern parts of the country, the hatred against Godoy ex-
ploded during the night of 17 March in Aranjuez. A mob took his house by as-
sault, and if Godoy had not hidden in a garret he would scarcely have survived.
To save his life the King ordered his arrest and deprived him of all his duties. On
the following day new disturbances occurred. In the streets the abdication of the
King was openly demanded. Charles IV was terrified. On 19 March in the evening
he abdicated.[4] All hopes were now built on his son, Ferdinand VII. But Napoleon
refused to acknowledge the new sovereign. He had announced his visit to the
Spanish capital and Ferdinand hoped that on this occasion he would express
the missing recognition. In the meantime, at French insistence, Charles IV retracted his abdication pretending that he had acted under pressure. In reality,
however, he did not wish to recover the throne. Instead, he and his wife pressed
upon the French Emperor in numerous letters to ensure that Godoy was released
from prison and to procure to all three of them in common a peaceful homestead
abroad.[5]

The further course of events placed several trumps into Napoleon's hands.
Both Charles IV and his son laid claim to the Spanish throne, Charles if not in
earnest, at least in appearance. Both expected the solution of their conflict
from the French Emperor at the visit he had announced several times. Unexpectedly Napoleon gained the role of an umpire between the quarrelling Kings, but
he did not intend to go to Spain. When on 2 April 1808 he made for the South, he
was not headed for Madrid but for Bayonne near the Spanish border. There, on
French soil, he desired to receive the Spanish monarchs. Charles and Luisa readily followed his invitation. Ferdinand however at first harbored misgivings. Hop-
ing that Napoleon would cross the border after all he left his capital on 10 April
in the intention to meet the Emperor in Northern Spain. When he couldn't find
Napoleon anywhere, two choices were left to him: to return to Madrid or to over-

---

3 Ibid., 89–90.
4 Ibid., 98–99.
5 Ibid., 107–108.

come his misgivings and proceed to Bayonne. At Vitoria he still hesitated but then decided to go ahead. On 21 April he arrived in Bayonne. Before long the Emperor disclosed his real intentions. Instead of acknowledging Ferdinand as King of Spain he demanded his resignation in favor of the Bonaparte dynasty. For days Ferdinand resisted the pressure. When Ferdinand's parents arrived at Bayonne Charles IV demanded that he return the crown to him. After a few days of fruitless confrontation Ferdinand gave in. By a letter of 6 May he returned the crown to his father, not knowing that Charles had, on the previous day, already renounced his rights to the Spanish throne in favour of Napoleon. The Emperor had attained his goal. Adding deceit to pressure he had succeeded in ousting the Spanish Bourbons from the throne. A few days later the two former Kings issued a proclamation to the Spanish people from Bordeaux and released them from their duties of obedience. The two monarchs were placed under confinement in France, Charles IV and his consort Luisa at the castle of Compiègne near Paris, Ferdinand VII at the castle of Valençay on the Loire.[6] The Spanish throne was handed over to Napoleon's brother Joseph who had since 1806 been King of Naples.

While at Bayonne negotiations were held on the future of the Spanish monarchy, heavy fighting was on the way in Madrid. On 2 May the population of the capital rose against the French army of occupation. Murat had the revolt bloodily suppressed. Hundreds of insurgents were arrested and shot overnight in Madrid and on the surrounding mountains by firing squads. Six years later both the revolt and the ensuing executions were captured in two large paintings by Francisco de Goya. The *Dos de Mayo* has remained till today a national day of remembrance. It marks the beginning of the Spanish War of Independence against Napoleon. During almost six years the Spanish people offered resistance against King Joseph who had been forced upon them. With a view to safeguarding the sovereignty of his brother Napoleon was incessantly obliged to station a substantial part of his forces in the country. When general Masséna in 1810 invaded Portugal the Imperial armies on the Iberian Peninsula numbered not less than 325.000 soldiers.[7] In their revolt against the superior French forces the insurgents developed the tactics of the "small war" (*guerilla*). They were supported by British forces under the command of Sir Arthur Wellesley, later Duke of Wellington. In no other country Napoleon met such fierce resistance as in Spain.

---

6 Ibid., 118–120; Charles and Luisa later proceeded via Marseille to Italy where they died almost simultaneously in 1819.

7 David Gates, *The Spanish Ulcer. A History of the Peninsular War* (Cambridge, Mass.: Da Capo Press, 1986), 34.

Even though Ferdinand had thoughtlessly given away his throne at Bayonne the Spanish nation adhered to him. The insurgents even interpreted their resistance as a fight for their imprisoned, their longed-for King (*el Rey deseado*). The political direction of the resistance was at first entrusted to a *Junta Suprema Central y Gubernativa del Reino*. On 31 January 1810 the Junta transferred power to another governing body, the Regency council (*Consejo de Regencia del Reino*). The chair was taken by general Francisco Javier Castaños, victor in the battle of Bailén in July 1808.[8] Not later than 5 May, Ferdinand had issued a decree from Bayonne convoking the Spanish estates (*Cortes*) in the intent of having them organize the resistance against the foreign occupants.[9] The Junta repeated the convocation in 1810. The Cortes assembled on 24 September 1810 on the Isle of León before Cádiz, but went far beyond the instructions of the King. They proclaimed national sovereignty and arrogated to themselves the constituent power (*poder constituyente*). They fought for the reform of the monarchy on democratic principles.[10] Thus far their efforts resembled the work of the French National Assembly in the summer of 1789. According to the preamble Ferdinand was expected to proclaim the constitution at his return as King of Spain "by the grace of God and on behalf of the constitution of the Spanish monarchy." The wording was a commitment to divine right, but it is obvious that the twofold foundation of monarchical authority deprived divine right of any significance in public law. As is demonstrated by the articles about the position of the King, he had been transformed, not unlike Louis XVI by the French constitution of 1791, from sovereign to a merely executive organ of the state. According to article 170 his essential task was to "provide for the execution of the laws," and his power extended "to everything that refers to the maintenance of order on the interior and to the safety of the state on the exterior, in line with the constitution and the laws."[11] On account of his detention in France Ferdinand had not been able to participate in the deliberation of the constitution, and when on 19 March 1812 the constitu-

---

8 Miguel Artola Gallego, *L'España de Fernando VII*, vol. 1: *La guerra de la independencia y los orígenes del constitucionalismo* (Madrid: Espasa-Calpe, 1996), 442; Lovett, *Napoleon*, vol. 1, 358; Gates, *Ulcer*, 53–56.

9 Andreas Timmermann, *Die "gemäßigte Monarchie" in der Verfassung von Cadiz (1812) und das frühe liberale Verfassungsdenken in Spanien* (Münster: Aschendorff, 2007), 26.

10 Constitucion española 1812, art. 3: "La soberanía reside esencialmente en la Nación, y por lo mismo pertenece a ésta exclusivamente el derecho de establecer sus leyes fundamentales."

11 Constitucion española 1812, art. 170: "La potestad de hacer ejecutar las leyes reside exclusivamente en el Rey, y su autoridad se extiende á todo cuanto conduce á la conservación del orden público en lo interior, y á la seguridad del Estado en lo exterior, conforme á la Constitución y á las leyes."

tion was adopted, it was unknown how long the King would still have to stay at Valençay. The Russian campaign which was to be the turning-point in Napoleon's rule lay still ahead.

It took indeed two more years before Ferdinand was allowed to return on his throne. The advance of the allied armies in Germany and on the Iberian Peninsula during 1813 caused Napoleon on 11 December 1813 to conclude with him the peace treaty of Valençay.[12] The Emperor recognized Ferdinand as King of Spain and promised to release him from captivity. He hoped that the treaty with Spain would procure to him the badly needed relief and enable him to reinforce his armies at the remaining theatres of war. On 13 March 1814 Ferdinand made for his realm. His departure had been delayed because Napoleon had at first intended to await ratification of the treaty by the Cortes.

Article 173 of the constitution of Cádiz of 1812 ruled that the King take an oath before ascending the throne. Thus, in April 1814, Ferdinand VII was in the same quandary as Louis XVIII at the same time. But his reaction to the demand of the assembly was exactly the opposite of Louis XVIII's. This results already from the declarations by which the monarchs on their way back to their capitals commented on the constitutions that had been elaborated during their absence: the Declaration of Saint-Ouen of 2 May and the Manifesto of Valencia of 4 May. Whereas Louis XVIII acknowledged the Senatorial constitution in principle, Ferdinand VII denied to the Cortes of Cádiz any authority and to their constitution any binding force. Whereas Louis did not dwell on the question of who possessed the constituent power, Ferdinand declared that the Cortes had divested "him of his sovereign power and had feigned to attribute it to the nation, only in order to appropriate it to themselves." By adopting the "revolutionary and democratic foundations of the French constitution of 1791" they had created "principles not of a limited monarchy but of a popular government with a president or a magistrate at the top" (*Gobierno popular con un Gefe ó Magistrado*). This magistrate, however, was nothing but a "delegated executor" (*mero egecutor delegado*) and no King, "even though he had received the name of King with a view to deceiving and misguiding the credulous and the nation." Unlike Louis XVIII Ferdinand would not even accept the work of the Cortes as a basis for the elaboration of a constitution that preserved the monarchical principle. Instead he declared the constitution of 1812 and the other decrees of the Cortes

---

12 J. Alberto Navas-Sierra, "El tratado de Valençay o el fracaso del pacto imperial napoleónico. El caso de la España peninsular," *Jahrbuch für Geschichte von Staat, Wirtschaft und Gesellschaft Lateinamerikas* 27 (1990), 259–261, 294–298.

"null and without any value and effect" (*nulos y de ningun valor ni efecto*).[13] Simultaneously he promised soon to convoke the Cortes in line with the ancient laws of Spain, a promise he never lived up to.[14]

Many historians call the reaction of the King a coup d'état (*golpe de Estado*). This verdict makes sense only if the regime the Cortes had set up during the absence of the King, had possessed legitimacy. Since Ferdinand VII denied the Cortes any legitimacy, he felt entitled to refuse them any share in the government. At any rate he could have pointed out that since he had never assented to the constitution of the Cortes, it had not attained force of law. But to the juridical argument must be added a moral point of view. Since Ferdinand's return on the throne was largely due to the Cortes, his attitude appears not only extremely ungrateful but also highly impolitic.

On the same 4 May 1814, the day when he published the Valencia manifesto, the King ordered the arrest of the members of the Regency, of the government, and of leading members of the Cortes, 38 persons in all.[15] Thereupon many other liberal leaders flew abroad. At the ensuing law-suits the courts were confronted with the difficulty that there was no norm in Spanish law that the defendants might have violated.[16] Nevertheless, by the middle of June a list of 28 accusations had been put up. The first three items contained the main charge that encompassed all the others: in the first place that the defendants had "violated the sovereignty of Sr. Don Fernando VII and the rights and prerogatives of the throne with a view to establishing a democratic government and divest him of his royal crown and his realms"; in the second place that by convoking the Cortes in 1810 they had usurped the King's sovereignty; in the third place that they had intended to make the principle of popular sovereignty (*soberania popular*) the foundation of government.[17] The ensuing law-suit dragged on for more

---

13 Manifiesto de 4 de mayo 1814, Gaceta Extraordinaria de Madrid del jueves 12 de mayo de 1814, 515–521, here: 517, 520; Manuel Pando Fernandez de Pinedo (Marqués de Miraflores), *Apuntes histórico-criticos para escribir la historia de la revolucion de España, desde el año 1820 hasta 1823*, vol. 1 (London: Taylor, 1834), 32–38, here: 34–35, 37. The manifesto is also printed in: Manuel Fernández Martín, *Derecho parlamentario español*, vol. 2 (Madrid: Espasa-Calpe 1992), 856–863.

14 Ibid., 518, 36; Artola Gallego, *España*, vol. 1, 527–528.

15 Ignacio Lasa Iraola, "El primer proceso de los liberales (1814–1815)," *Hispanica* 30 (1970), 328, 336–367.

16 Ibid., 341–342.

17 Quoted from: Manuel Fernández Martín, *Derecho parlamentario español*, vol. 3 (Madrid: Espasa-Calpe, 1992), 106–107: "Cargo 1.° Lo es, el haber atentado contra la soberania del Sr. Don Fernando VII y contra los derechos y regalias del trono para establecer un gobierno democrát-

than 18 months. At last, the King lost patience. On 15 December 1815 he issued the sentences himself by royal decree. They provided for prison of between six and ten years.[18]

The trial was political. The charge that the defendants had tried to transfer sovereignty from the King to the nation, was justified. But this charge, quite apart from the fact that in Spanish penal law it did not exist, would of right have to be directed not only against the 38 defendants, but against all the other deputies of the Cortes as well who had voted for the constitution of Cádiz. Because of this omission the limitation of the accusation on 38 persons only was arbitrary. Incompatible with any rightful procedure was issuing the sentence by royal decree.

The fact that the defendants had for six years, during the absence of the lawful monarch who had frivolously gambled it away, defended the guideless country against the imposed King Joseph and the French army of invasion, did not play any role in the law-suit, notwithstanding the fact that the revolt of the Spanish people since 1808 fully justified the policies of the *Junta Suprema* and the *Consejo de Regencia*, and likewise the Cortes of Cádiz. The writer Ramón de Mesonero Romanos called Ferdinand's proceedings against the liberals in his "Memoirs of a Septuagenarian" a symptom of "political ingratitude and dullness" of a kind that the history of modernity had not known yet (*ingratitud y torpeza politica que no tiene semejante en la historia moderna*). The numerous "futile revolts" of the following period and the "terrible reactions" directed against them had "ensanguined" his government. Ferdinand had impregnated the next two generations with a "spirit of discord, of intolerance, and of wrath." From this had resulted "three civil wars, half a dozen constitutions, and innumerable *pronunciamientos* and crises" which had procured to the Spaniards the reputation of "an ungovernable people" and of "a rebellious race that was condemned to incessant struggle and to senseless and feverish agitation."[19]

By persecuting the leaders of the national resistance against Napoleon Ferdinand deprived himself of a social élite that could after his return have assisted him in the restoration of his government. And that was not all: He also drove another élite to emigration, namely the large number of those who had collaborated with Joseph Bonaparte, the so-called *afrancesados*. When after the battle of Vitoria in June 1813 King Joseph sought refuge in France he was followed by about 12.000 families of Spanish collaborators who wanted to escape persecu-

---

ico, privarle de su Corona Real y de la posesion de sus Reinos"; see also: Lasa Iraola, "Proceso," 356–357.

18 Artola Gallego, *España*, vol 1, 531, 533–534; Lasa Iraola, "Proceso," 379.

19 Ramón de Mesonero Romanos, *Memorias de un setentón* (Madrid: Tebas, 1975), 129.

tion by the returning monarch.[20] At this time Ferdinand VII was still a French prisoner at Valençay. When he returned to Spain the refugees hoped for an amnesty. By decree of 30 May 1814, however, Ferdinand barred to all those who had supported Joseph Bonaparte in the public service or in the army, the way back to Spain. The prohibition included the spouses. An amnesty was issued to rank and file only.[21] By the expatriation of the afrancesados Ferdinand VII broke the promises he had given to Napoleon in the treaty of Valençay in December 1813. He could have referred to the fact that this treaty had not been ratified by either party.[22] Other than Ferdinand, Louis XVIII in article 11 of the charte constitutionnelle granted amnesty to those who in 1792 had participated in the overthrow of the monarchy, and in this way excluded political purges.

Ferdinand's return to absolutism and the relentless persecution of the liberals and the collaborators severely strained the assent to the monarchy. The liberal opposition went underground and hid to a great extent in the various secret societies. In the following years criticism of the King found expression in several unsuccessful rebellions of officers, the so-called *pronunciamientos*. According to José Luis Comellas a "pronunciamiento" was "a kind of military insurrection peculiar to 19th century Spanish history and directed against the power of the state with a view to bringing about political reforms."[23] The phenomenon originated between 1814 and 1820 from the discontent of a minority that felt slighted by Ferdinand VII's government in its dignity and rights.[24] All pronunciamientos of the period served liberal objectives. Before Napoleon's intervention officer's posts had in the main been reserved to the aristocracy in line with Ancien Régime practice. During the war against the French invasion many non-noble officers distinguished themselves by their prowess and made a career in the army.[25] After his return from exile the King was forced to reduce armaments. Since he set about restoring the structures of the ancient professional army, he dismissed even war heroes of great merit or displaced them to the provinces for garrisonduties. Because of these measures discontent if not hostility shortly piled up among the dismissed and side-lined officers. Among the military personnel con-

---

20 Miguel Artola Gallego, *Los afrancesados* (Madrid: Soc. De Estudios y Publ., 1953), 236.

21 Decreto de 30 de mayo de 1814, Artt. 1, 6 e 7, ibid., 268–269.

22 Navas-Sierra, "Tratado," 262, n. 8.

23 José Luis Comellas, *Los primeros pronunciamientos en España 1814–1820* (Madrid: Consejo Superior de Investigaciones Científicas, 1958), 23: "Una forma de golpe militar asestado contra el poder para introducir en él reformas politicas, propia de la Historia española del siglo XIX."

24 Ibid., 31.

25 Julio Busquets, *Pronunciamientos y golpes de Estado en España* (Barcelona: Ed. Planeta, 1982), 52.

cerned three groups can be distinguished: the former members of the guerillas, mostly coming from the peasantry or from the working classes; the young officers of bourgeois origin who during the war had entered into the military academies and whose opportunities of advancement were now restricted by the restoration of aristocratic privileges; finally the officers, approximately 4.000, who had after the conclusion of the peace returned from captivity in France where they had become acquainted with the liberal institutions of the restored Bourbon monarchy.[26] A great many officers entered Freemasonry and hoped that the regime would shortly turn liberal and restore the constitution of Cádiz. The mood within the officer corps is best characterized by a sentence in a letter that General Pedro Augustín Girón on 30 August 1814 sent to his father. Girón writes he despised the officers in the entourage of the King, because "they were better acquainted with the promenades of Ceuta and Cádiz than with the battlefields on which Spanish independence had been won."[27] Behind the pronunciamientos, however, there was no solid organization. Therefore in the first years all of them collapsed after a short period of time. It was only the pronunciamiento of colonel Rafael del Riego on new year's day of 1820 in Las Cabezas de San Juan that produced far-reaching consequences. Riego was one of the prisoners of war who had returned from France. Near Cádiz troops had been gathered for embarkation to America where they should fight the independence movement in the Spanish colonies. Since the preparations for embarkation were delayed the opposing officers were offered opportunities for conspiracy.[28] The rebellion soon extended to large sections of the realm. Ferdinand VII had no choice but to swear the constitution of 1812 and to convoke the Cortes again.[29] For three years he ruled as head of a democratic monarchy. At the elections to the Cortes the liberals gained the majority. Before long, however, the liberal camp split into two wings that fiercely fought each other, the so-called *doceañistas* or *moderados* (moderates) on the one hand and the *exaltados* (radicals) on the other. The conflict was sparked off by the question whether the army near Cádiz from which the revolution had originated, was to be kept in readiness or dissolved, and by the plans of the moderate government, to dis-

---

26 Ibid., 52–55.

27 Quoted from: Comellas, *Pronunciamientos*, 50.

28 Charles J. Esdaile, *Spain in the Liberal Age. From Constitution to Civil War, 1808–1939* (Oxford: Blackwell, 2000), 48; Artola Gallego, *España*, 634–635.

29 Ibid., 543–547; Walther L. Bernecker and Horst Pietschmann, *Geschichte Spaniens. Von der frühen Neuzeit bis zur Gegenwart*, 4th ed. (Stuttgart: Kohlhammer, 2005), 249.

solve the Patriotic Societies. The moderates were afraid that the army or the Societies exert pressure on the organs of the constitution and control the proceedings of the Cortes.[30] In the last resort the question was, whether the revolution had attained its objectives or whether it had to continue in order to protect its achievements against reaction. At the elections of February 1822 the exaltados obtained the majority.[31] Rafael del Riego, symbol of democratic resistance, was elected president of the Cortes. The conflict between the two fractions of liberalism impaired the government's ability to act. In particular by his personnel policy the King intensified the conflict, apart from the fact that he sued the conservative great powers for help at restoring absolutism.[32] In 1823 constitutional France of all powers terminated the constitutional interlude by military intervention. On 1 October Ferdinand VII revoked the constitution of Cádiz and annulled all acts of the liberal government of the *trienio*.[33] Again many liberals flew abroad, the majority of them to France, whereas the leaders of liberalism repaired to England.[34] Once more, as with respect to 1814, the question arises, why Ferdinand had not taken advantage of the French intervention to combine the repeal of the democratic constitution of Cádiz with the imposition of a constitution framed in accordance with the monarchical principle, and thus to transfer the monarchy by way of an organic restoration and without infringement of its traditional legitimacy carefully and under control into the age of democracy. Twice this opportunity was offered to Ferdinand and both times he failed to seize it.

Until Ferdinand's death on 29 September 1833 the country was subjected to the most severe reaction. In Spanish collective memory these ten years have been preserved as the "ominous decade" (*década ominosa*).[35] Only half a year later the country again received a constitution, the *Estatuto Real*. This unforeseen turn of events resulted from the dynastic crisis into which Ferdinand's death had precipitated the country. Ferdinand left behind two daughters but no son. Since 1713 the *lex salica* had been in force in Spain which excluded female succession.

30 Christiana Brennecke, *Von Cádiz nach London. Spanischer Liberalismus im Spannungsfeld von nationaler Selbstbestimmung, Internationalität und Exil (1820–1833)* (Göttingen: Vandenhoeck & Ruprecht, 2010), 60–64.

31 *Esdaile*, Spain, 58.

32 Charles Wentz Fehrenbach, "Moderados and Exaltados: The Liberal Opposition to Ferdinand VII, 1814–1823", *Hispanic American Historical Review* 50 (1970), 67; Manuel Espadas Burgos and José Ramón de Urquijo Goitia, *Guerra de la Independencia y época constitucional (1808–1898)* (Madrid: Ed. Gredos, 1990), 49.

33 Ibid., 141.

34 Ibid., 142–147.

35 Angélica Sánchez Almeida, *Fernando VII. El deseado* (Madrid: Alderabán), 1999, 141.

To be sure, the Cortes had in 1789 adopted a Pragmatic Sanction permitting female succession, but the then reigning King Charles IV had not signed the decree. His son and successor had in three marriages remained without issue. When his fourth consort, Maria Cristina, princess of the Two Sicilies, in 1830 got pregnant, he made good his father's omission and signed the Pragmatic Sanction of 1789. In October a daughter was indeed born to the couple, María Isabel Luisa. Upon Ferdinand's death the infant succeeded her father on the throne at the age of only three years as Isabella II. By will Ferdinand had appointed his consort Maria Cristina regent and had ordered the formation of a regency council (*Consejo de Gobierno*) in her support. Ferdinand's brother, Don Carlos María Isidro, however, contested the succession settlement arguing that the signature under the Pragmatic Sanction, rendered forty years later by the successor of the King who had issued it, was invalid. On 4 October 1833 he declared himself the lawful King of Spain by the manifesto of Santarém.[36] Since Don Carlos shared the reactionary views of Ferdinand VII, all liberal-minded Spaniards, in particular among the high aristocracy, the public servants and the educated middle classes, not to mention the middle classes of the coastal cities, supported Isabella and the regent. During the Queen's minority the regent was dependent on the support of these social groups. The consequence was a liberalization of the regime and the renewed transition of the country to constitutionalism.[37]

After Ferdinand's death the regent had at first tried to continue the absolute government of the deceased King. On 4 October 1833, the same day that Don Carlos raised his claim to the throne, she published her program of government in a manifesto that her first minister Cea Bermúdez had drawn up. Therein she declared it her duty not to tolerate any limitation of the royal power entrusted to her and not to admit any "dangerous innovations."[38] Instead she announced reforms of the administration. Against this program resistance emerged from various parts and soon became public. One of the most prominent opponents of Cea Bermúdez' policy was the Marqués de Miraflores. A critical memorandum he sent on 15 November 1833 to the regent, was spread without his involvement.[39]

---

36 Joaquin Tomás Villarroya, *El sistema politico del Estatuto Real (1834–1836)* (Madrid: Inst.de Estudios Politicos, 1968), 21.

37 José Luis Commellas, *Isabel II. Una reina y un reinado* (Barcelona: Editorial Ariel, 1999), 27–28.

38 Manifiesto de S. M. la Reina Gobernadora, Palacio, 4 de octubre de 1833, quoted from: [Don Manuel Pando Fernández de Pinedo], Marqués de Miraflores, *Memorias del reinado de Isabel II*, vol. 1 (Madrid: Ed. Atlas, 1964), 197.

39 Tomás Villarroya, *Sistema*, 30; the text of the memorandum in: Miraflores, *Memorias*, vol. 1, 32–33.

When the regency council also advocated a change of policy, the regent dismissed Cea Bermúdez and in January 1834 appointed the writer Francisco Martínez de la Rosa, a man in whose biography is reflected the history of Spanish liberalism since 1814. Martínez had been a member of the second Cortes that assembled at Cádiz in the autumn of 1813.[40] After Ferdinand's return from exile he shared the fate of many other liberals. During the night of 10 March 1814 he was arrested at Madrid and imprisoned at the barracks of the royal guard where he remained for about 20 months under indescribable conditions.[41] On 15 December 1815 he was by the above mentioned royal decree sentenced to eight years of hard labour in the fortress of Peñon de Vélez de la Gomera on the Moroccan cost of the Mediterranean. Thanks to the revolt of Cádiz he regained his liberty ahead of time in March.[42] Immediately upon his return he was elected to the restored Cortes. On 9 July he presided their solemn opening.[43] After the split of the liberal camp into *moderados* and *exaltados* Martínez developed into one of the most prominent spokesmen of the moderates. In February 1822 he followed an invitation of the King and formed a cabinet.[44] Only a few months later, however, the government succumbed in the July troubles short of civil war.[45] After the French intervention had terminated the trienio liberal in April 1823, Martínez de la Rosa asked for asylum in France. On 24 June he arrived at Bayonne.[46] On 26 September he settled in Paris. He remained there for seven years before he returned home in the autumn of 1831.[47]

The critics of the minister Cea Bermúdez had unanimously demanded the convocation of the Cortes. As results from the memoirs of the Marqués de Miraflores they regarded this step as the only method by which the endangered monarchy could be placed again on secure foundations. The monarchy appeared endangered by the controversy over the succession, by the minority of the Queen and by the high-wrought expectations of many liberals who hoped, after Ferdinand's disappearance, for the restoration of the constitution of Cádiz. Miraflores considered it an illusion to expect the resolution of the crisis from an absolute regime. He was convinced that for this task a man was required who by his "au-

---

40 Jean Sarrailh, *Un homme d'état espagnol: Martínez de la Rosa (1787–1862)* (Poitiers: Féret, 1930), 41–42.
41 Ibid., 50.
42 Ibid., 55.
43 Ibid., 103.
44 Ibid., 116.
45 Ibid., 121.
46 Ibid., 163.
47 Ibid., 170, 183.

thority" and by his "moral and material force" filled the "great gap" [...] "the late King had left. This man should either be of royal descent or base his power on the sword."[48] Cea Bermúdez had not been that man. Instead of resolving the crisis he had by adhering to absolutism estranged from the party of the Queen many personalities of moderately liberal ideas whose support the regent should in her contest with the pretender under no circumstances have renounced. Like many others Miraflores also advised her immediately to convoke the Cortes, but he admonished her to take this step "very tactfully." The Cortes she convoked must in no case resemble those which had assembled on the basis of the constitution of 1812. The least suspicion that she was about to restore the regime that had fallen in 1823, would only engross the files of the pretender. If however she proceeded with adequate caution she could assemble the sober-minded members of the liberal party behind the Queen. These included many men of fortune and prestige who were only waiting for an opportunity "to join the cause of Her Majesty."[49]

Even if Miraflores at the moment did not expressly mention the imposition of a new constitution, by pleading for the convocation of the Cortes he did not demand anything else but a constitutional restoration of the endangered monarchy. At the same time he defined the conditions for an attempt to secure the power of the crown. In the civil war that was on the verge of breaking out the Queen was in need of support. From the partisans of absolutism she could not expect assistance, because these sided with the pretender. Neither could the regent count on the adherents of the constitution of 1812. On the one hand this constitution was based on popular sovereignty and therefore incompatible with monarchical restoration. On the other it had in the eyes of many Spaniards proved impracticable during the trienio liberal.[50] Therefore the monarchy was obliged to strive for an alliance with the composed and moderate forces of liberalism and to seek a course between the extremes.

Francisco Martínez de la Rosa who was appointed first minister, embodied this policy. Accordingly, only a few days after his taking up government preparations were initiated for the imposition of the *Estatuto Real*, a constitution based on the monarchical principle. At first a draught was worked out on the ministerial level. On 7 March 1834 Martínez de la Rosa forwarded it to the regency council (*Consejo de Gobierno*). In his accompanying note he justified it with the care of Her Majesty for "the stability of the throne and the general well-being of the na-

---

48 Miraflores, *Memorias*, vol. 1, 28.
49 Ibid., 29 – 30.
50 Tomás Villarroya, *Sistema*, 49.

tion."[51] From 9 to 24 March the regency council deliberated in no less than sixteen sessions on the draught of the ministers, before it transmitted to the council of ministers a detailed comment.[52] The most important objection of the regency council referred to type and legal weight of the proposed Estatuto. The regency council recognized in the draught only the torso of a constitution. Therefore it proposed "to name" it instead of an Estatuto Real simply a "royal decree concerning the convocation of the Cortes."[53] Eventual supplements if required could easily be worked out later on by the government themselves in collaboration with the Cortes. Of this recommendation the government gave no heed. The crown claimed sovereign power for itself and was not ready to share it with the nation. Therefore it refused to assign to the Cortes the right to cooperate in the revision of the constitution. But it followed the suggestion to grant to the Cortes the right of petition. The regency council did not oppose the limitation of the right to initiate legislation to the crown. On 10 April 1834 the regent signed the Estatuto.[54]

The Estatuto Real has indeed remained a torso in many respects. It is limited to composition and procedure of the chambers and does not include the formation of the government and the position of the ministers or of the judiciary. In particular, there is no catalogue of basic rights. Unusual in the text of a constitution is the first article. It informs that the Queen-regent had on behalf of her daughter Isabella II, referring to the pertinent articles in the "new Spanish collection of laws of Castile" (*Nueva recopilación de las leyes de Castilla*) of 1567 resolved to convoke the *Cortes generales* of the realm. A date for the assembly is not indicated. The constitutional norms for the Cortes are listed only afterwards, beginning with the second article. But even in this part of the constitution more than once reference is made to the Castilian collection of laws of 1567, namely in the articles 27, 30, and 34. Instead of introducing new law, at these points the Estatuto only confirms the already existing law. Article 27, for example, calls to memory that "after the King's death Cortes should be convoked in order that his successor swear observance of the laws and receive from the Cortes the oath of fidelity and allegiance due to him." The wording shows that the Estatuto Real was expressly inserted in the tradition of Spanish public law. The Cortes had from of old been an institution of the Spanish monarchy and did not have to be introduced anew. But the Estatuto Real reorganized division and composition of the Cortes. In the Ancien Régime the assembly had consisted

---

51 Quoted from ibid., 57.
52 Ibid., 62.
53 Ibid., 63.
54 Ibid., 77. Text of the Estatuto Real ibid., appendix, 635–642.

of three *curiae* that represented the clergy, the aristocracy, and the cities. The constitution of Cádiz had put in the place of the three curiae a single chamber. In article 2 of the Estatuto the Cortes were divided into two chambers, the *Estamento de Próceres* and the *Estamento de Procuradores*. The Estamento de Procuradores was to be composed of the representatives of the high clergy, of the grandees of Spain, the titulars of Castile, merited public servants and rich landowners, industrialists, merchants, university professors, scientists, and writers. The grandees should be members by heritage, the other *próceres* should be appointed by the King for life. The *procuradores* were to be elected by a high census for a period of three years. The suffrage was limited to the 16.000 most heavily taxed subjects.[55]

The announcement of the impending convocation of the Cortes and the limitation of the Estatuto to their composition and procedure are to be explained from the preconditions of the imposition. As has been shown, in view of the critical situation of the monarchy after the death of Ferdinand VII several authors had demanded the convocation of the Cortes. A constitution they had not expressly asked for. However, the convocation of the Cortes required a foundation in constitutional law. If the constitution of Cádiz should not be brought into force again, a new foundation had to be created. That was the purpose of the imposition of the Estatuto Real. Since no binding procedures could have been deduced from the constitutional tradition of the realm, the Estatuto had to settle structure and procedure of the future Cortes. In all matters it did not touch, the traditional law should be observed. This rule corresponded to the principle that sovereignty remained with the monarch and was subjected to those limitations only that were expressly enumerated in the constitution.

The fact that the Estatuto presupposed the existence of Cortes as a matter of course corresponded to the intention to let it appear, in relation to the Ancien Régime, as little as possible as an innovation. The designation of Cortes alone referred to the monarchy in an estates-based society. *Estamento* was the traditional term for "estate." The use of the term *estatuto* instead of *constitución* with its revolutionary connotations points in the same direction. It is as plain as can be that by these linguistic regulations the government wanted to emphasize that the legitimacy of the crown was not based on the national will but on the ancient laws of the monarchy. In accordance with this principle in the letter by which the council of ministers transmitted to the regent the Estatuto it is written that it was to her that "had been reserved the glory of restoring our ancient fundamental laws of which the non-observance had during three centuries

---

55 Comellas, *Isabel II*, 33; Estatuto Real, Art. 17, in: Tomás Villarroya, *Sistema*, Apéndice IV, 638.

caused so much trouble and of which the restoration by the august hand of Her Majesty will be the happiest omen for the government of Her elevated daughter."[56]

The obvious incompletion of the Estatuto has caused not only the Regency council but modern authors as well to deny it the quality of a constitution and to interpret it merely as a decree for the convocation of the Cortes. Such an interpretation is indeed suggested by the first article in which the Regent announces her intention to convoke them. But essential features of a convocation decree are missing in the document, namely place and date of the proposed meeting. Joaquín Tomás Villarroya in his treatise on the Estatuto Real has raised two further objections to the supposition that it was merely a letter of convocation and no constitution. In the first place he points out that the Estatuto does not refer to a single case but expresses general norms. Article 25 is a case in point. It rules that the Cortes assemble on the basis of a royal letter of convocation at the place and on the day determined therein.[57] This alone shows that the Estatuto itself cannot have been regarded as a letter of convocation. Accordingly the Regent issued a formal letter of convocation for the assembly of the Cortes on 20 May 1834 in which reference was made to the Estatuto by saying the Regent convoked the Cortes "according to the principles contained in the Estatuto Real."[58] Joaquín Tomás Villarroya's second objection to the thesis that the Estatuto was merely a letter of convocation, consists in pointing out that renowned contemporaries had indubitably regarded it as a constitution and discussed it as such, no matter whether they consented to it or criticized it.

The expectations, with which the Estatuto was received in Spain, are documented in the Madrid newspaper *La Revista* of 16 April 1834. The delivery of the printed copies had been announced for 10 o'clock in the morning of the day before. In the early hours already the royal printing-office had been thronged by a great number of people who were waiting for the text: "Within a few moments they snatched thousands of copies and distributed them in every corner of the capital; reading it was the exclusive and coveted pursuit of all citizens [...]."[59]

---

56 Exposicion preliminar al Estatuto real, in: Tomás Villarroya, *Sistema*, Apéndice III, 621: "A V. M. está reservada la gloria de restaurar nuestras antiguas leyes fundamentales, cuyo desuso ha causado tantos males por el espacio de tres siglos, y cuyo restablecimiento por la augusta mano de V. M. será el más prospero presagio para el reinado de su excelsa Hija."

57 Estatuto Real, Art. 25: "Las Cortes se reunirán, en virtud de Real Convocatoria, en el pueblo y en el día que aquélla señalare."

58 Quoted from Tomás Villarroya, *Sistema*, 105: the entire debate ibid., 102–106.

59 La Revista, 16 April 1834, quoted from ibid., 80.

The paper continues: "It was not a novel by Walter Scott that aroused public curiosity; it was and is the sacred claim to our civil rights and our future security."[60]

Soon however curiosity and joy increasingly yielded to disappointment. Only
a short time after their opening there was initiated in the Cortes a lively debate
on an extension of the Estatuto.[61] Several members of the Estamento de procuradores demanded that a catalogue of basic rights be drawn up, including primarily the freedom of the press. On 28 August a group of procuradores directed
a petition to the government according to article 32 of the Estatuto and attached
to it the draught of a catalogue of basic rights. After a vivid discussion the second
chamber adopted the petition with a few amendments.[62] For the time being the
resolution remained without consequences. In 1835 the demands of a revision of
the Estatuto grew more insistent. During the summer several provinces rose and
demanded a reform of the constitution. Some of them proposed the reintroduction of the constitution of Cádiz. In September Prime Minister Juan Álvarez Men-
dizábal promised a revision of the Estatuto. However he was not able to keep his
promise before his fall from office in May 1836. His successor Francisco Javier de
Istúriz took the project up again. A draught of 55 articles was adopted by the
council of ministers.[63] The draught took the demands of reform which had
been voiced since the promulgation of the Estatuto Real, largely into account.
It contained a list of basic rights such as freedom of the press (art. 3) and the
right of property (article 6). Expressly stated was the separation of powers
(art. 8–10). The legislative power was to be exercised in common by the two
chambers and the King (art. 13). The right to initiate legislation was conferred
to either chamber separately and to the King (art. 12). The question of sovereignty
was not touched. Before Istúriz could introduce the draught into the Cortes, a
military revolt at La Granja, the summer residence of the Kings of Spain, forced
the Regent to reintroduce the constitution of Cádiz. The constitutional restoration
of the Spanish monarchy had failed.

To an explanation of this failure might contribute a comparison with the restoration in France. Both the Estatuto Real and the Charte constitutionnelle were
imposed in the hope to meet the expectations of the citizens. In either country
these expectations resulted from incisive historical experiences, of the Revolution in France, of the war of independence against Napoleon in Spain. Both in

---

60 Quoted from ibid.: "No era una novela de Walter Scott la que excitaba la curiosidad pública;
era y es el título sagrado de nuestros derechos civiles y de nuestra seguridad venidera."
61 For a summary of the criticism at the Estatuto see ibid., 86–91.
62 Ibid., 537–543.
63 Ibid., 547–552; the text of the draft in: Miraflores, *Memorias*, vol. 1, 264–269.

Spain and in France the impositions wrecked the hopes of attaining democratic constitutions. In France Louis XVIII had replaced the Senatorial constitution of 6 April 1814 by the Charte. In Spain there existed at the death of Ferdinand VII neither a constitution nor the draught of a constitution, but the *exaltados* set their hopes upon the reintroduction of the constitution of Cádiz. The constitution of Cádiz was a myth. It was connected with the memories both of the sacrifices during the resistance to Napoleon and of the humiliating suppression of the trienio with the help of French troops in 1823. The Estatuto Real was measured against the constitution of Cádiz no less than the Charte constitutionnelle was measured – going further back – against the constitution of 1791. As compared to the democratic constitutions the imposed constitutions were impaired by a structural deficit which they could not overcome and which they tried all the more diligently to compensate by concessions regarding content. Missing was the declaration of national sovereignty.

As to content the Charte constitutionnelle differed as little as possible from the Senatorial constitution. In the declaration of Saint-Ouen Louis XVIII had emphasized that in principle he consented to the constitution. If only to avoid calling this statement into question, he was interested in minimizing the changes effected in the Senatorial constitution. Many articles, especially those that were meant to confirm the achievements of the Revolution and the Empire were indeed literally inserted in the Charte. But the Charte is much more detailed and therefore more precise than the Senatorial constitution. While the Senatorial constitution only contains 29 articles, the Charte numbers as many as 76. This may be called an improvement.

A comparison of the Estatuto Real with the constitution of Cádiz, however, reveals at once the great difference between the two texts. In the first place they differed extremely by dimension. Whereas the Estatuto contained 50 articles, the constitution of Cádiz extended to no less than 384. As far as the resolution of crucial questions is concerned, the most conspicuous deficiency is the absence of essential traits which are ordinarily expected from a constitution, most seriously the failure to state fundamental rights. Precisely in Spain which under Ferdinand VII had two times – in 1814 and in 1823 – experienced the repeal of the constitution of Cádiz and the return to unlimited despotism, legal guarantees were indispensable. In this respect the Regent had disregarded a crucial prerequisite of the success of any restoration when it imposed the Estatuto Real. Since the country still kept in mind the democratic constitution of 1812 which was widely regarded as a model, the imposition should have taken into account to a much larger extent the demands of the radical liberals in order to ensure at least a moderate chance of success.

It should not be overlooked that the forced reintroduction of the constitution of 1812 by the Regent on 13 August 1836 was subjected to the condition that government and Cortes cooperated in the elaboration of a new constitution. The Cortes were convoked for 24 October. A committee was entrusted with the elaboration of a draught. The new constitution was put into force on 18 June 1837. In determining the role of the Crown at the creation of the constitution the preamble returned to the formula of the constitution of 1812. Isabella II proclaimed the constitution as "Queen by divine right and by the constitution of the Spanish monarchy." Notwithstanding the formal appeal to divine right she simultaneously declares: "Since it is the national will to revise, in application of its sovereign rights, the constitution of Cádiz of 19 March 1812, the *Cortes generales,* having assembled for the purpose, decree and sanction the following constitution of the Spanish monarchy."[64]

The first title of the constitution contains a catalogue of fundamental rights which largely corresponds to the government draught of the preceding year. Legislation is entrusted to the two houses of Parliament, to the Senate and the Congress of deputies, on the one hand, and to the King on the other. The King is inviolable. The ministers are responsible. Without ministerial countersignature royal ordinances are ineffectual. Ministers may be members of either chamber. Both houses separately and the King have the right to initiate legislation.

By the preamble the Cortes placed the new constitution unmistakably on the foundation of national sovereignty. As compared to the Estatuto Real the definitely liberal character of the constitution of 1837 is also shown by the articles on the right to initiate legislation. Following the Charte constitutionnelle it was characteristic of imposed constitutions that they reserved this right to the crown and granted to parliament only the right of petition. In this way parliament should be prevented from infringing on the prerogatives of the Crown either by legislating or by changing the constitution. This protecting wall of the monarchical principle had disappeared through the repeal of the Estatuto Real, and the constitution of 1837 only underscored this change. The abrogation of the Estatuto Real confirmed the failure of constitutional restoration in Spain.

As compared to the other European monarchies the constitutional restoration in Spain was only of very short duration, and more than that: The imposed constitution of April 1834 was opposed from the outset by many citizens. Some explanations of this have already been given. On the whole it appears that the backwards oriented policies of Ferdinand VII had polarized Spanish society to a degree that after the two decades of his reign a constitutional compromise

---

64 Constitución de la Monarquía Española, 18 June 1837, Preamble.

had become impossible. If the imposition of the Estatuo Real was an attempt to attain the impossible the odds notwithstanding, it was clearly a much too half-hearted and thus unsuitable attempt. The incompletion of the Estatuto, the omission of a catalogue of fundamental rights, and the severe restrictions of the suffrage demonstrate a degree of timidity on the part of the Regent and her government which is hard to understand. It should not be overlooked, however, that she had taken over the government under extremely difficult circumstances. Ferdinand had severely undermined confidence in the monarchy. Upon his death a civil war broke out over the succession. The Queen was a three year old child, her mother a foreigner.

In comparison to the French restoration of 1814 the Spanish restoration of 1834 resembles a two-act play with a long break in between. The constellations after the breakdown of the Napoleonic Empire resembled each other. In both countries the monarchs were presented with a constitution based on national sovereignty when they returned from exile. But whereas Louis XVIII immediately subjected the Senatorial constitution to a revision and promulgated the revised version as an expression of monarchical sovereignty only a few weeks after his return, Ferdinand VII restored absolutism. It was only his widow Maria Cristina in her capacity as Queen Regent for his daughter Isabella II who finally decided to impose a constitution which remained, however, in many respects rudimentary, the Estatuto real. As it soon became clear, this concession came too late. Even the Regent's attempt of 1836 to impose a far more liberal constitution, proved unable to save monarchical sovereignty. There was no margin left for compromise. At last the Regent had no choice but to swear the democratic constitution of 1837.

Italy 1848

When the French Empire broke down Italy was divided into four areas of dominion.[1] A broad strip of territory along the Western coast of the Apennine Peninsula from Piedmont to Latium and including the city of Rome had been annexed by France and was governed from Paris. To the East it bordered on the Kingdom of Italy (*Regno d'Italia*) which had been founded in 1805 with Milan as capital. It was composed in the main of Lombardy, Venetia, Istria and Dalmatia, the Legations around Bologna, and the Marche region. Napoleon had himself crowned King and connected the Kingdom by personal union with the French Empire. His stepson Eugène de Beauharnais was made Viceroy. The Kingdom of Naples in the South was since 1806 a French satellite. At first governed by Napoleon's brother Joseph it was in 1808, after Joseph's takeover of the Spanish throne, placed under the government of Napoleon's brother-in-law Gioacchino Murat. The fourth area was formed by the Isles of Sicily and Sardinia which Napoleon had not been able to conquer, since they were shielded by the British fleet. On Sicily King Ferdinand IV of Naples had found refuge, on Sardinia King Victor Emanuel I of Sardinia. Upon the end of Napoleonic domination the former multiplicity of states was restored. But there were exceptions. The Republic of Genoa was annexed by the Kingdom of Sardinia, because the great powers wanted to erect a bulwark against new French expansionist tendencies at this point. The Republic of Venice was united with Lombardy in a Lombardo-Venetian Kingdom and in the interest of the European balance of power incorporated into the Habsburg monarchy. Possession of this Kingdom should secure to Austria the hegemony over the Italian peninsula and in this way stabilize the European states system as it had been renewed at the congress of Vienna. In the South the personal union of the Kingdom of Naples and Sicily was restored. But in 1816 King Ferdinand abrogated Sicilian autonomy and changed the personal union into a real union by the name of a Kingdom of the Two Sicilies (*Regno delle due Sicilie*), which he governed henceforth as King Ferdinand I from Naples. This step had major consequences for the interior structure of the Isle of Sicily: In the Kingdom of Naples incisive reforms had been carried through during the *Decennio francese* (French decade). These reforms, among other things the introduction of the *Code civil*, were from 1816 onwards transferred step by step to Sicily, whereas the con-

---

1 Alfonso Scirocco, *L'Italia del Risorgimento 1800–1871*, 2nd ed. (Bologna: Il Mulino, 1993), 14; see also Volker Sellin, "Die Restauration in Italien," in: Rainer Marcowitz and Werner Paravicini, eds., *Vergeben und Vergessen? Vergangenheitsdiskurse nach Besatzung, Bürgerkrieg und Revolution* (Munich: Oldenbourg, 2009), 126.

DOI 10.1515/9783110524536-005

stitution that had in 1812 been created on the English model under the patronage of the British plenipotentiary Lord Bentinck, was tacitly rendered inoperative.

From now on the Apennine Peninsula was subjected to Austrian hegemony for four and half decades. Until the revolution of 1848 Austrian policy was in the hands of State Chancellor Clemens Metternich. Under his leadership the Imperial government both in interior and in foreign relations persistently defended the Status quo. Wherever revolutionary tendencies made themselves felt, Metternich sought to intervene either by diplomatic or, if need should be, by military means, appealing to the alliance of the four great powers which had been concluded against France at Chaumont in March 1814 and renewed a year later. In addition he had secured himself against liberal reforms in the Kingdom of the Two Sicilies by the treaty of 12 June 1815 by which King Ferdinand was obliged not to admit any political changes that went beyond the principles governing in the Austrian provinces of Italy.[2] In Lombardy and in Venetia as well as in all other provinces of the Habsburg Empire Metternich opposed the introduction of constitutions for fear of encouraging the struggle for independence of the various nationalities. By the treaty just mentioned King Ferdinand was prevented from according a constitution to his subjects. When however during the revolution of 1820 the citizens of his realm forced him to adopt the constitution the Spanish *Cortes* had voted in 1812, Austrian troops marched in and compelled him to return to absolutism, and when in 1821 the Spanish constitution was introduced in Piedmont, Austria again intervened militarily.[3]

The introduction of the Spanish constitution in the Kingdom of the Two Sicilies and in the Kingdom of Sardinia was no more than its introduction in Spain itself an act of restoration on the model of the imposition of the *Charte constitutionnelle* in France. The three monarchs, to be sure, acted under the pressure of the revolutionary movement like Louis XVIII. The constitution of Cádiz which was forced upon them, however, was not based on divine right like the Charte, but on the sovereignty of the people. Its introduction did not aim at strengthening the monarchical principle, but placed monarchy in the three countries at the disposition of the nation.

In Metternich's eyes the revolutions in the Kingdom of the Two Sicilies and in Piedmont were a consequence of injudicious policies. After the breakdown of

---

2 Traité d'Autriche et le roi des Deux-Siciles, 12 June 1815, articles séparés et secrets II, in: *Recueil des traités, conventions et actes diplomatiques concernant l'Autriche et l'Italie* (Paris: Amyot, 1859), 203.

3 For the revolutions of 1820/21 in Italy see Jens Späth, *Revolution in Europa 1820–23. Verfassung und Verfassungskultur in den Königreichen Spanien, beider Sizilien und Sardinien-Piemont* (Cologne: SH-Verlag, 2012).

Napoleonic domination in Italy these countries had restored the bureaucratic absolutism of the Ancien Régime and had not even preserved the council of State
characteristic of the Napoleonic constitutional system. The returning princes
thus renounced an institution which could have promoted the acceptance of
the monarchy among the population. The Napoleonic council of State had
been an institution independent from the bureaucracy and in which not only
highly placed state's servants but also representatives of the social elites advised
the ruler und reported regularly on the needs of the country.[4] The *Supremo con-*
siglio di cancelleria which King Ferdinand I had created in December 1816 instead of the council of State did not possess the independence from the governing organs which had characterized the Napoleonic model. Accordingly the new
council was presided over not by the first minister as had been the case with the
council of State, but by the monarch.[5] In order to forestall further revolutions
Metternich obliged King Ferdinand on the congress of Laibach in 1821 to reintroduce independent advisory bodies. He called to mind the experiences Austria
had made in the government of the Lombardo-Venetian Kingdom, where as
early as 1815 advisory bodies consisting of elected representatives of the country
had been established: two general congregations seated in Milan and Venice re-
spectively and a provincial congregation in each province.[6] On 26 May 1821 Ferdinand I issued a decree which transformed the obligations imposed on the
Kingdom of the Two Sicilies at Laibach, into law. It provided for the creation
of two advisory bodies by the name of *Consulte di Stato* with far-reaching competences. The *Consulte* were to have their seats at Naples and Palermo. Besides,
in every province was to be created a provincial advisory body (*Consiglio provin-*
ciale).[7]

Metternich expected that by establishing Consulte the monarchy would be
strengthened, because they would, not unlike the Napoleonic Council of State,
enable representatives of the social elites to cooperate at the formation of public
policy. The Consulte were characteristic instruments of restoration, because they
were meant to contribute to the acceptance of monarchy, even if in political effi-
cacy they remained naturally far behind a constitution. But constitutions were
excluded by Metternich. That the advisory bodies had to exercise a restorative

---

4 On the Napoleonic Council of State see: Jacques Godechot, *Les institutions de la France sous la*
Révolution et l'Empire, 2nd ed. (Paris: Presses Universitaires de France, 1968), 561–563.
5 Carlo Ghisalberti, "Dalla monarchia amministrativa alla monarchia consultiva," in: Ghisalberti, *Contributi alla storia delle amministrazioni preunitarie* (Milan: Giuffrè, 1963), 155; Marco Meriggi, *Il Regno Lombardo-Veneto* (Turin: UTET, 1987), 42–62.
6 Ghisalberti, "Monarchia," 161.
7 Ibid., 162–164.

function, is demonstrated by a letter of the Austrian envoy to Naples, count Karl Ludwig von Ficquelmont, of 1 April 1824, to the State chancellor. The Consulte, he writes, are nothing but "an additional instrument in the hands of the King" that was to help him "reconstruct the monarchy" (*à reconstruire la monarchie*); their task was to inform the government of "the requirements and the truth." If "the concentration of power in the hands of the King" would constitute by itself already "the veritable monarchy" (*la véritable monarchie*), nothing would have to be changed at Naples, because since 1815 the King had had a free hand to do everything that he had deemed useful in the interest of the well-being of his subjects, and he had been able to do it again since 1821. In this respect "the monarchical principle" was valid without any limitation. In other words: The King of Naples ruled absolute, his will knew no limits, but still Ficquelmont would not regard the regime as a perfect monarchy. He maintained that it was not the will (*volonté*) of the King to which something had to be added. Missing was force (*force*). The Consulte or other advisory bodies could not by themselves provide him with force, if it was lacking, but they could show him how to find and use it. Only in this way "the real restoration of monarchy" (*la véritable restauration de la monarchie*) could begin.[8] But the government of Naples was not ready to follow Metternich's suggestions without reservation. They delayed even the application of their own decree of 1821. In the law of 1824 on the *Consulta generale del Regno* only a shadow remained of the original concept. The Consulta for Sicily was not established at Palermo but at Naples. Moreover, the tasks of the two bodies were reduced. By the decree of 1821 they would have been called to give an opinion on every draught law of the government, but the law of 1824 permitted them to give comments only at request.[9]

After Ferdinand I of Naples and Sicily the next Italian monarch to introduce an advisory body was King Carlo Alberto of Sardinia. By edict of 18 August 1831 he established a State council which in composition and attributions exceeded by far the Neapolitan Consulte. As is explained in the preamble to the edict the King expected from this institution that it disclose to him the needs of the population in the various parts of his country, make proposals for improvements and discover abuses if need should be. Accordingly, here as well a provision was made that to the general assembly of the State council were appointed, apart from senior officials, also leading representatives of society from all over the

8 Ruggero Moscati, ed., *Il Regno delle Due Sicilie e l'Austria. Documenti dal marzo 1821 al novembre 1830* (Naples: Presso la R. Deputazione, 1937), vol. 2, 238–239.
9 Ghisalberti, "Monarchia," 163, 169–171.

country. This norm, however, was already suspended for an indefinite period of time in September 1831. Maintained was the regulation that the council of State would give an opinion on every bill before its enactment.[10]

In other States of the Peninsula the introduction of consultative bodies was delayed. Obviously, measures for the stabilization of thrones at the moment were not considered urgent. The reason was less a belief that the monarchies were stable than Austrian hegemony in Italy. Since military interventions of the Habsburg monarchy were to be expected, as soon as revolution appeared imminent anywhere, the Italian princes did not feel obliged to secure their thrones in the long term by way of concessions. Quite to the opposite, after the experience of 1821 they had to reckon with Austrian intervention just as well, if they tackled liberal reforms in their countries by themselves. Under these circumstances the concession of constitutions and thus the only efficient type of a long-lasting restoration was out of the question until 1848.

The political stagnation was drawing to a close only after Cardinal Giovanni Mastai Ferretti had been elected to the Holy See on 16 June 1846. On 21 June the new Pope was inaugurated and adopted the Papal name of Pius IX. Four weeks later, following an ancient custom, he proclaimed an amnesty thanks to which in the States of the Church hundreds of political prisoners were released and hundreds of fugitive and exiled persons were invited to return home.[11] As never before, the amnesty of 1846 was hailed enthusiastically, even far beyond the borders of the Papal States. In numerous cities of the Peninsula joyous demonstrations took place. The Papal action was everywhere understood as a harbinger of liberty, of political unity and of Italian national independence. In the words of Giacomo Martina the amnesty was "the spark" that "carried the fire all over Italy and into a great part of Europe." It had even aroused a "collective fever."[12] The governments felt threatened by the public stir Pius IX had created by his amnesty, since everywhere the demonstrations of joy and gratitude were mixed with demands of political reforms.[13] To what degree the demonstrations were coordinated across the borders of the single States is shown by a sym-

---

10 Ibid., 175–180; Paola Notario and Narciso Nada, *Il Piemonte sabaudo. Dal periodo napoleonico al Risorgimento* (Turin: UTET, 1993), 210–213.

11 Giacomo Martina, *Pio IX*, vol. 1 (1846–1850) (Rome: Ed. Pontificia Univ. Gregoriana, 1974), 97–100. Martina estimates that about 400 prisoners had been released; the number of exiled and fugitive persons who were invited to return appears to have been similar.

12 Ibid., 101.

13 Narciso Nada, "Le riforme carlo-albertine del 1847," *Rassegna storica toscana* 45 (1999), 262; for developments in the Regno delle Due Sicilie see: Alfonso Scirocco, "Il 1847 a Napoli: Ferdinando II e il movimento italiano per le riforme," *Archivio storico per le province napoletane* 115 (1997), 437–438.

bolic act of national protest during the night of 10 December 1846, when on the highest summits of the Apennines from Liguria down to Calabria gigantic fires were lit.[14] The authors of the action are unknown.

By the election of Pius IX and the ensuing amnesty the whole of Italy had over night got into a revolutionary situation. Most of the governments sought to obviate the menace by reforms. It is obvious that all of a sudden they no longer were sure that they could rely on the military power of Austria alone for protection. Therefore the year of 1847 was to become in all States of the Peninsula, with the exception of Lombardy and Venetia, a year of reforms from above.[15] But the idea that the absolute monarchs even now still had the chance to calm down the aroused spirits by introducing reforms without renouncing the monarchical principle was questionable. This is illustrated by a satirical article of 21 June 1848, published in the democratically oriented *Gazzetta del Popolo* of Turin, in which the "moderate monarchy" (*monarchia moderata*) is said to be "not only just as despotic," but "dissimulated over and above" that it was not.[16]

Forerunner in the policy of reform of 1847 was again Pius IX whose country, to be sure, of all Italian monarchies required modernization by far the most urgently. The press law of 15 March 1847 introduced the most liberal censorship in contemporary Italy.[17] On 19 April 1847 the Papal government issued a circular by which the institution of a *Consulta di Stato* was initiated.[18] From each province of the Papal States should be elected and sent to Rome a person who "excelled by his social position, by his wealth and by his knowledge" and who "was devoted to the government and enjoyed public reputation and the trust of his fellow citizens." With the help of the appointed person the public administration should be improved.[19] When the news of the Papal initiative became known to the public the citizens of Rome thronged Piazza del Popolo and from there marched to Quirinal Palace where the Pope resided. Their route was illuminated by thousands of torches fixed to the balconies of the houses. The procession carried with it a poster on which in big letters was reproduced the Papal circular.[20] By

---

14 Nada, "Riforme," 254–255.

15 On 20 and 21 March 1998 a congress was held in Florence that was devoted to the reforms of 1847; see "Le riforme del 1847 negli Stati italiani," *Rassegna storica toscana* 45 (1999).

16 Quoted from: Filippo Mazzonis, "La monarchia sabauda," in: Umberto Levra, ed., *Il Piemonte alle soglie del 1848* (Rome: Carocci, 1999), 151–152.

17 Martina, *Pio IX*, 125.

18 Alberto Maria Ghisalberti, *Nuove ricerche sugli inizi del pontificato di Pio IX e sulla Consulta di Stato* (Rome: Vittoriano, 1939), 34, 39 and passim; Martina, *Pio IX*, 129–130.

19 Quoted from: Angelo Ara, *Lo Statuto fondamentale dello Stato della chiesa (14 marzo 1848)* (Milan: Giuffrè, 1966), 38.

20 Ibid.

his decision to institute a Consulta di Stato Pius IX not only introduced a reform of the State but permitted for the first time the participation of laymen in the administration of the States of the Church. Under the chairmanship of a cardinal to whom was adjoined a prelate as vice-chairman, the 24 ordinary members of the body assembled on 15 November in Rome for their inaugurating session. They had been chosen by the sovereign from proposals transmitted to him by the provincial councils, each one containing three names. The Roman aristocracy was as well represented in the Consulta as the landed nobility of the provinces. Members of the agricultural bourgeoisie were seated next to representatives of the educated and the economic middle-classes of the towns. Among the members there were numerous lawyers.[21] The high-pitched expectations the public connected with the Consulta caused the Pope in the very first session to make it clear that even though he loved to stand up for his subjects, he would not tolerate that from "the supreme rights of his Papal office, as he had received it from God and his predecessors," the least part be curtailed. The attributions of the Consulta were limited to advising his conscience and to discussions with the ministers and the Holy Office. Those who expected that the Consulta would put into practice "any private utopia" and the foundation-stone of an institution "incompatible with Papal sovereignty," deceived themselves.[22] Obviously the Pope was afraid to be driven by the wave of consent with which the first reforms were greeted, from one concession to the next. The Austrian state chancellor Metternich belonged to the number of those who, nevertheless, regarded the establishment of the Roman Consulta as a first step towards the overthrow of the existing political system. On 2 November 1847 he wrote to the Austrian envoy at Paris that the Roman Consulta contained the germ of a representative system that was compatible neither with the sovereignty of the head of the catholic world nor with the constitutions of the church.[23]

Like a confirmation of Metternich's apprehensions appears a heated discussion of December within the Consulta itself about the publication of their debates. In the final analysis the question touched upon the nature of the institution. The Pope insisted on secrecy. To him the Consulta was a body to advise the ruler. The advocates of publication on the other hand argued that its members had emerged from elections, and the electors ought to have the opportunity to inform themselves on the performance of the elected. By this argument the Con-

---

21 A list of the members ibid., 54.

22 Quoted from ibid., 55–56.

23 Metternich to Apponyi, 2 November 1847, in: [Clemens Metternich], *Aus Metternich's nachgelassenen Papieren*, ed. Richard Metternich-Winneburg, vol. 7 (Vienna: Braumüller, 1883), no. 1617, 436.

sulta was looked upon as something close to a representation of the people. Whereas Pius IX regarded the Consulta as the utmost concession he was ready to make, the discussion about the publicity of their debates shows how a demand of reform, once fulfilled, brought forth further demands.[24] Not without reason Carlo Ghisalberti has defined the consultative monarchy (*monarchia consultiva*) as a mere intermediate stage in the development from bureaucratic absolutism (*monarchia amminstrativa*) to constitutional monarchy (*monarchia rappresentativa* or *costituzionale*). Conservatives regarded the consultative monarchy as a welcome alternative, liberals as a prelude to monarchical constitutionalism.[25]

On 7 May 1847 Grand-Duke Leopoldo II of Tuscany enacted a law on the freedom of the press on the model of the Roman press law of 15 March. On 24 August a Consulta was established in Florence as well.[26] The creation of a militia followed. Towards the end of the year the call for a constitution intensified. But the government hesitated because it was afraid that political concessions might provoke Austria to a new intervention.[27] Carlo Alberto of Sardinia on 29 October 1847 also ordered a series of reforms on the example of the States of the church and Tuscany. A press law reformed censorship; the competences of the police were restricted. A new criminal procedure was introduced. The people greeted the measures with demonstrations.[28] On 27 November an edict on the reform of the communal and provincial administration was issued. In the future the communal councilors (*consiglieri comunali*) should be elected. The mayor (*sindaco*) should be chosen by the King from among the elected communal councilors. The provincial councilors should be determined by the King from a list of candidates presented to him by the communal councilors. In the same way he was to proceed in the appointment of the divisional councilors. The whole of the communal reform, however, remained a dead letter, because in March 1848 it was rendered obsolete by the imposition of the constitution.[29]

On 12 January 1848, on the 38th anniversary of Ferdinand II, King of the Two Sicilies, a riot broke out at Palermo, the first revolution of 1848 in Europe. The aims of the revolt were political autonomy and the restoration of the Sicilian constitution of 1812 with timely adjustments. Within only seventeen days the garrison was driven out of the city. By the middle of February the government of

---

24 On the debate see: Ara, *Statuto*, 67–75.
25 Ghisalberti, *Monarchia*, 174, 182.
26 Luigi Lotti, "Leopoldo II e le riforme in Toscana," *Rassegna storica toscana* 45 (1999), 248.
27 Ibid., 245, 249–250.
28 Nada, "Riforme," 263–264.
29 Ibid., 264–267.

the Bourbons on the Island had broken down. Only the city of Syracuse and the citadel of Messina had withstood the assaults.[30] The unrest soon extended to the mainland. Following revolts in Cilento in the province of Salerno, on 27 January at Naples a demonstration took place with thousands of participants.[31] Repeatedly the people shouted: "Long live Pius IX! Long live Italy! Long live the constitution!"[32] Thereupon on 29 January the King promised to impose a constitution.[33] The year before, Ferdinand had repeatedly refused to cede to the pressure of his first minister, the Marquis of Pietracatella, and embark on reforms like the other Italian monarchs in order to meet the expectations of the public. No later than 8 September 1846 Pietracatella had warned the King not to put his trust exclusively on the army: "Instead of waiting weapons at the ready for the revolution everything must be done to prevent it."[34] At that time the minister had already pointed out the critical situation especially in Sicily: "Sicily perspires discontent from all pores: Even benefits remain without effect. Sicily is a case like Ireland and Poland."[35] In the provinces of the mainland the danger was just as great. Among the measures Pietracatella had proposed with a view to appeasing the citizens, were the restoration of the Consulte in the manner, in which they had originally been conceived, and the establishment of the Consulta for Sicily at Palermo, as Metternich had demanded at the congress of Ljubljana. In addition he had recommended a far-reaching autonomy for the Island and a greater degree of liberty of the press on the Prussian model.[36] At that time the King had disregarded Pietracatella's admonitions. Now the revolution had indeed broken out and had compelled Ferdinand on 29 January to promise a constitution. Two days earlier

---

30 Giorgio Candeloro, *Storia dell'Italia moderna*, vol. 3: *La rivoluzione nazionale (1846–1849)*, 3rd ed. (Milan: Feltrinelli, 1995), 120–123.

31 Kerstin Singer, *Konstitutionalismus auf Italienisch. Italiens politische und soziale Führungsschichten und die oktroyierten Verfassungen von 1848* (Tübingen: Niemeyer, 2008), 196–197.

32 Luigi Parente, "Francesco Paolo Bozzelli e il dibattito sulla costituzione," *Archivio storico per le province napoletane* 117 (1999), 78.

33 Singer, *Konstitutionalismus*, 195, 252ff.

34 Pietracatella to Ferdinand II, 8 September 1846, in: Alfonso Scirocco, "Il 1847 a Napoli: Ferdinando II e il movimento italiano per le riforme," Appendix, *Rassegna storica toscana* 45 (1999), 294: "Invece di aspettare la Rivoluzione con le armi al braccio, bisogna far di tutto per prevenirla"; idem in: *Archivio storico per le province napoletane* 115 (1997), 457.

35 Scirocco, "*1847*," *Rassegna storica toscana* 45 (1999), 296: "La Sicilia traspira da tutti i suoi pori il malcontento: gli stessi benefizi sono inefficaci. La Sicilia è un stereotipo dell'Irlanda, della Polonia."

36 Ibid., 297–298: "Vorrei come in Prussia permettere alla stampa di esaminare e discutere le quistioni d'interesse pubblico, ponendoci i limiti e le garanzie esistenti in Prussia."

he had dismissed Pietracatella and appointed the Duke of Serracapriola prime minister. On 30 January Francesco Paolo Bozzelli was made the new minister of the Interior.[37] Bozzelli was directed to present a draught constitution within ten days. The King signed the constitution on 10 February and proclaimed it on the next day. Bozzelli had entered the public service of Naples under the government of Joseph Bonaparte. Following his participation in the rising of 1820 he had been arrested and exiled in 1821. During his exile he had got to know the political systems of England, France, and Belgium.[38] This explains why his draught was heavily influenced by the Charte constitutionnelle of 1814 and 1830 and by the Belgian constitution of 1831. Other than the revised Charte of 1830 and the Belgian constitution Bozzelli's draught was based exclusively on the monarchical principle. King Ferdinand declared in the preamble, to be sure, that he had promised a constitution because of the "unanimous desire of his dearly beloved peoples," but he added that this promise had originated from his "full, free, and spontaneous will." To this corresponded the way in which the constitution was made. No body, elected by the nation, took part in its elaboration. The King alone imposed it, Ferdinand II, by divine right *Re del Regno delle Due Sicilie.*[39] The constitution did not grant autonomy to Sicily. The island did not receive its own parliament.

As late as 1847 Ferdinand II had felt so secure on his throne that, other than the rest of the Italian monarchs, he had not considered it necessary to take account of the public criticism the political torpidity had aroused. Now it was him who by the precipitate imposition of 11 February foiled the attempts of the governments at Rome, Florence, and Turin, to weaken the revolutionary movement by initiating moderate reforms. Ferdinand's rushing ahead left to the other monarchs no choice but to impose constitutions as well.

From the point of view of a lasting restoration of monarchy, to the *Statuto albertino* must be given precedence over the other three constitutions. When the revolution was over, the monarchs at Naples, Rome, and Florence restored absolutism and thereby entirely jeopardized their credibility. By consequence they lost their thrones in the process of national unification between 1859 and 1861. Only in the Kingdom of Sardinia the constitution was retained beyond the year of 1849. Since between 1859 and 1870 the King of Sardinia annexed one after the other all other States of the Peninsula, the Statuto albertino became

---

37 Romualdo Trifone, "La costituzione del Regno delle Due Sicilie dell'11 febbraio 1848," *Archivio storico per le province napoletane* 70 (1947–1949), 28.

38 Parente, "Bozzelli," 82–83.

39 Costituzione del Regno delle Due Sicilie, 11 Febbraio 1848, in: Alberto Aquarone et al., eds., *Le costituzioni italiane* (Milan: Ed. di Comunità, 1958), 565.

the constitution of the Italian national State and remained in force until the end of the monarchy in 1946.

By imposing the Statuto the government in Turin responded to the crisis that had unexpectedly broken upon the monarchy in the beginning of 1848. In reaction to the demonstrations that followed the amnesty of Pius IX neither King Carlo Alberto nor the other monarchs had let themselves be induced to share power with a representative assembly. His ideal remained bureaucratic absolutism, a monarchy possessing an administration that was enlightened but in no ways hostile to innovation. The reforms he carried through in October and November 1847, corresponded to this conception. It should be noted, however, that even before the announcement of a constitution at Naples it had become evident that the reforms only stimulated the citizens to expect further concessions. Several political newspapers of various tendencies were founded in Turin at the end of 1847 following the relaxation of censorship. By their reports and commentaries they accompanied from now on the political development. One of the newspapers was *Il Risorgimento*, organ of moderate liberalism, of the *moderati*. Director of *Il Risorgimento* became Cesare Balbo. But the driving force in the background was Camillo di Cavour.[40]

Within the monarchy the strongest impulses towards a continuation of the reforms came from Genoa. On 4 and 5 January at mass demonstrations in the city the expulsion of the Jesuits and the creation of a civil guard were demanded. Cesare Cabella drafted a petition to this effect and collected at least fifteen thousand signatures. In the evening of 5 January at Marquis Andrea Doria's house a deputation of nine men was elected and charged to transmit the petition to the King. The next morning the deputation left for Turin. But the King would not allow himself to be pushed on the way of reforms by his subjects and refused to receive the deputation. Instead he ordered the minister of the Interior, Giacinto Borelli, to point out to them the lawlessness of their undertaking and to send them back home. Meanwhile the Genovese initiative was taken over by the citizens of the capital as well. In the evening of 7 January the representatives of the Turin newspapers assembled at Hotel Europa and discussed possibilities of supporting the deputation from Genoa.[41] Whereas democratically-oriented participants of the assembly proposed to make one's own the demands of the Genovese, Camillo di Cavour proposed on behalf of the moderate wing of the liberals (*moderati*) at the assembly, to chose a different path and invite the

---

40 Rosario Romeo, *Cavour e il suo tempo*, vol. 2 (1842–1854) (Bari: Laterza, 1977), 272–278.
41 [Camillo Cavour], *Tutti gli scritti di Camillo Cavour*, ed. Carlo Pischedda and Giuseppe Talamo, vol. 3 (Turin: Centro Studi Piemontesi, 1977), 1030, n. 1.

King to grant a constitution.[42] In the beginning of November 1847, immediately after Carlo Alberto's reform edicts of 29 October, Cavour had already declared that the introduction of the representative system was ineluctable, but had expected it to come only after a couple of years.[43]

The explanation of his unforeseen proposal is to be found in an unsigned article Cavour published on 8 January in the newspaper *Il Risorgimento*. The article begins by a harsh criticism of the events at Genoa. They threatened the public order and endangered the continuation of the policy of reform. Most of all they put at risk the "harmony between monarch and citizens." Demonstrations as those of Genoa endangered "the foundation of any free government." Freedom of opinion presupposed debate. But debates were made impossible "if the clamour of masses of men in the streets and on the squares of a city dictates the law to the State."[44] However, Cavour warned the government to counteract unrest with coercive measures: "Violence breeds more violence." The demands of the citizens had to be examined. For the sake of examinations of this kind the Council of State (*Consiglio di Stato*) had been established. However, in its present composition the Council of State was not able truly to represent national opinion. Therefore the appointment of additional individuals was required – in the interest of the continuation of the reforms, for securing the independence and freedom of the fatherland, for the well-being of the citizens and for the stabilization of the throne of Savoy on which all Italians placed their hopes.[45]

The terms constitution and representative system do not appear in the article. But its recommendations were tantamount to replacing the Council of State that had been created on the model of the consultative monarchy, by a real representation of the people and to creating a constitutional monarchy. By his explicit reference to the establishment of the Council of State Cavour sought to insert his espousal of institutional reform in the political course the King had already adopted. That was a clever assessment of the King's cast of mind, all the more so since Cavour simultaneously distanced himself emphatically from the disturbances at Genoa. The King should not allow the street to force upon him a policy. Instead it should result from his free decision. At the end of the article the motif of the advice emerges: restoration and stabilization of the monar-

42 Narciso Nada, *Dallo Stato assoluto allo Stato costituzionale. Storia del Regno di Carlo Alberto dal 1831 al 1848* (Turin: Istituto per la storia del Risorgimento italiano, Comitato di Torino, 1980), 163; Romeo, *Cavour*, vol. 2, 282–283.
43 Cavour to Émile de la Rüe, [6 November 1847], in: Camillo Cavour, *Epistolario*, vol. 4 (1847), ed. Narciso Nada (Bologna: Zanichelli, 1978, 371; Romeo, *Cavour*, vol. 2, 280–282.
44 [Camillo Cavour], ["I fatti di Genova"], in: idem, *Scritti*, vol. 3, 1030–1031.
45 Ibid., 1031.

chy in the long term. The unimpaired political debate with "free, educated, and enlightened citizens" protected "the prince from the revolt of the people in exactly the same way as it protected the people from arbitrary actions of the men in power."[46]

However, Carlo Alberto was not yet ready to take such a step. For the time being the reforms of 1847 had touched upon the limits of his readiness for concessions. Meanwhile the development in the South of Italy came to a head. To the imposition of a constitution by King Ferdinand II Carlo Alberto reacted with deep resentment. In a personally hand-written letter to the minister of the Interior Borelli he pointed out that the King of Naples could not have done greater harm to the repose of Italy. It was to be expected that the success of the opposition in the Kingdom of the Two Sicilies would encourage the opposition in other States as well to enhance their activities. But this was no reason for the government in Turin to lose courage, quite the contrary. If at Genoa, as the general governor of the City, Marchese della Planargia, foresaw, a demonstration of joy should be organized, patience was required. If, however, the demonstrators should demand a constitution for Piedmont-Sardinia as well, he was determined to fight to the bitter end.[47] But on 2 February the King believed the situation to be critical to a degree that he considered laying down his crown.[48] But his ministers entreated him to stay. At a session of the *Consiglio di conferenza*, the council of ministers, Borelli declared that the abdication of the King would be the greatest misfortune for the country. His name alone was a power. If he abdicated, everything would fall down, and even the cause of the dynasty would be compromised.[49] Therefore he asked the King to reconsider his attitude towards the constitutional question. The decision of Ferdinand of Naples had indeed brought about a new situation. The demand of a representative form of government would soon be made in

---

46 Ibid., 1032.

47 Emilio Crosa, "Lo Statuto del 1848 e l'opera del ministro Borelli. Con lettere inedite di Carlo Alberto," *La Nuova Antologia*, vol. 177, 5th series, 16 June 1915, 538–539.

48 Nada, *Stato*, 164.

49 Consiglio di Conferenza presieduto da Sua Maestà. Processo verbale della seduta del 3 febbraio 1848, in: Luigi Ciaurro, ed., *Lo Statuto albertino illustrato dai lavori preparatori* (Rome: Dipartimento per l'informazione e l''editoria, 1996), 119; the minutes of the Consiglio di Conferenza are published also in: Domenico Zanichelli, ed., *Lo Statuto di Carlo Alberto secondo i processi verbali del Consiglio di Conferenza dal 3 febbraio al 4 marzo 1848* (Rome: D. Alighieri, 1898); and in: Adolfo Colombo, ed., *Dalle riforme allo Statuto di Carlo Alberto. Documenti editi ed inediti*, Casale: Società per la Storia del Risorgimento Italiano. Pubblicazioni del Comitato Piemontese, 1924; see also: Alessandro Luzio, "Dalle riforme allo Statuto di Carlo Alberto," *Archivio storico italiano* 84 (1926), 92–93.

Piedmont as well.[50] On 3 February 1848, at a meeting of the Consiglio di conferenza under the chairmanship of the King, Borelli recommended openly the imposition of a constitution. The arguments by which he tried to win over the King,
underscore the restorative motif of the proposal. The point of departure of his
reasoning was the idea that an uprising would take place, unless it was prevented in time: "Refusing a constitution could provoke unrest, a revolt, perhaps
bloodshed and at last anarchy."[51] If the King waited, until the constitution was
forced upon him by the revolution, he inevitably risked weakening the monarchy. If, however, he granted it of his own accord, before it was demanded
from him, he would strengthen the throne and monarchy and neutralize the advance of the agitators, and the formation of the constitution would remain in his
own hands. Openly Borelli threatened the resignation of the entire cabinet if the
King insisted on his point of view.[52] After Borelli the other ministers spoke one
after the other. Unanimously they underlined the gravity of the situation and endorsed the advice of the minister of the Interior. Only by granting a constitution
could the King save the State and the dynasty, the minister of public works, Des
Ambrois, added.[53] Several ministers did not believe that the country was ready
for constitutionalism. After the latest developments in Sicily and Naples, however, revolt and anarchy threatened if the Crown refused to make the necessary
concessions.

On 5 February at an extraordinary meeting the municipal council of the city
of Turin resolved to send a petition to the King asking for a constitution. The cav-
alier Derossi di Santa Rosa had introduced the proposal. In the petition reference
is made to the demonstrations not only in Naples, but in Genoa, Turin, and many
other cities of Piedmont as well, and it was asserted that the constitution would
complete the reforms of the previous autumn, fortify the government and render
the throne more secure.[54]

At the next meeting of the Consiglio di conferenza on 7 February it was resolved that the King publicly promise on the next day to grant a constitution. It is
a symptom of the general sensation of crisis that the government tried to inform

---

50 See Borelli's undated letter to Carlo Alberto in: Crosa, "Statuto," 540–541.
51 Consiglio di Conferenza, 3 febbraio 1848, in: Ciaurro, *Statuto*, 119: "Il rifiuto di una costituzione potrebbe portare a dei moti, ad una insurrezione, forse a dei massacri e in seguito all'a-
narchia."
52 Ibid., 114: "Bisogna darla, non lasciarsela imporre; dettare le condizioni, non riceverle; bisogna avere il tempo di scegliere con calma i modi e l'opportunità, dopo aver promesso di impie-
garli."
53 Ibid., 116.
54 Consiglio generale straordinario di Torino, 5 February 1848, in: Colombo, *Riforme*, 168–169.

the public as comprehensively as possible of its intentions. In this way the decision fitted in well with the restorative tenor of the discussions in the Consiglio di conferenza. In all contributions it was pointed out that Carlo Alberto governed his country excellently and that therefore there was in fact no reason to introduce a new system of government. The question of imposing a constitution was discussed exclusively from a tactical point of view. The debate did not center on the advantages or disadvantages of constitutionalism in contrast to bureaucratic absolutism, but on the best method of steering the monarchy as uninjured as possible through the crisis and to preserve power and authority of the Crown.

A few days later Cavour commented on the events in a letter to Giacomo Giovanetti, writing of "the so happily mastered crisis." The King had ceded "to the necessity of the times." A constitution had become unavoidable in order to prevent the unrest from spreading and to stop the radical party that strove towards an "ultra-democratic constitution." Cavour continued that the situation required the formation of a "conservative liberal party" (*un partito liberale conservatore*). He expected that soon an "extreme, impatient party" (*un partito estremo, impaziente*) would be formed. One had to get ready to fight it and to support the government in this struggle.[55] On 13 February 1848 Cavour wrote to Mathilde de La Rive, in few weeks the political institutions of the country had experienced a "complete revolution." He called it a "happy revolution," because it had cost neither tears nor blood, and above all, because the Crown had neither been humiliated nor deprived of its moral authority. The hitherto existing institutions had no longer been in accord with the development of society: The new institutions would, so he hoped and believed, "satisfy the overwhelming majority of the country." He was convinced that there was no reason to fear "further upheavals."[56]

Indeed: Monarchical sovereignty had been maintained. No concessions had been made to democracy. Accordingly, Carlo Alberto on 4 March proclaimed the *Statuto albertino* in his capacity of King by the grace of God. He retained Ancien Régime language also in that in the preamble he addressed not the citizens but

---

55 Cavour to Giacomo Giovanetti, [after 8 February 1848], in: Camillo Cavour, *Epistolario*, vol. 5 (1848), ed. Carlo Pischedda (Bologna: Zanichelli, 1980), 55.

56 Cavour to Mathilde de La Rive, 13 February 1848, ibid., 64: "Dans quelques semaines une révolution complète s'est opérée dans nos institutions politiques. Révolution heureuse, car elle n'a coûté ni larmes ni sang et surtout parce qu'elle s'est accomplie sans que le pouvoir se soit avili ou dépouillé de son autorité morale. Les anciennes institutions étaient en désaccord complet avec notre état social; les nouvelles satisferont, je l'espère et le crois, la grande majorité du pays. Aussi je suis convaincu que nous n'avons pas d'autres bouleversements à craindre."

his "well-beloved subjects" (*i nostri amatissimi sudditi*).[57] The concept of subject was unfit for the constitutional age.[58] But the wording is not strictly upheld in the text of the constitution. The section on the fundamental rights is devoted to the rights and duties of the "citizens" (*cittadini*). Article 24 states that all inhabitants of the Kingdom (*regnicoli*) are equal before the law. But beyond such terminological variations the constitution was without doubt liberal. Article 10 placed the right to initiate legislation into the hands both of the monarch and of the two chambers, and article 67 limited the monarch's freedom of discretion by the prescription, central in all monarchical constitutions, that acts of government would only be valid if they were countersigned by the responsible minister.

In the meantime in Tuscany as well unrest had attained a degree that Grand-Duke Leopoldo II no longer could avoid promising to his country a constitution. During the whole of 1847 the government in Florence had reacted to the repeated demands of reform with utmost restraint. A disappointing press law, the creation of a civil guard and the institution of a Consulta with limited advisory competence had not been sufficient to subdue the growing excitement.[59] In September 1847 the Grand-Duke was told by his own foreign minister, Neri Corsini, that "the only means" that had remained, "to replace the government on secure foundations was the transition from pure monarchy (*monarchia pura*) to moderate monarchy (*monarchia temperata*)." If Leopoldo did not grant "a reasonable constitution," he ran into the danger that a constitution would be forced upon him which was essentially determined by the "democratic principle."[60] On 13 February Bettino Ricasoli warned the government in his paper *La Patria* not to delay the unavoidable step any longer. The longer the government hesitated, the weaker the monarchy became.[61] In the meantime this admonition had become obsolete, because at court by order of the Grand-Duke for two days a committee of five notables had been busy elaborating the text of a constitution. The committee had been instituted through highest resolve (*motuproprio*) of 31 January and was orig-

---

57 Statuto del regno di Sardegna, 4 March 1848, preamble, in: Aquarone, *Costituzioni*, 662; also in: Wilhelm Altmann, ed., *Ausgewählte Urkunden zur außerdeutschen Verfassungsgeschichte seit 1776* (Berlin: R. Gaertners Verlagsbuchhandlung, 1897), 227.

58 See: Volker Sellin, "Regierung, Regime, Obrigkeit," in: Otto Brunner, Werner Conze, and Reinhart Koselleck, eds., *Geschichtliche Grundbegriffe. Historisches Lexikon zur politisch-sozialen Sprache in Deutschland*, vol. 5 (Stuttgart: Klett-Cotta, 1984), 411–412.

59 Antonio Chiavistelli, "Toscana costitutionale: La difficile gestazione dello statuto fondamentale del 1848," *Rassegna storica del Risorgimento* 84 (1997), 345–347.

60 Quoted from ibid., 351.

61 Ibid., 353–354: "Quanto più si tarda a stipulare questo patto fra Principato e Popolo tanto più il Principato si indebolisce."

inally meant only to prepare a reform of the existing press law and of the Consulta di Stato. There had at first been no mention of a constitution.[62] Obviously, Leopoldo had still hoped to avoid this concession. His change of mind was caused by the news of Carlo Alberto's promise of a constitution for the Kingdom of Sardinia of 8 February. This is shown already by the dates, since on 11 February the Grand-Duke enlarged the task of the committee by an additional *motuproprio* in which the creation of a national representation (*rappresentanza nazionale*) was announced. All at once time appeared essential for the defense of the throne. To the citizens of Tuscany, however, the Grand-Duke appealed by his second *motuproprio* not to lose patience: "Wait calmly only a few more days until the projects which are meant to secure your future, are ready."[63]

The committee fulfilled its new task within four days. Therefore the Grand-Duke was able to proclaim the *Statuto fondamentale* as soon as 15 February.[64] The constitution provided for two chambers, a Senate to be appointed by the Grand-Duke for life, and a Chamber of deputies (*Consiglio generale*), the 86 members of which were to be elected.[65] The right to initiate legislation was reserved to the government (Art. 50). With this constitution Tuscany placed itself on the level of the Charte constitutionnelle of 1814. The Grand-Duke was not prepared as yet to make a single step beyond absolute necessity.

In the Papal States as late as January 1848 the impression had prevailed as though the public were satisfied by the reforms of the year 1847. But the promises of the King of the Two Sicilies gave a new impulse to the opposition. In early February there were demonstrations for a constitution in the streets and on the squares of Rome and in other cities of the States of the Church.[66] The demonstrations were mixed up with anti-clerical elements. On 8 February at a great gathering at Rome people shouted: "Death to the government of priests!" (*Morte al ministero de' preti*).[67] Obviously, the demand of a constitution in the States of the Church aimed not only at political participation but also at the secularization of the State. If the Pope hesitated longer than all the other Italian sovereigns, before he promised a constitution, one of the reasons was certainly the difficulty to separate spiritual and secular power in a constitutional system. On 12 February he appointed a commission of ten members and ordered it "to propose systems

---

62 Ibid., 359–360.
63 Quoted from: Statuto del Granducato di Toscana (1848), in: Aquarone, *Costituzioni*, 631.
64 Chiavistelli, "Toscana," 369–370.
65 Statuto del Granducato di Toscana, Titolo III, in: Aquarone, *Costituzioni*, 636–637.
66 Ara, *Statuto*, 85–86, 93–94.
67 Quoted from ibid., 96.

of government compatible with Papal authority."[68] Members of the commission were exclusively clergymen, among them seven cardinals.[69] Obviously, the Pope was afraid that the participation of laymen would lead to the demand that he share sovereignty with them.[70] On 12 March the commission adopted a constitution. On 14 March it was proclaimed by Pius IX. In the preamble the Pope recalled that in the preceding year he had instituted an "advisory representative assembly" (*rappresentanza consultiva*) and expected that it support his government in legislating and in the administration. But since the neighbouring countries had deemed "their peoples" mature enough to receive "the blessing of a not only advisory but decision-making representation," he did not want to demonstrate less respect towards his subjects than those. The constitution declared the "holy college of cardinals who elected the Pope" the Senate. Besides, provision was made for a parliament consisting of two chambers, a "High Council" (*Alto consiglio*) and a "Council of Deputies" (*Consiglio dei Deputati*). The right to initiate legislation was reserved to the government and to each of the two houses, provided that at least ten members supported an initiative of their respective chamber (Art. 35).

With the proclamation of the constitution of the Papal States all four of the Italian States not belonging to the house of Habsburg had adopted constitutionalism. The history of the impositions in the four States shows characteristic parallels in essential respects. Under the protection of the great powers and especially of Austria the governments concerned had been able until the beginning of 1848 to defend absolutism. The constitutions were imposed from fear of revolution as political demonstrations increased rapidly. The demonstrations were triggered by the amnesty Pope Pius IX had proclaimed after entering upon office in the summer of 1846. With the exception of Ferdinand II the Italian princes had at first tried to contain the revolutionary movement by reforms. Among the most important measures were a relaxation of censorship, the admission of civil guards, and the institution of advisory bodies (*Consulte*) of the kind the congress of Ljubljana had first imposed on the Kingdom of the Two Sicilies in 1821. In the beginning of the year 1848, however, it had become clear that the reforms were not sufficient to satisfy the citizens. The outbreak of the revolution at Palermo and the extension of the disturbances to the mainland caused King Ferdinand II to a precipitate promise of a constitution. In this way he triggered a chain reaction that within two months spread to the whole of Italy. Every success of the

---

68 Quoted from ibid., 108.
69 The names in: Aquarone, *Costituzioni*, 597.
70 Ara, *Statuto*, 110.

opposition in one State immediately encouraged the demonstrators in all others States to demand the same concession from their monarchs. Following the imposition of a constitution in Naples the monarchs feared for their thrones if they refused to cede to the demands. Only by imposing constitutions they hoped to save the monarchy, and the constitutions were just liberal enough to grant the attainment of this objective. In Sicily in particular, however, the constitution of 11 February for the Neapolitan-Sicilian composite State failed to satisfy the opposition, because it did not grant autonomy to the Island.

On 12 March 1849 Ferdinand II dissolved the parliament at Naples not to convoke it again. But the 1848 constitution was not expressly abrogated. Formally revoked instead was the constitution of Tuscany. In his memoirs Grand-Duke Leopoldo justifies this decision by the political change-over that had taken place in Europe. The *coup d'état* of Louis-Napoléon Bonaparte of 2 December 1851 had driven away "the spectre of revolution": "France and Europe respired." On 31 December 1851 Emperor Francis Joseph had revoked the Austrian constitution. Thus the moment had arrived "to do away with the Tuscan constitution."[71] In November 1848 the Pope had fled from Rome. Thereupon elections to a constituent assembly had been held in the city. The assembly convened and proclaimed a republic. When in May 1849 the Pope returned on his throne with French help he did not restore the constitution of 1848. Only in the Kingdom of Sardinia the Statuto albertino of 4 March 1848 remained in force beyond the abortive revolution.

The impositions of constitutions in early 1848 were measures aimed at the restoration of the monarchies threatened by revolution. Each of the four sovereigns acted under the pressure of demonstrations and from fear of losing his throne. An imposed constitution is no less a contract between monarch and subjects. If a monarch revokes it one-sidedly or renders it tacitly inoperative, he commits a *coup-d'état*. Whereas the imposition was meant to strengthen the monarchy, the breach of the given promise was bound irrevocably to weaken it. This was revealed in 1860, when the citizens who had been cheated out of their constitutions, in their overwhelming majority valued the attainment of national unity under the Statuto albertino and King Victor Emanuel II of Sardinia higher than loyalty to their traditional rulers.

---

71 Franz Pesendorfer, ed., *Il governo di famiglia in Toscana. Le memorie del granduca Leopoldo II di Lorena (1824–1859)* (Florence: Sansoni, 1987), 397: "Era manifesto che era venuto il tempo di abolire lo Statuto toscano"; ibid., 399: "Il 6 maggio 1852 firmai il decreto d'abolizione dello Statuto."

Russia 1906

On 9 October 1905, at 6 o'clock in the evening, Tsar Nicholas II received his first minister, count Sergej Jul'evič Vitte, at Peterhof Palace for a conversation. Vitte had requested the audience on 6 October in a letter to the Tsar. He had been motivated to take this step by count Dmitrij Martynovič Sol'skij, president of the economic department of the Council of State.[1] Vitte had justified his request with the political demonstrations and strikes that had troubled the country for days. He pointed out that he agreed with Sol'skij in that "into the actions of the State life had to be breathed" and that "fundamental reforms of the whole administrative mechanism" had to be tackled.[2] It is characteristic of the situation of the Russian monarchy in these days that Vitte had to cover the distance of 30 kilometers from Sankt Petersburg by boat on the Neva, because the railways were on strike.[3] Vitte, born in Tiflis in 1849, had from 1892 to 1903 been Russian minister of finance. In this capacity he had, in accordance with Friedrich List's "National System of Political Economy," energetically espoused the development of the infrastructure and the rapid industrialization of Russia. Among his chief accomplishments were the introduction of the gold standard in 1897 and the construction of the Trans-Siberian Railway.[4] In August 1903 the Tsar unexpectedly released him from his office and appointed him president of the committee of ministers instead.[5] Since every minister possessed access to the sovereign his new position did not offer additional opportunities to influence policy.[6] Another important political commission was entrusted to Vitte only in June 1905. In February 1904 Japan had attacked Port Arthur on Liaodong peninsula which Russia had leased in 1898 for a period of 25 years, and by this act triggered the Russo-

---

1 Vladimir Josifovič Gurko, *Features and Figures of the Past. Government and Opinion in the Reign of Nicholas II* (Stanford: Stanford University Press, 1939), 92.

2 Sergej Jul'evič Vitte, *Vospominanija (Memoirs)* (Moscow: Izd. social'no-economičeskoj literatury, 1960), vol. 3 (17 October 1905 – 1911), 24. For the complicated history of the making and publication of Vitte's memoirs see Sidney Harcave, ed., *The Memoirs of Count Witte* (Armonk, N. Y./ London: M. E. Sharpe, 1990), Introduction, XIII-XXII.

3 Vitte, *Vospominanija*, vol. 3, 24: "The trains did not move, and the connection to New-Peterhof was maintained only by steamships on the Neva."

4 Sidney Harcave, *Count Sergei Witte and the Twilight of Imperial Russia. A Biography* (Armonk, N. Y./London: M. E. Sharpe, 2004), 3, 49 – 50, 68, 52 – 55, 60 – 64; Theodore H. von Laue, "Count Witte and the Russian Revolution of 1905," *American Slavic and East European Review* 17 (1958): 26.

5 Vitte, *Vospominanija*, vol. 2 (1894-October 1905), 244: "Ja vas prošu prinjat' post predsedatelja Komiteta ministrov (I am asking you to accept the post of president of the committee of ministers)"; Harcave, *Count Sergei Witte*, 102.

6 Ibid., 43.

DOI 10.1515/9783110524536-006

Japanese war for supremacy in Manchuria. In the course of the war the Tsarist Empire proved unequal to the new great power in the Far East. Symptomatic of Russian inferiority was the fate of its Baltic fleet. In order to employ it against Japan it had to be sent to the theatre of war through the Belt and around the Cape of Good Hope. Immediately upon arrival it was almost entirely annihilated on 14 May 1905 in the naval battle of Tsushima. From now on Russia's will of war was broken. On the invitation of the President of the United States, Theodore Roosevelt, plenipotentiaries of the two warring States in August met at Portsmouth, New Hampshire, for peace negotiations. Vitte had been appointed head of the Russian delegation. In recognition of his success in the negotiations the Tsar conferred the earldom upon him.

In the meantime the interior situation of Russia came to a head. Since the beginning of the year the country had been shaken by a series of severe crises. The 9 January 1905 is remembered in history as Bloody Sunday of St. Petersburg. A peaceful demonstration of workers who had come to hand over a petition to Tsar Nicholas II in the Winter Palace, ended up in a blaze of army gunfire. At least 130 people died, about a thousand were wounded.[7] The consequences for the autocracy were drastically represented to the Tsar only a few days later by the minister of Agriculture, Aleksej Sergeevič Ermolov, in a personal encounter. As Ermolov pointed out, the protest movement had already spread to other cities. An extension to the countryside could not be excluded. If it should come to extremes, the Tsar could no longer depend on the army. After all, the demonstrators originated from the same people as his soldiers. In spite of these warnings the Tsar did not heed Ermolov's advice to pronounce a public regret and to look after the families of the victims.[8] On 12 January Petr Struve wrote in a leading article of the paper *Osvoboždenie:* "In this way one cannot live on!"[9] On 4 February Grand-Duke Sergej Aleksandrovič, General Governor of Moscow and uncle of Nicholas II, fell victim to an assassination. It was the first mortal attempt upon the life of a member of the Tsar's family since the assassination of Alexander II in 1881. Bloody Sunday had triggered a series of strikes that exceeded everything that had been seen so far. In January alone, there were more workers on strike in Russia than in the previous ten years combined.[10] During the first

---

7 Manfred Hildermeier, *Die Russische Revolution 1905–1921* (Frankfurt: Suhrkamp, 1989), 51.
8 [Aleksej Sergeevič Ermolov], "Zapiski A. S. Ermolova" (Notes of A. S. Ermolov), *Krasnyj Archiv* 8 (1925): 51–53; see Volker Sellin, *Gewalt und Legitimität. Die europäische Monarchie im Zeitalter der Revolutionen* (Munich: Oldenbourg, 2011), 38–39.
9 Quoted from: Nathan Smith, *The Constitutional-Democratic Movement in Russia 1902–1906*, PhD Thesis, University of Illinois, Urbana 1958, 283: "Tak dal'še žit' nel'zja."
10 Ibid., 289.

quarter of 1905 more than twenty times the number of workers participated in strikes than in any one year since 1895. The strike movement spread to provinces which during the previous ten years had either not known any labour disputes at all or very few only.[11] At Ivanovo-Voznesensk, a center of the textile industry, 250 kilometers east of Moscow, the strike carried on for over two months, from May to July 1905.[12] In the course of the year numerous unions and professional associations were founded, even by members of the liberal professions. In May delegates of fourteen associations assembled in Moscow and created an umbrella organization, the "Union of Unions" (*sojus sojusov*). The liberal historian Pavel Miljukov was made president of the umbrella organization.[13] Society, separated from the State, was about to organize themselves.

During the first half of the year the strikers' demands were chiefly economic. But since strikes, regardless of their purpose, were against the law, every strike was a rebellion against the political authorities. Bloody Sunday had an impact on politics also in the narrow sense of the term. The Tsar realized that he had to approach society. In a ukase for the Senate of 18 February he encouraged authorities and citizens in the whole Empire to make proposals for the improvement of the political structures, a reverence to public opinion that was scarcely compatible with the claim to autocratic power.[14] Simultaneously he directed a rescript to the minister of the Interior, Aleksandr Grigor'evič Bulygin, and ordered him to form a commission and charge it to make plans for a representative body that was to discuss legislative proposals before they were adopted by the government.[15] The message for the Senate triggered a veritable flood of petitions during the ensuing months. The authors were in the main private associations of all kinds and several government agencies. The demands included the appointment of the members of the Bulygin committee by election, social and political reforms, and the convocation of a constituent assembly.[16] By calling a constituent assembly the Tsar would have acknowledged revolution. That was exactly what he sought to avoid. The empire-wide petition campaign, however, resulted in an unexpected politicization of the citizens, all

---

11 Abraham Ascher, *The Revolution of 1905*, vol. 1: *Russia in Disarray* (Stanford: Stanford University Press, 1988), 138.

12 Ibid., 145–150.

13 Ibid., 143.

14 Immenoj vysočajšij ukaz dannyj Pravitel'stvujuščemu Senatu (Highest order for the governing Senate), 18–20 February 1905, in: Zakonodatel'nye akty perechodnago vremeni 1904–1906 gg (Legislative acts of the period of transition 1904–1906) (Sankt Petersburg: Pravo, 1906), 23.

15 Vysočajšij reskript dannyj na imja Ministra Vnutrennich Del Aleksandr Grigor'evič (Highest rescript, directed to the minister of the Interior Aleksandr Grigor'evič), 18 February 1905, ibid., 27–28.

16 Smith, *Movement*, 299–300.

the more so since the proposals were for the most part published in the local news-papers with the consequence that the awareness of the need of reform spread every-where. The "consultative State Duma" (*Soveščatel'naja Duma*) was introduced on 6 August by a "Highest Manifesto" to which were attached a statute of the State Duma and an electoral law.[17]

Louis XVIII had represented the imposition of the Charte constitutionnelle as a bestowal of privileges in the tradition of the Kings of the Middle Ages in order to counteract any impression as though he had made concessions to the Revo-lution, incompatible with the ancient right of the monarchy. A similar endeavour is discernible in the manifesto by which the introduction of the consultative State Duma was announced. The Tsar maintains in the document "concord and unity" (*soglasie i edinenie*) of Tsar and people were "the great moral force that had created Russia in the course of the centuries." As early as 1903 he had appealed to the country to coordinate elected bodies and organs of the gov-ernment in the sphere of local administration with a view to overcoming conflicts among them. "The autocratic Tsars, our predecessors, have never ceased to re-flect upon this." Now time had come to follow their example. Nicholas expressly emphasizes that the introduction of a consultative Duma would not affect the "autocratic power" (*samoderžavnaja vlast'*) which was imbedded in the funda-mental law of the Empire.[18] Like Louis XVIII Nicholas placed the greatest empha-sis on retaining public power in its entirety, notwithstanding the concessions he had proclaimed. From 19 to 26 July he had invited the cabinet and high public officials along with several respected notables to a conference under his chair-manship at Peterhof Palace to discuss the proposals of the Bulygin commission. The central issue was the question whether a merely consultative State Duma was compatible with the Tsar's claim to unlimited possession of autocratic power.[19] Baron Schwanebach, one of the liberal-minded participants in the con-ference, felt very strongly about this. Turning to the Tsar who presided over the conference, he declared that it was natural that the reform in question would re-

---

17 Vysočajšij manifest, 6 August 1905, in: Zakonodatel'nye akty, 129–131; Učreždenie Gosu-darstvennoj Dumy (Institution of a State Duma), ibid., 131–145; Položenie o vyborach v Gosu-darstvennuju Dumu (Ordinance concerning the elections to the State Duma), ibid., 145–190; the manifesto and extracts of the elections order in English translation in: Marc Raeff, *Plans for Political Reform in Imperial Russia, 1730–1905* (Englewood Cliffs: Prentice Hall, 1966), 141–152; see also: Vitte, *Vospominanija*, vol. 2, chap. 49: "Bulyginskaja Duma" (Bulygin Duma), 482–489.
18 Vysočajšij manifest, 6 August 1905, in: Zakonodatel'nye akty, 129–130.
19 Andrew M. Verner, *The Crisis of Russian Autocracy. Nicholas II and the 1905 Revolution* (Princeton: Princeton University Press, 1990), 205; Bernard Pares, "The Peterhof Conference," The Russian Review 2/4 (1913): 87–120.

sult in "a limitation of your autocratic rights," but since it is a "self-limitation," it will "strengthen your Majesty's hallowed authority."[20] Thus he coined the basic idea of restoration into a single sentence: the forced cession of rights weakened, whereas the voluntary renunciation strengthened monarchy.

The electoral law that was proclaimed on 6 August along with the Imperial Manifesto and the statute of the State Duma, provided for an extremely complicated indirect procedure of elections to the Duma. High property qualifications excluded the working class and a large part of the agricultural population from the suffrage. At St. Petersburg out of a population of approximately 1,4 million only 7.130 persons had the right to vote, at Moscow 12.000 out of 1,1 million. For the population of the extra-European parts of Russia only unsatisfactory allowance was made.[21] The Duma was to meet no later than the middle of January of 1906.[22]

In June the doubts about the reliability of the armed forces which Ermolov had pronounced after Bloody Sunday, seemed to be confirmed when on the battleship Potemkin that belonged to the Black Sea fleet of Russia, a mutiny broke out. Triggered by a complaint of the cooks about rotten meat the revolt ended up at Odessa on 15 June in a new bloodshed. Thousands of Odessans had assembled at the port where members of the crew had deposited the corpse of their killed speaker Grigorij Nikitič Vakulenčuk upon a bier. Before long, agitators mixed with the crowd. Grief and protest turned into revolt. People marched plundering through the streets of the city. In the evening troops began to fire on the crowd. It is estimated that 2.000 people were killed, 3.000 were wounded.[23]

During the summer months the strike movement that had begun in January gradually subsided. But already in early autumn new conflicts were in the making. On 20 September in Moscow the printers downed tools, and in the beginning of October the Union of Railroad Employees proclaimed a general strike. On 10 October there was no more train from and to Moscow. The railroaders of St. Petersburg joined the strike. Within a short period of time food prices soared in Moscow and St. Petersburg. In Moscow the deceased could no longer be buried.[24]

That was the state of affairs when Vitte was received by Nicholas II on 9 October. In preparation for the encounter Vitte had asked Vladimir Dmitrjevič Kuzmin-Karavaev, a right-wing liberal exponent of the *zemstvo* movement, to draft a memorandum with a comprehensive program of government on the basis of fun-

20 Quoted from ibid., 97.

21 Ascher, *Revolution*, vol. 1, 179.

22 Vysočajšij manifest, 6 August 1905, 130.

23 Ascher, *Revolution*, vol. 1, 170 – 74; Jan Kusber, *Krieg und Revolution in Rußland 1904 – 1906. Das Militär im Verhältnis zu Wirtschaft, Autokratie und Gesellschaft* (Stuttgart: Steiner, 1997), 96 – 98.

24 Ascher, *Revolution*, vol. 1, 211– 15.

damental reflections on political philosophy.[25] Vitte's report at the audience was an abridged version of the memorandum. The point of departure was a phrase in the second paragraph: "Thinking Russia has outgrown the existing structures." The "exterior forms of Russian life" must be assimilated to the ideas with which the reasoning majority of society is imbued.[26] Vitte explained carefully that it was only through comprehensive reforms that the indispensable transformation of the country could be achieved. It required "labour, steadfastness, and circumspection," but most of all "time."[27] Nicholas listened to Vitte without making any comment, but asked him to come back the next day.[28]

The memorandum, on which Vitte's report had been based, begins by the statement that the "watchword which lay at the basis of the present social movement in Russia," was "freedom."[29] The roots of the liberation movement "reached down into the depths of the centuries" and in the last analysis "into human nature."[30] With this wide-ranging introduction Vitte obviously hoped to convince the Tsar that the movement could not be stopped and that therefore it was imperative not to delay the reforms any further. Until now the demands of the opposition had remained within the sphere of what appears "feasible and reasonable." Meanwhile however the "evil symptoms of a terrible and stormy outbreak" were increasing every day. In broad layers of society the government was losing support, and the authorities were showing day by day their "weakness, incompetence, and helplessness." The institution of the consultative Duma on 6 August had remained almost without any effect. Therefore, the Tsar was left with no other choice but to take the government into his own hands: "A government that does not direct events but is directed by them, plunges the State into ruin."[31] But as soon as the government takes the lead it will recover the support of society and in this way the ability to control the movement. If in the beginning of his exposition Vitte had declared freedom the watchword of the present social movement, he now demanded that

---

25 [Sergej Jul'evič Vitte], "Zapiska Vitte ot 9 oktjabrja" (Vitte's Memorandum of 9 October), *Krasnyj Archiv* 11–12 (1925): 51–61; Harcave, *Count Sergei Witte*, 168–169; on Kuzmin-Karavaev see Gurko, *Features*, 662.
26 [Sergej Jul'evič Vitte], "Černovik vsepoddannejšego doklada Vitte" (Konzept von Vittes aller-untertänigstem Vortrag), *Krasnyj Archiv* 11–12 (1925): 62.
27 Ibid., 64.
28 Vitte, *Vospominanija*, vol. 3, 11; according to Verner, *Crisis*, 228, n. 25, the two audiences took place on 8 and 9 October already.
29 [Vitte], "Zapiska," 51: "Osnovnoj lozung sovremennogo obščestvennogo dviženija v Rossii – svoboda."
30 Ibid., 52.
31 Ibid., 55: "Pravitel'stvo, kotoroe ne napravljaet sobytija, a samo sobytijami napravljaetsja, vedet gosudarstvo k gibeli."

the government make freedom the guiding principle of their policy as well. But this presupposed the introduction of a constitution (*konstitucija*). There was "no other expedient for the rescue of the State." Progress in history was irresistible. "The idea of civil liberty" will at any rate prevail, "if not by way of reform, certainly by way of revolution."[32] A revolution in Russia however would, Vitte continued prophetically, assume apocalyptic dimensions and lay "everything in ashes, without sense and without mercy." In what shape Russia would emerge from such an ordeal, transcended every power of imagination; "the horrors of the Russian Revolution" might "surpass everything" that hitherto "had been recorded in history."[33] All the more urgent it was to overcome the actual crisis by an efficient policy of reform. To this effect Vitte had outlined a program expressly aimed at "saving the fatherland" (*spasti otečestvo*).[34]

In his memoirs Vitte quotes a report of Prince Nikolaj Dmitrjevič Obolenskij of the summer of 1906 in which the dramatic events of October 1905 are recorded. According to Obolenskij during the encounter of 9 October Vitte had declared to the Tsar that there were only two ways to overcome the crisis. The first solution was conferring "unlimited dictatorial power" (*neograničennaja diktatorskaja vlast'*) on a trustworthy personality, and authorizing it to break every resistance by force, "even if it should cost immense bloodshed," a policy, for which he, Vitte, would not accept responsibility. The second solution was "following public opinion" and "embark upon the constitutional path": "In other words, Your Highness decides upon imposing a constitution (*darovanie konstitucii*) and confirms count Vitte's program."[35]

The constitution Vitte had in mind, provided for a State Duma that in legislating possessed not only advisory, but deciding vote. Besides, it should have budgetary power and control public administration. Vitte tried to overcome the Tsar's opposition to the introduction of a constitution by affirming that even the deciding vote of the Duma would not limit the power of the Tsar since he re-

---

32 Ibid., 53–55; ibid., 55: "Ideja graždanskoj svobody vostoržestvuet esli ne putem reformy, to putem revoljucii."

33 Ibid., 55–57.

34 Ibid., 59.

35 Zapiska Knjasja N. D. Obolenskogo, in: Vitte, *Vospominanija*, vol. 3, 25. Obolenskij's version is confirmed by a note of an employee of the committee of ministers, Nikolaj I. Vuič, of December 1906: [Nikolaj I. Vuič], "Zapiska Vuiča," *Krasnyj Archiv* 11–12 (1925), 66–69. According to Vuič in the critical days between the end of September and the beginning of October Vitte had "all the time" been "extremely concerned and had repeated several times how confused the interior situation had become and that he was convinced that only one of two solutions had remained: either everywhere to proclaim the state of war (*voennoe položenie*) or to grant a real constitution (*nastojaščaja konstitucija*)."

tained the absolute veto power with the consequence that no resolution of the assembly would obtain force of law without his sanction.[36] Vitte urgently recommended a reform of the electoral law. The law that had been introduced in August for the advisory Duma had created an "artificial system of representation," and the restrictions on the franchise and other regulations had excluded from the elections to the Duma whole categories of citizens.[37]

The imposition of a constitution, Vitte hoped, would restore confidence in the Tsar and thus renew monarchical legitimacy. To Vitte's concept of governmental reform also belonged the institution of a cabinet under the presidency of a responsible first minister possessing the exclusive right to report to the monarch. Hitherto every minister had been free to pursue his own policies and had thus been in a position to induce the Tsar repeatedly to contradictory actions.[38]

How the country could the easiest be turned around, was controversial within the government. Whereas Vitte tried to persuade the Tsar to assuage public excitement by promising a constitution, the deputy minister of the Interior, General Dmitrij Fedorovič Trepov, simultaneously General Governor of St. Petersburg, on 14 October issued a proclamation to the population of the capital prohibiting every demonstration and procession. In case people who had assembled in the streets or on public squares would not disperse upon demand, police and army were instructed not to use blanks and not to spare bullets.[39]

Vitte's assurance that the institution of a deciding Duma would not reduce the power of the Tsar, as long as he disposed of the absolute veto, was certainly incorrect. To be sure, by his veto power the Tsar could block every single project, but if legislating should not cease, he had to acknowledge that henceforth he would no longer legislate all by himself. By imposing a constitution in time he would for the time being at least prevent the usurpation of the constituent power by the people.

On 14 October Prince Orlov phoned Vitte from Peterhof to inform him that the Tsar wanted to meet him on the following day at 11 a. m. He was asked to bring with him the draft of a manifesto which was to be worded in such a way that all promises contained therein would appear as given by the Tsar personally. In the draft Vitte's recommendations of 9 October should be listed as "facts granted by the Tsar."[40] For

---

36 [Vitte], "Zapiska," 57.

37 Ibid.

38 The reform of the cabinet had been discussed since February; see Marc Szeftel, "Nicholas II's Constitutional Decisions of Oct. 17–19, 1905, and Sergius Witte's Role," in: *Album J. Balon* (Namur: Les Anciens Établissements Godenne, 1968), 485–487.

39 Ascher, *Revolution*, vol. 1, 223.

40 Vitte, *Vospominanija*, vol. 3, 14.

the sake of prudence Vitte would have preferred that the Tsar limit himself to sanctioning the text of his report instead of publishing a manifesto in his own name.[41] He does not explain his doubts about the manifesto more in detail. But it is to presume that by the ministerial countersignature he wanted to exonerate the Tsar from the responsibility of the risky move. After all, the imposition aimed at splitting the opposition. Whether the concessions went far enough for this purpose, was not sure. After Bulygin's project of August had already missed its political objective, the Tsar could not again risk a failure. Nicholas and his entourage appear not to have understood that much, however. The obvious lack of comprehension of what constitutionalism meant, was no propitious omen for the success of the constitutional system in Russia.

Vitte asked Prince Aleksis Dmitrjevič Obolenskij, member of the State Council, who happened to be present, to draft a text by next morning.[42] His unmistakable order to Vitte notwithstanding the Tsar was considering as late as 16 October to renounce concessions and struggle through the crisis, if need should be, by applying force. This was one of the two expedients that Vitte had sketched out. The Tsar would have been obliged to appoint a new Minister if he considered applying force and to confer full dictatorial power to someone who was ready to steer the government through the state of emergency because Vitte had declined the responsibility of such a course. As a candidate for the office of dictator Nicholas had in mind his cousin, Grand-Duke Nikolaj Nikolaevič. When the minister of the Imperial household, Baron Vladimir Borisovič Frederiks, revealed this plan to him, the Grand-Duke is reported to have taken his revolver out of his pocket and to have shouted:

> "You see this revolver. I shall presently go the Tsar and beseech him to sign the manifesto and the program of count Vitte. Either he will sign, or I shall shoot myself a bullet into the forehead in his presence."[43]

Vitte was not the only person the Tsar had asked to draft a manifesto. Several versions have long been known that the former minister of the Interior, Ivan L. Goremykin, had presented together with the head of the petition chancellery, Baron Aleksandr A. Budberg. Recently a further draft has been discovered that Budberg had written by himself und which provided for concessions that surpassed by far Vitte's

---

41 Ibid.; the text of the report in: [Vitte], "Černovik," 62–66; the content of the report is discussed in: Szeftel, "Decisions," 477–483.
42 Vitte, *Vospominanija*, vol. 3, 14.
43 Quoted from ibid., 41.

manifesto. According to this draft the chamber of deputies should be elected by universal suffrage. The members of the upper chamber were to be appointed by the Tsar. The president of the council of ministers and on his proposal the other ministers should also be appointed by the Tsar. It was expressly stated that they would be responsible to both chambers "for the overall performance of the government of the State."[44] Budberg's proposals show that even within the closest entourage of the Tsar the situation of the country was considered dramatic to a degree that some of his advisors went so far as to recommend the introduction of parliamentary government in order to preserve the monarchy.

The Tsar decided in favour of Vitte's draft, all the more so since Vitte had declared that he would remain in the cabinet only if the Tsar supported his course. On 17 October the Tsar finally made up his mind and signed. The manifesto was a mile-stone in the history of Russian constitutionalism, comparable to the promises of constitutions given by Charles Albert of Sardinia in February and Frederick William IV of Prussia in March 1848. The purpose of the October manifesto is said to be "the improvement of public order."[45] The preamble once more cites the two methods of resolving the crisis which the government has in mind: Either repression of the unrest or pacification of the State (*umirotvorenie gosudarstva*). With a view of overcoming the crisis without resorting to violence the Tsar reports to have given to the government three instructions: first, to grant to the citizens the imperturbable foundations of civil liberty, i.e. personal inviolability and freedom of conscience, of speech, of assembly, and of association; second, to grant also to those classes of citizens the suffrage to the State Duma who had not received it yet; thirdly, to stipulate that every legislative project had to be approved by the State Duma, and to insure that the members of the Duma were entitled to control the legality of public administration.

The October manifesto brought Russian absolutism to an end. The Empire turned constitutional. The history of the making of the manifesto and the circumstances of its proclamation leave no doubt that the Tsar had decided upon this step because he believed that it was the only way to recover freedom of action. He was ready to dispense with part of his prerogative and to share power with a popular representation in order to stabilize his hold on the government. The success of this policy depended to a great extent on the degree of firmness with which it was pursued. It remained to be seen whether the Tsar was moved to

---

44 Proekt manifesta A. A. Budberga (A. A. Budberg's draft of a manifesto), in: A. V. Ostrovskij and M. M. Safonov, eds., "Neizvestnyj proekt manifesta 17 oktjabrja 1905 goda" (Unknown draft of a manifesto for 17 October 1905), *Sovetskie Archivy* 2 (1979), 63–65.
45 Text of the manifesto in: *Krasnyj Archiv* 11–12 (1925), 46–47, in: *Pravo. Eženedel'naja Juridičeskaja Gazeta*, 25.10.1905, 3395–3397, and in: Zakonodatel'nye akty, 237–238.

it by a momentary embarrassment only or by the conviction that in Russia as elsewhere the development of society demanded the transition to constitutionalism. As Vitte reports in his memoirs, in October 1905 he regarded the monarchy as endangered for other reasons as well:

"When I took over the government, I was fully aware that two things were required if Russia were to overcome the revolutionary crisis and if the house of Romanov were left unshaken – to obtain a great amount of money in order to be relieved from all financial anxieties, and" – after the end of the Russo-Japanese war – "to relocate the chief part of the army from beyond Lake Baikal into the European part of Russia."[46]

During the crisis the troops were badly needed for the maintenance of internal security, and from the disposal of liquidity the freedom of action of the government depended. After tough negotiations with an international consortium an agreement was signed in Paris on 3 April 1906 providing for a loan of two and quarter milliards of Francs.[47]

In Nicholas' diary there are only three sentences under the 17 October 1905: "I signed the manifesto at five o'clock. At the end of a day like this the head grew heavy, and the mind got confused. Lord, help us, save Russia and give her peace!"[48] The meagerness of the note stands in no relation to the political significance of the occurrence, but it corresponds to the Tsar's habit to limit himself in his diary to the registration of external processes. In detail, however, he expressed himself in the letters to his mother, Marija Fedorovna, a Danish princess, daughter of King Christian IX. In the days under discussion she was with her family at the court of Copenhagen at Amalienborg Castle. In a letter of 19 October Nicholas revealed the motives which had been at the bottom of his decision to sign the October manifesto.[49]

---

46 *Vitte*, Vospominanija, vol. 3, 219.
47 Ibid., 247; *Harcave*, Count Sergej Witte, 219.
48 K. F. Šacillo, ed., *Dnevniki Imperatora Nikolaja II (Diaries of Emperor Nicholas II)* (Moscow: Orbit, 1991), 285.
49 M. Pokrovskij, ed., "Perepiska Nikolaja II i Marii Fedorovny (1905–1906 gg.)" (Correspondence of Nicholas II and Marija Fedorovna (1905–1906)), *Krasnyj Archiv* 22 (1927), 153–209; the numerous passages of Marija Fedorovna's letters written in French are reproduced in the original wording. The collection contains 45 pieces from the period between 18 May 1905 and 10 November 1906. In 1928 a French translation of the Russian edition was published with explanatory notes: see Paul L. Léon, ed., *Lettres de Nicolas II et de sa mère, l'Impératrice douairière de Russie* (Paris: Les Documentaires, 1928). An English edition of the correspondence was arranged by Edward J. Bing, ed., *The Letters of Tsar Nicholas and Empress Marie, being the confidential correspondence between Nicholas II, last of the Tsars, and his mother dowager Empress Maria Feodorovna*, London 1937. The letters published by Bing, all in English translation, cover a much longer

The Tsar begins by describing the strikes and the unrest, first in Moscow, then in St. Petersburg as well. As a consequence the two cities had been "cut off" from "the interior governments" of the country. For a week already the Baltic railway had been on a standstill. The only connection between Peterhof castle and the capital was by sea. When "at meetings" – *na mitingach*, "a new vogue expression," as the Tsar added in brackets – an armed uprising had been decided upon, he had ordered General Trepov, General Governor of St. Petersburg, to put the troops of Petersburg garrison in standby and to order them to repel every attack by force of arms. Only by this peremptory order had he succeeded in bringing the "movement or revolution" (*dviženie ili revoljucija*) to a halt. "Terrible days of quiet" (*groznye tichie dni*) had ensued, and one had had a feeling as it precedes "a strong thunderstorm" in summertime. Everybody's nerves had been strained to the extreme, and "naturally such a situation could not be borne for a long time."[50]

During these "terrible days" he had regularly met Vitte. The conversation had begun in the morning and had ended only in the evening at nightfall. Obviously in the face of the immediate menace which was directed against the autocracy, Vitte had succeeded in convincing the Tsar of the ineluctability of the measures he had proposed, since Nicholas continues by pointing out that two ways out had been envisaged. The first one was "the appointment of an energetic military man and to try with all disposable forces to quell the sedition." In this way, however, peace would have been restored only for a certain period of time; "streams of blood" would have run, and the urgent reforms would not have been tackled. This was the resort to dictatorship that Vitte had already mentioned in his memorandum of 9 October as an alternative which however he did not advocate. The second alternative which was indeed chosen, was granting "civil rights" (*graždanskie prava*) to the population – "freedom of speech, of the press, of assembly, and of association and the inviolability of the individual"; besides the obligation that every project of law was brought before the State Duma.

---

period of time than the edition by Pokrovskij. The first letter dates from 1879, the last one from 21 November 1917. As the editor explains in the preface, only those letters have been included in the volume of which he believed they "were of the relatively greatest human and historical interest," and frequently the letters have not been reproduced in their entirety (see: The Editor's Foreword, ibid., 19–20). The German edition of the correspondence – Wladimir von Korostowetz, ed., *Der letzte Zar. Briefwechsel Nikolaus' II. mit seiner Mutter* (Berlin: Metzner, 1938) – is a translation of Bing's English edition. The omissions are not indicated. For scientific purposes the French edition appears to be the most adequate, apart from the Russian original.
50 Nicholas II to Marija Fedorovna, 19 October 1905, in: Pokrovskij, *Perepiska*, 167: "Čuvstvo bylo, kak byvaet letom pered sil'noj grozoj!"

This, however, was the essence of a "constitution" (*konstitucija*).[51] Vitte had passionately defended this course of action and declared, if it was risky, it was also the only one that was feasible. In his report Nicholas continues by saying that almost everyone he had asked, was of the same opinion.[52]

As the Tsar continues in his report to his mother, the search for a way out of the crisis was interlocked with the problem of the relationship between the Tsar and his first minister and thus of the preconditions of government efficiency. As has been pointed out, since 1903 Vitte's position was "president of the committee of ministers." The committee was not a cabinet. The president's freedom of action was limited. Every minister possessed personal access to the monarch. Under these circumstances neither could be achieved discipline within the cabinet nor did the president dispose of the necessary support for winning the Tsar over to his ideas. But constitutionalism required ministerial solidarity. Therefore count Sol'skij had recommended in August, on behalf of a special conference he had presided, the transformation of the committee of ministers into a cabinet. This transformation would be connected with the creation of the office of prime minister who would in the future preside at cabinet meetings in the place of the Tsar.[53] The transformation was in fact commissioned by the highest order of 19 October. The third article of the order demanded that the council of ministers (*sovet ministrov*) work under the presidency of a personality appointed by the monarch and chosen primarily among the ministers.[54] From now on the cabinet was an autonomous institution, separate and distinct from the Tsar. On 18 October, the day after signing the October manifesto, the Tsar appointed count Vitte the first prime minister in Russian history.[55] Vitte had signified to the Tsar that he could accept the charge only on condition that the Tsar assent to his program and refrain from interfering with his governance.[56] The fact that the Tsar accepted Vitte's conditions indicates the gravity of the situation.

The Tsar's letter to his mother is a unique document. In no other case of an imposition exists a comparable personal statement of the imposing monarch about his decision making process. A few statements give the impression as though Nicholas wanted to justify his actions opposite his mother, for instance at the very start where he writes he did not know how to begin.[57] After all, she was the widow of Alexander

---

51 Ibid., 167–168.
52 Ibid.
53 Szeftel, "Decisions," 484–488.
54 "Imennoj vysočajšij ukaz," *Zakonodatel'nye Akty*, 244.
55 Harcave, *Count Sergei Witte*, 177; Szeftel, "Decisions," 487.
56 Nicholas to Marija Fedorovna, 19 October 1905, in: Pokrovskij, *Perepiska*, 168.
57 Ibid., 166.

III who had been a determined and firm defender of autocracy. On the other hand Marija Fedorovna had declared Vitte when he urged Nicholas to sign the October manifesto, in a letter to the Tsar of 16 October the "only person who can help you and can be of use to you" – *un homme génial énergique et qui voit clair.*[58] And her later letters do not reveal any criticism regarding her son's decision. Quite the contrary: On 1 November she assured him that he could not have acted otherwise at all.[59] Therefore the helplessness which the Tsar's letter is conveying appears in fact to be genuine. Ultimately, so Nicholas interprets his action, he signed the manifesto for the only reason that he had not found anybody who was able to show him an alternative way out of the severe crisis of the autocracy and dissuade him from attaching his signature. On the other hand, it is obvious that he did not possess the least understanding of the development of Russian society as it was rapidly advancing on the road to industrialization. Besides, the political calculation that underlay the manifesto, namely that its most important aim was to recover the confidence of the partisans of the monarchy, is not mentioned in his letter at all. Granting basic rights to the citizens and giving to the State Duma a share in legislation to him obviously was not part of a vision of a free and lawful society. He did not even attempt to veil that he had not acted from personal conviction but exclusively under the compulsion of the circumstances. This, however, gives rise to the question how determined he was to abide by the constitution once it had been introduced.

The October manifesto was only a promise. Now it was the government's turn to insert the promises into a constitution. The elaboration took until the spring of 1906. On 23 April the Tsar put it into effect under the name of "fundamental laws of the State" (*osnovnye gosudarstvennye zakony*). The name recalled the codification of the Russian laws that Michail Speranskij had carried through in 1832. The term *konstitucija* was avoided on purpose because it would have evoked associations with Western revolutionary ideas. Resorting to existing legal traditions at the same time was meant to counteract the impression as though the Tsar had allowed himself to get carried away to unheard of innovations. By its name alone the new Russian fundamental law thus resembled the *Charte constitutionnelle* of 1814 which had been inserted by Louis XVIII into the tradition of medieval privileges.

One of the promises contained in the October manifesto was the elaboration of an electoral law that corresponded to the criteria indicated therein. Since the

---

58 Marija Fedorovna to Nicholas II, 16 October 1905, in: Pokrovskij, *Perepiska*, 166.
59 Marija Fedorovna to Nicholas II, 1 November 1905, ibid., 171: "Enfin tu ne pouvais pas agir autrement, le bon Dieu t'a aidé à sortir de cette terrible et plus que pénible situation [...]."

council of ministers was unable to agree on a draft, Vitte proposed to the Tsar on 30 November to invite the cabinet, members of the State council, and other public figures for deliberations to Carskoe Selo.[60] After the July conference at Peterhof castle this was already the second time within the year that Nicholas convened the highest dignitaries of the State.[61] Two more periods of deliberations were to follow, the first one in February, and another one in April. In the meantime it became clear that Vitte's hopes that the interior situation would rapidly ease, were fulfilled only in part. On 27 October Nicholas wrote to his mother Vitte had not expected to get confronted with so many difficulties. It appeared strange that "such an intelligent man" had let deceive himself in his confidence in a "rapid calming down."[62] All the more urgent was the swift adoption of an electoral law. The secret deliberations of Carskoe Selo began on 5 December and were presided over by the Tsar.[63] The deliberations were based on two alternative drafts. One of the two, in the minutes called project no. 1, had been approved by the council of ministers and was an improvement of Bulygin's electoral regulation in that the right to vote was extended to further classes of society. Depending on the category to which a citizen was assigned, his vote possessed more or less weight. The other draft, called project no. 2 in the minutes, had been worked out by two renowned public figures who were not members of the government – Aleksandr Ivanovič Gučkov, son of a Moscow industrialist and member of the city council there, and Dmitrij Nikolaevič Šipov, an exponent of *zemstvo* liberalism. The council of ministers had asked them to elaborate electoral rules based on universal suffrage.

At Carskoe Selo Šipov and Gučkov spoke first and defended their draft. Šipov began by remembering that Russia was in the middle of a severe crisis. "Between government and society" an "abyss" (*propast'*) had opened which it was urgent to close again. It is true that by the October manifesto a basis for the pacification of the country had been laid. But now it mattered to publish as soon as possible an electoral law and to fix the date for the convocation of the State Duma. The Duma had to be composed in a way to gain "the confidence (*doverie*) of all well-in-

---

60 Harcave, *Count Sergei Witte*, 194.

61 Verner, *Crisis*, 205–217; Pares, "Conference," 87–120.

62 Nicholas II to Marija Fedorovna, 27 October 1905, in: Pokrovskij, *Perepiska*, 169.

63 The minutes of the deliberations on the reform of the electoral law have been published in: V. Vodovozov, ed., "Carskosel'skija soveščanija. Protokoly sekretnago soveščanija pod predsedatel'stvom byvšago imperatora po voprosu o rasširenii izbiratel'nago prava" (Deliberations at Carskoe Selo. Unpublished protocols of the secret deliberation chaired by the former Tsar on the question of suffrage extension), *Byloe* no. 3 (25), September 1917, 217–265.

tentioned subjects of your imperial Majesty."[64] In this respect the electoral law of 6 August had been imperfect. It had taken into account only the wealthy classes and had therefore not received the required consent (*sočuvstvie*) in society. On the other hand the law had permitted the extremist parties to strengthen the "revolutionary movement among the masses." With the help of the Duma it was now to be attempted to tie the citizens again to the state. But the Duma would enter upon a conservative course only on condition that the entire people of Russia and not only certain classes were enfranchised.[65] To what degree the electoral regulation of August had missed this mark was demonstrated by the next speaker, Gučkov. In Moscow only 8.200 citizens were permitted to vote. Under universal suffrage voters would have numbered 300.000.[66]

When Šipov contended that there was an abyss between government and society, he alluded not predominantly to the council of ministers who could easily have been replaced, but to the monarchy itself and to the whole apparatus of state. Basically he was concerned about the abyss between a society without political participation worth mentioning, and a state that was separated from it and governed it like a foreign conqueror. By this diagnosis Šipov tried not only to explain the revolutionary disturbances in the country, but also to show a way out of the crisis. Closing the abyss appeared to be possible only by creating a national representation elected by all classes of society. Šipov was convinced that the monarchy could recover support in society only on the basis of a democratic electoral law.[67] The terms confidence and consent that were used in this connection, had from the beginning belonged to the discourse of restoration. Confidence and consent are only synonyms of legitimacy, and without legitimacy no government could persist. Therefore the extension of the suffrage to include all segments of the population appeared as a means to restore monarchical legitimacy and, considering the deep crisis of the country, as the most important instrument to restore monarchical authority in Russia. The fact alone that the autocrat Nicholas invited the leading public figures to Carskoe Selo for extraordinary deliberations on the right of electing to the Duma, shows how central a significance was attributed at court to the cooperation of the people in the formation of policy.

Gučkov joined Šipov in advocating a democratic electoral law: "In my opinion granting universal suffrage (*vseobščee izbiratel'noe pravo*) is inevitable," and

---

64 Ibid., 238: "Sostav eja dolžen pol'zovat'sja doveriem vsech vernopoddannych v[ašego] i [mperial'nogo] v[eličestva]."

65 Ibid., 239.

66 Ibid., 240.

67 Ibid., 239: "V osnovanie izbiratel'noj sistemy dolžen byt' položen princip demokratičeskij" (The electoral system must be based on the democratic principle).

if it is not conceded voluntarily it will in the very near future be extorted by the revolutionary movement.[68] It seems that the assembly was unanimous in the opinion that the Duma was to be organized and composed in such a way as to guarantee the maintenance of monarchy and state. Baron Pavel Leopol'dovič Korf declared himself to be sure that the masses would vote conservative, and Šipov agreed with him: "If universal suffrage is introduced, our candidates will be elected, if not [...], our opponents."[69] Vitte who had originally advocated project no. 1, meanwhile also advocated universal suffrage. He justified his position by the argument that the revolutionary fermentation (*smuta*) had by all means to be overcome. This could not be done by force. There were not enough troops. Therefore there was no choice but to "take the road of moral appeasement." The electoral law had to satisfy "the whole population, the whole people," and "not this, a second, or a third category, each one of them separately."[70] Prince Aleksis Dmitrjevič Obolenskij proposed a middle-way between the two projects by introducing universal suffrage on the one hand, but attributing different weight to the single voters on the other. This should be made possible by making the people vote within one of three categories: farmers, land-owners, and at last those who were neither farmers nor landowners, in other words, essentially the population of the cities.[71] With a view to creating a counterweight to the elected chamber Vitte recommended, not unlike Budberg had done in his draft of the October manifesto, to create side by side with the lower chamber a State council forming a first chamber.[72] Nobody doubted the critical state of affairs in the country. "At present Russia is experiencing a revolution," Vitte declared.[73] The demands of the revolutionaries must be anticipated by adequate policies. Therefore, Šipov explained, it was imperative to remedy the grievances which had turned out a "suitable breeding ground" for revolutionary propaganda.[74] Baron Korf was optimistic that the convocation of the State Duma would put an end to the revolution.[75]

Overcoming the crisis into which Russia had plunged, and restoring monarchical authority were the primary issues in every contribution. On the second day

---

68 Ibid., 241.
69 Ibid., 241–242.
70 Ibid., 248: "vstupit' na put' nravsvtvennago uspokoenija."
71 Ibid., 256.
72 Ibid., 245.
73 Ibid., 244–245.
74 Ibid., 244.
75 Ibid., 243: "Sozyv gosudarstvennoj dumy – eto konec revoljucii" (The convocation of the State Duma – that is the end of the revolution).

of the deliberations, on 7 December, the Tsar terminated the discussion of the two projects and declared that only the first one was acceptable. He added that he had been wavering during the two sessions. "But this morning it has become clear to me that the first project is better, less dangerous and more adequate to Russia. As to the second project I feel that it cannot be adopted. It is impossible to go ahead by steps too great. If one concedes universal suffrage today, the democratic republic has come close. That would be unreasonable and a crime. The first project contains more guarantees of implementation of the reforms proclaimed in the manifesto of 17 October."[76] More guarantees of implementation meant more security that the crisis could be mastered by the promised reforms and that the monarchy would in the end be stronger. In other words: The Tsar regarded universal suffrage as a concession that exceeded by far the purpose of restoration, namely the preservation of monarchical prerogative. This explains his observation that along this road the democratic republic was not far. Obviously, he could not imagine for Russia a combination of monarchism and universal suffrage on the model of the German Reich.

By decree of 11 December 1905 the new electoral law was proclaimed. As Andrew M. Verner points out, it was neither universal nor equal nor direct, but it admitted a greater number of people to elections than the electoral regulation of 6 August had done.[77] The population was divided into four groups – landowners, farmers, town dwellers, and workers. Those having the right to vote elected electors and these in turn elected the deputies. The inequality of the suffrage is expressed by the regulation that one elector was elected by every 2.000 landowners, 4.000 town dwellers, 30.000 farmers and 90.000 workmen. Women, agricultural labourers, and day-labourers did not receive the right to vote.[78]

The expansion of the suffrage required a reform of the Council of State. If it had so far been a body to advise the Tsar and his government, it was now to be transformed into an upper chamber. One half of its members should from now on be elected. A deliberation on the reform of the Council of State took place on 14 and 16 February 1906 at Carskoe Selo at another extraordinary conference. The Tsar had ordered count Sol'skij to draft a proposal.[79] At the very beginning of the first meeting count Ignat'ev stated that the transformation of the Council of State into a first chamber (*verchnjaja palata*) was a "decisive step towards con-

---

76 Ibid., 258–259.

77 Verner, *Crisis*, 290; the text of the new electoral regulation in: Imennoj vysočajšij ukaz, 11 December 1905, in: *Zakonodatel'nye akty*, 282–295.

78 Abraham Ascher, *The Revolution of 1905*, vol. 2: *Authority Restored* (Stanford: Stanford University Press, 1992), 43.

79 Verner, *Crisis*, 293.

stitutionalism." Vitte confirmed this statement indirectly by pointing out that the first chamber was to form a counterweight to the second chamber. "A first chamber only" could "save from the unpredictability of the second chamber." Hence it was required "with a view to preserving the conservative structure of the State." The first chamber served "to protect from all extreme opinions" that could easily carry the majority in the second chamber. It was to function as a "buffer" between the second chamber and the monarch. In order to live up to this task it had to be composed of "the most conservative elements possible." Therefore it was provided that among the 26 elected members there should be eighteen from the aristocracy, six from the orthodox clergy and twelve from industry.[80] In the constitution, as adopted on 23 April 1906, it was left open how many members the State Council would have. But article 58 ruled that the number of appointed members must not exceed the number of elected members.[81] In the constitution the body is still named Council of State, but at the same time its functions of a first chamber are unmistakably defined. Accordingly, article 64 rules that Council of State and Duma disposed of the same rights in legislation, and article 7 determined that the Tsar exercised legislative power in cooperation with the Council of State and the Duma.[82]

From the point of view of restoration the fourth article of the fundamental laws deserves particular attention. According to its first sentence the Tsar possessed "supreme autocratic power" (*verchovnaja samoderžavnaja vlast'*). In the fundamental laws of 1832 his power had still been defined as "autocratic" and "unlimited" (*neograničennaja*). Since from now on the Tsar depended in legislating on the cooperation of State Council and Duma he no longer disposed of unlimited power. Nobody denied him the title of "autocrat" (*samoderžec*), however. It designated the possessor of supreme power and thus corresponded to the

---

80 V. Vodovozov, ed., "Carskosel'skija soveščanija. Protokoly sekretnago soveščanija v fevrale 1906 goda pod predsedatel'stvom byvšago imperatora po vyrabotke Učreždenij Gosudarstvennoj Dumy i Gosudarstvennago Soveta" (Deliberations at Carskoe Selo. The minutes of the secret deliberation of February 1906 chaired by the Tsar on the institution of a State Duma und of a State Council), *Byloe* 4 (26) (October 1917), 293.

81 Osnovnye Gosudarstvennye Zakony (Fundamental Laws of the State), 23 April 1906, no. 27805, § 58, in: *Polnoe Sobranie Zakonov Rossijskoj Imperii* (Complete collection of the laws of the Russian Empire), *Sobranie tret'e* (Third collection), vol. 26 (1906), St. Petersburg 1909, 460; for the fundamental law of 1906 see: Marc Szeftel, *The Russian Constitution of April 23, 1906. Political Institutions of the Duma Monarchy*, Brussels: Éd. de la Librairie Encyclopédique, 1976; therein contained is an English translation of the articles 1–124 of the fundamental laws and a commentary; a German translation of the fundamental laws and a detailed commentary in: Anton Palme, *Die russische Verfassung* (Berlin: Reimer, 1910).

82 Osnovnye Gosudarstvennye Zakony, 23 April 1906, § 64, ibid., 460; § 7, ibid., 457.

Western term of sovereign. By insisting on autocracy the Tsar disclosed the same interpretation of his legal position as Louis XVIII and every monarch that had imposed a constitution. All of them had steadfastly retained the understanding that even under constitutionalism they had remained in full possession of public power. When, however, Nicholas II at Carskoe Selo, during deliberations on the fourth article, doubted if he was permitted to consent that his power was no longer unlimited, Vitte responded dryly, unlimited power was possessed by the Turkish Sultan alone.[83]

The episode illuminates the lack of willingness at court to make concessions. The crisis of October 1905 appears to have been forgotten. Under the new constitution Duma and government faced each other from the beginning in a hostile mood. The government's policy of conflict culminated as early as 8 July 1906 in the premature dissolution of the Duma. The second Duma assembled in February 1907 but was again dissolved in June. By taking advantage of the emergency article of the constitution the Tsar simultaneously imposed a new electoral law by which the representatives of the aristocracy and the middle classes obtained the majority in the Duma. Under these circumstances there was no chance to integrate increasing sections of society into the State, and the monarchy proved less and less able to base its legitimacy on social consent. The restoration of monarchy in 1906 had produced, in Max Weber's words, only the appearance of constitutionalism.[84]

---

83 V. Vodovosov, ed., "Carskosel'skija soveščanija. Protokoly sekretnago soveščanija v aprele 1906 goda pod predsedatel'stvom byvšago imperatora po per smotru osnovnych zakonov" (Minutes of the secret deliberation of April 1906 presided by the former Tsar, on the revision of the fundamental laws), 9 April 1906, *Byloe* 5 – 6 (27 – 28), November-December 1917, 206; on the deliberations at Carskoe Selo see: Sellin, *Gewalt*, 191 – 198.

84 Max Weber, "Rußlands Übergang zum Scheinkonstitutionalismus" (1906), in: id., *Zur Russischen Revolution von 1905. Schriften und Reden 1905 – 1912*, ed. Wolfgang J. Mommsen, in cooperation with Dittmar Dahlmann (Tübingen: Mohr, 1989), 280 – 684 (Max Weber Gesamtausgabe, part I, vol. 10).

Conclusion

The triumph of democratic constitutionalism in North America and in France was a result of the modern revolution. By contrast, the restoration that followed upon the fall of Napoleon is often regarded as an attempt to transfer Ancien Régime principles to the 19th century. An entire period of European history is named after this attempt. The period is said to have lasted in France until the July revolution of 1830 and in Germany and Italy until the revolutions of 1848.

This understanding of restoration is fraught with difficulties. To begin with, it is open to discussion whether restoration can be conceived as a uniform epoch in European history. The conditions, from which the various attempts at restoration originated, differed. In France the nation itself had abolished monarchy. In Italy and in Spain the dynasties had been deposed by Napoleon without consulting the subjects. In Germany the dethronement of princes by the emperor of the French had remained the exception. When by the treaty of Paris of 30 May 1814 the left bank of the Rhine was returned to Germany, there were no princes who had the right to recover their ancient possessions. The ecclesiastical territories of the Empire had been dissolved in 1803 and the secular princes of the left bank of the Rhine had been indemnified on the right bank. Obviously, after Napoleon's fall the political development in the countries of Europe pointed in different directions. Only in France with its revolutionary tradition did the restoration of monarchy require the imposition of a constitution. The other monarchs who had lost their thrones, returned in 1814 without making concessions to their subjects. The French restoration thus differed from the restorations in all other monarchies. The Prussian general and politician Joseph Maria von Radowitz called the French type of restoration organic. To the historian is thus left the choice between two concepts of monarchical restoration. By restoration is either understood the return of dethroned dynasties after the fall of Napoleon, no matter what kind of government they established, or the term refers more specifically to the renewal and consolidation of monarchical legitimacy by imposing a constitution whenever the need was perceived.

Taken in its organic conception restoration is no longer exclusively attached to the period of 1814 but includes every imposition of a constitution in the course of the century that was meant to consolidate monarchical legitimacy. In this sense monarchical restorations took place in Poland in 1815, in Spain in 1834, in Prussia, in Austria, and in the Italian states in 1848, and in Russia in 1906. Restoration is then no longer a period of European history, but a period within the history of every single monarchy, and restorations are no longer limited to cases where the dynasty had been expelled or the monarchy abolished.

The imposition of a constitution turned restoration into a device to promote freedom and to grant the subjects a degree of participation in government. In this respect it resembled revolution. With regard to the stability of the changes they caused, restorations were more successful than revolutions. The French constitutional monarchy of 1791 lasted but one year. The constitution the Prussian National Assembly elaborated during the revolution of 1848 failed. By contrast, the Charte constitutionnelle remained in force during 16 years at first and after its revision in the July revolution for another 18 years, and the Prussian constitution that had been imposed in December 1848 and revised in 1850, persisted until the end of the monarchy in 1918. When during the constitutional conflict of the early 1860's the Prussian House of Deputies was on the verge of extracting parliamentary government from the monarchy, the new prime minister Otto von Bismarck managed to safeguard the preponderance of the Crown. He argued that since the constitution had been imposed by the King, the King alone was in the position to resolve conflicts over its interpretation. In the same way as the Charte constitutionnelle resulted from a revision of the Senatorial constitution the Prussian constitution of 1848 and 1850 originated from a revision of the constitution the Prussian National Assembly had elaborated during the revolution. Since after the wars of 1866 and 1870/71 the new German Empire was founded by Prussia, it was natural that the monarchical principle became the cornerstone of the constitutional framework of Germany as well, thus making restoration the foundation of the new German monarchy.

Restoration differs from stagnation. Still, its readiness to embrace change referred not primarily to the realization of new, but to the protection of long established values. Its objectives were essentially defensive in nature. It aimed at the preservation of monarchy and of the monarchical principle in the face of revolution. By their ability to assert themselves through change Dieter Langewiesche has recently explained the astonishing staying power of the European monarchies in the 19th century.[1] Change required readiness to adopt aims of the revolution. Written constitutions had been an essential concern of both the American and the French Revolution. Hence the most important instrument of monarchical restoration was the imposition of a constitution. Whereas revolutions determined their course of action by themselves, restorations reacted to the challenges of democracy. The appeal to what had been proven beneficial always remained the strongest argument in favour of restoration. Therefore in spite of their readiness for change, restorations sought to insert their program in established traditions.

---

1 Dieter Langewiesche, *Die Monarchie im Jahrhundert Europas. Selbstbehauptung durch Wandel im 19. Jahrhundert*, (Heidelberg: Winter, 2013).

This is revealed by the terms by which the imposed constitutions were designated: *Charte constitutionnelle* in France, *Estatuto real* in Spain, *Osnovnye Gosudarstvennye Zakony* (Fundamental laws of the State) in Russia. Terms of this kind served as linguistic barriers to revolution.

Even if the transition of monarchies to constitutionalism in the long run did not succeed thanks to revolution but to restoration, it remains nevertheless true that restorations were but reactions to the pressure of revolution, either to steal a march on anticipated revolutions or to mitigate revolutions already under way. Restorations did not follow political visions, but were tactical maneuvers by which sovereigns sought to preserve their claim to dynastic legitimacy in the age of democratic revolution. Accordingly, the readiness of monarchs to make concessions was determined by this tactical aim. It was not uncommon for monarchs to withdraw the concessions made, either in part or in their entirety, as soon as the pressure of revolution subsided. Emperor Francis Joseph and all Italian princes except the King of Sardinia revoked the constitutions they had imposed in 1848, when the revolution was over.

If the policy of restoration had everywhere been implemented consistently, in present day Europe there would exist only monarchies. Their legitimacy, however, would most probably be, if not by law, at least in fact, no less democratic than if they had, in the age of revolution, expressly been based on the constituent power of the people. In the long run monarchical and democratic principle approached each other. They differed only in the method by which they admitted a steadily increasing degree of political participation. The advantages of restoration as against revolution consisted in the preservation of continuity in promoting constitutionalism. The continuity was rendered possible through the monarch's formal retention of sovereignty while political participation was extended to a growing number of subjects. The monarchical principle admitted concessions without shaking monarchy to the core.

The origins of restoration go back to the French Revolution. The memorandum that Louis XVI left in the Tuileries in the night of 20 June 1791 before his attempt at flight, contains an early program of monarchical restoration. In the memorandum the King promised "a constitution" that will guarantee "that our holy religion will be respected, that government will stand on safe and beneficial grounds, that property and everybody's rights will be protected from encroachments, that laws cannot be violated with impunity, and that freedom will rest on safe and unshakable foundations."[2] Since the flight failed and the King

---

2 Archives parlementaires, series I, vol. 27, 21 June 1791, 383; see Volker Sellin, *Gewalt und Le-*

was returned to Paris ahead of time, he did not get the opportunity to put into practice his program of restoration. In 1814 his brother was unexpectedly given a new chance to restore monarchical legitimacy. The Charte constitutionnelle merges the two aspects of restoration policy in an exemplary way: the preservation of monarchical sovereignty and the qualified acknowledgement of revolution. By its two-faced nature the Charte became the widely imitated model of 19th century constitutionalism. But whereas during the July Revolution of 1830 parliamentary government was introduced in France, Article 57 of the Final Act of the Vienna ministerial conferences of 1820 had introduced the monarchical principle into the public law of the German Confederation. The revolution of 1848 sought to put the democratic principle in its place, both within the single states and on the national level. The national assembly of Frankfurt aimed at a democratic monarchy and parliamentary government. But the revolution failed, and the attempt of the Prussian Progressive Party in the early sixties to make the government of Berlin dependent on Parliament, was thwarted by prime minister Otto von Bismarck. After the Prussian victory over Austria and the breakdown of the German Confederation in 1866 the new National Liberal Party supported Bismarck for more than a decade, regardless of the fact that there was no hope to introduce parliamentary government into the constitution of the new German Empire. Germany remained a restoration type monarchy with an Imperial Diet that failed to obtain the decisive influence on the national government. The Imperial Chancellor was appointed by the Kaiser alone and was not responsible to the Diet. Thus the monarchical principle remained in force almost until the end of the First World War, and parliamentary government was introduced only in 1917.

---

gitimität. Die europäische Monarchie im Zeitalter der Revolutionen, (Munich: Oldenbourg, 2011), 186–190.

Bibliography

Ajrapetov, Oleg. *Vnešnjaja politika Rossijskoj Imperii (1801–1914)*. Moscow: Evropa, 2006.

Album J. Balon [Hommage à Monsieur Joseph Balon]. Namur: Les Anciens Établissements Godenne, 1968.

Altmann, Wilhelm, ed. *Ausgewählte Urkunden zur außerdeutschen Verfassungsgeschichte seit 1776*. Berlin: R. Gaertners Verlagsbuchhandlung, 1897.

Álvarez Junco, José, and Adrian Shubert, eds. *Spanish History since 1808*. London: Arnold, 2000.

Ambrosini, Filippo. *Carlo Alberto Re*. Turin: Edizioni del Capricorno, 2004.

Andreas, Willy. *Die Entstehung der badischen Verfassung*. Marburg and Leipzig: Quelle & Meyer, 1912.

Andreas, Willy. *Geschichte der badischen Verwaltungsorganisation und Verfassung in den Jahren 1802–1818*, vol. 1. Leipzig: Quelle & Meyer, 1913.

Angeberg, comte de (Leonard Jakob Borejko Chod'zko), ed. *Le congrès de Vienne et les traités de 1815, précédé et suivi des actes diplomatiques qui s'y rattachent*, 2 vols. Paris: Amyot, 1863.

Angeberg, comte de (Leonard Jakob Borejko Chod'zko), ed. *Recueil des traités, conventions et actes diplomatiques concernant la Pologne 1762–1862*. Paris: Amyot, 1862.

Angermann, Erich, "Ständische Rechtstraditionen in der amerikanischen Unabhängigkeitserklärung." *Historische Zeitschrift* 200 (1965): 61–91.

Anschütz, Gerhard, *Die Verfassungs-Urkunde für den Preußischen Staat vom 31. Januar 1850. Ein Kommentar für Wissenschaft und Praxis*, vol. 1. Berlin: Häring, 1912.

Anweiler, Oskar, "Die russische Revolution von 1905. Aus Anlaß ihres 50. Jahrestages." *Jahrbücher für Geschichte Osteuropas* 3 (1955): 161–93.

Aquarone, Alberto et al., eds. *Le costituzioni italiane*. Milan: Ed. di Comunità, 1958.

Ara, Angelo, *Lo Statuto fondamentale dello Stato della Chiesa (14 marzo 1848): Contributo ad uno studio delle idee costituzionali nello Stato Pontificio nel periodo delle riforme di Pio IX*. Milan: Giuffrè, 1966.

Archives du Ministère des Affaires Étrangères, Paris (MAE), Mémoires et Documents (MD) France, vol. 646 (Fonds Bourbon); vol. 668.

Archives Nationales. Paris, CC 986; 40 AP 7.

Archives parlementaires. Paris.

Artola Gallego, Miguel. *Los afrancesados*. Madrid: Sociedad de Estudios y Publicaciones, 1953.

Artola Gallego, Miguel. *Los orígenes de la España Contemporánea*, 2 vols. Madrid: Instituto de Estudios Politicos, 1959.

Artola Gallego, Miguel. *La España de Fernando VII*, vol. 1: *La guerra de la independencia y los orígenes del constitucionalismo*. Madrid: Espasa-Calpe, 1996 (Historia de España. Edited by Ramón Menendez Pidal. 32).

Ascher, Abraham. *The Revolution of 1905*, vol. 1: *Russia in Disarray*. Stanford: Stanford University Press, 1988; vol. 2: *Authority Restored*. Stanford: Stanford University Press, 1992.

Bailleu, Paul, ed. *Briefwechsel König Friedrich Wilhelm's III. und der Königin Luise mit Kaiser Alexander I.* Leipzig: Hirzel, 1900.

Bernecker, Walther L., and Horst Pietschmann. *Geschichte Spaniens: Von der frühen Neuzeit bis zur Gegenwart*, 4th ed. Stuttgart: Kohlhammer, 2005.

Bing, Edward J., ed. *The Letters of Tsar Nicholas and Empress Marie: Being the confidential correspondence between Nicholas II, last of the Tsars, and his mother, dowager Empress Maria Feodorovna*. London: Ivor Nicholson, 1937.

Blackwell, William L. *Alexander I and Poland: The Foundations of His Polish Policy*, Ph. D. Dissertation, Princeton University 1959.

Böckenförde, Ernst-Wolfgang. "Der deutsche Typ der konstitutionellen Monarchie im 19. Jahrhundert." In *Beiträge zur deutschen und belgischen Verfassungsgeschichte im 19. Jahrhundert*. Edited by Werner Conze, 70–92. Stuttgart: Klett, 1967.

Bojasiński, Józef. *Rządy tymczasowe w królestwie polskiem. Maj-grudzień 1815*, Warsaw: P. Laskauer, 1902.

Botzenhart, Manfred. *Deutscher Parlamentarismus in der Revolutionszeit 1848–1850*. Düsseldorf: Droste, 1977.

Branch, Michael, Janet M. Hartley, and Antoni Mączak, eds. *Finland and Poland in the Russian Empire. A Comparative Study*. London: School of Slavonic and East European Studies, University of London, 1995.

Brandenburg, Erich. *Untersuchungen und Aktenstücke zur Geschichte der Reichsgründung*. Leipzig: Quelle & Meyer, 1916.

Brandt, Hartwig, and Ewald Grothe, eds. *Rheinbündischer Konstitutionalismus*. Frankfort: Lang, 2007.

Brennecke, Christiana. *Von Cádiz nach London: Spanischer Liberalismus im Spannungsfeld von nationaler Selbstbestimmung, Internationalität und Exil (1820–1833)*. Göttingen: Vandenhoeck & Ruprecht, 2010.

Brunov, F. M. "Aperçu des principales transactions du cabinet de Russie sous les règnes de Cathérine II, Paul I et Alexandre I." In *Gody učenija ego imperatorskago naslednika cesareviča Aleksandra Nikolaeviča*, vol. 2. St. Petersburg, 1880, 197–416 (Sbornik Imperatorskago Russkago Istoričeskago Obščestva, vol. 31).

Bulletin des lois du Royaume de France, cinquième série.

Busquets, Julio. *Pronunciamientos y golpes de Estado en España*. Barcelona: Ed. Planeta, 1982.

Bußmann, Walter. *Zwischen Preußen und Deutschland: Friedrich Wilhelm IV: Eine Biographie*. Berlin: Siedler, 1990.

Candeloro, Giorgio. *Storia dell'Italia moderna*, vol. 2: *Dalla restaurazione alla rivoluzione nazionale*, 4th ed. Milan: Feltrinelli, 1994; vol. 3: *La rivoluzione nazionale (1846–1849)*, 3rd ed. Milan: Feltrinelli, 1995; vol. 4: *Dalla rivoluzione nazionale all'unità 1849–1860*, 3rd ed. Milan: Feltrinelli, 1995.

Cavour, Camillo. *Tutti gli scritti*. Edited by Carlo Pischedda and Giuseppe Talamo, 4 vols. Turin: Centro Studi Piemontesi, 1976–1978.

Cavour, Camillo. *Epistolario*, vol. 4 (1847). Edited by Narciso Nada. Bologna: Zanichelli, 1978; vol. 5 (1848). Edited by *Carlo Pischedda*, Bologna: Zanichelli, 1980.

Châteaubriand, François René de. *De la monarchie selon la charte*. Paris: Le Normant, 1816.

Chiavistelli, Antonio. "Toscana costituzionale: La difficile gestazione dello statuto fondamentale del 1848." *Rassegna storica del Risorgimento* 84 (1997): 339–74.

Ciaurro, Luigi, ed. *Lo Statuto albertino, illustrato dai lavori preparatori*. Rome: Dipartimento per l'informazione e l'editoria, 1996.

Coigny, Aimée de, duchesse de Fleury, *Mémoires*. Edited by Étienne Lamy. Paris: Calmann-Lévy, 1906.

Colombo, Adolfo, ed. *Dalle riforme allo Statuto di Carlo Alberto. Documenti editi ed inediti*, Casale: Società per la storia del Risorgimento Italiano. Pubblicazioni del Comitato Piemontese, vol. 5, 1924.

Colombo, Paolo. *Il re d'Italia: Prerogative costituzionali e potere politico della Corona (1848–1922)*. Milan: Angeli, 1999.

Colombo, Paolo. *Storia costituzionale della monarchia italiana*, 2nd ed. Bari: Laterza, 2003.

Comellas, José Luis. *Los primeros pronunciamientos en España 1814–1820*. Consejo Superior de Investigaciones Cientificas, Escuela de Historia Moderna, Madrid 1958.

Comellas, José Luis. *Isabel II: Una reina y un reinado*. Barcelona: Editorial Ariel, 1999.

Connelly, Owen. *Napoleon's Satellite Kingdoms*. New York: The Free Press, and London: Macmillan, 1965.

Constant, Benjamin. *Œuvres*. Paris: Gallimard, 1957.

Conze, Werner, ed. *Beiträge zur deutschen und belgischen Verfassungsgeschichte im 19. Jahrhundert*. Stuttgart: Klett, 1967.

Crosa, Emilio. "Lo Statuto del 1848 e l'opera del ministro Borelli, con lettere inedite di Carlo Alberto." *Nuova Antologia*, Series 5, vol. 177, 16.6.1915, 533–41.

Czartoryski, Adam. *Mémoires et correspondance avec l'empereur Alexandre Ier*, 2 vols. Paris: Plon, 1887.

Davies, Norman. *Heart of Europe: The Past in Poland's Present*, 3rd ed. Oxford: Oxford University Press, 2001.

Davion, Isabelle, Jerzy Kłoczowski, and Georges-Henri Soutou, eds. *La Pologne et l'Europe du partage à l'élargissement (XVIIIe-XXIe siècles)*. Paris: Presses de l'Université Paris-Sorbonne, 2007.

Diwald, Hellmut, ed. *Von der Revolution zum Norddeutschen Bund: Politik und Ideengut der preußischen Hochkonservativen 1848–1866*. Aus dem Nachlaß von Ernst Ludwig von Gerlach, 2 vols. Göttingen: Vandenhoeck & Ruprecht, 1970.

Doeberl, Michael. *Ein Jahrhundert bayerischen Verfassungslebens*, 2nd ed. Munich: Landauer, 1918.

Doeberl, Michael. *Rheinbundverfassung und bayerische Konstitution*. Munich: Bayerische Akademie der Wissenschaften, 1924.

Dundulis, Bronius. *Napoléon et la Lituanie en 1812*. Paris: Presses Universitaires de France, 1940.

Elm, Veit. *Die Moderne und der Kirchenstaat. Aufklärung und römisch-katholische Staatlichkeit im Urteil der Geschichtsschreibung vom 18. Jahrhundert bis zur Postmoderne*. Berlin: Duncker & Humblot, 2001.

[Ermolov, Aleksej Sergeevič]. "Zapiski A. S. Ermolova." *Krasnyj Archiv* 8 (1925): 49–69.

Esdaile, Charles J. *Spain in the Liberal Age. From Constitution to Civil War, 1808–1939*. Oxford: Blackwell, 2000.

Espadas Burgos, Manuel, and José Ramón de Urquijo Goitia. *Guerra de la independencia y época constitucional (1808–1898)*. Madrid: Ed. Gredos, 1990 (Historia de España. 11).

Fehrenbach, Charles Wentz. "Moderados and Exaltados: The Liberal Opposition to Ferdinand VII, 1814–1823." *Hispanic American Historical Review* 50 (1970): 52–69.

Fehrenbach, Elisabeth. *Wandlungen des deutschen Kaisergedankens 1871–1918*. Munich and Vienna: Oldenbourg, 1969.

Fehrenbach, Elisabeth. *Traditionale Gesellschaft und revolutionäres Recht. Die Einführung des Code Napoléon in den Rheinbundstaaten.* Göttingen: Vandenhoeck & Ruprecht, 1974.

Fernández Almagro, Melchor. *Orígenes del régimen constitucional en España.* Barcelona and Buenos Aires: Labor 1928.

Fernández Martín, Manuel. *Derecho parlamentario español,* 3 vols. Madrid: Congreso de Los Diputados, 1992.

Fournier, August. *Der Congress von Châtillon. Die Politik im Kriege von 1814. Eine historische Studie.* Vienna: Tempsky, 1900.

Frahm, Friedrich. "Entstehungs- und Entwicklungsgeschichte der preußischen Verfassung (vom März 1848 bis zum Januar 1850)." *Forschungen zur Brandenburgischen und Preußischen Geschichte* 41 (1928): 248–301.

Furtwängler, Martin. *Die Standesherren in Baden (1806–1848). Politische und soziale Verhaltensweisen einer bedrängten Elite.* Frankfort: Lang, 1996.

Gaceta Extraordinaria de Madrid del jueves 12 de mayo de 1814.

Gates, David. *The Spanish Ulcer. A History of the Peninsular War.* Cambridge, Mass.: Da Capo Press, 1986.

Geheimes Staatsarchiv Preußischer Kulturbesitz, Berlin, I. HA Rep. 92, Nachlaß Albrecht, no. 56.

[Gentz, Friedrich von]. *Briefe von und an Friedrich von Gentz.* Edited by Friedrich Carl Wittichen and Ernst Salzer, vol. 3, part I. Munich: Oldenbourg, 1913.

Gerlach, Lepold von. *Denkwürdigkeiten.* Edited by his daughter, vol. 1. Berlin: Hertz, 1891.

Gerner, Joachim. *Vorgeschichte und Entstehung der württembergischen Verfassung im Spiegel der Quellen (1815–1819).* Stuttgart: Kohlhammer, 1989.

Ghisalberti, Alberto Maria. *Nuove ricerche sugli inizi del pontificato di Pio IX e sulla Consulta di Stato.* Rome: Vittoriano, 1939.

Ghisalberti, Carlo. "Dalla monarchia amministrativa alla monarchia consultiva." In *Contributi alla storia delle amministrazioni preunitarie.* Edited by Carlo Ghisalberti, 145–83. Milan: Giuffrè, 1963.

Ghisalberti, Carlo. *Dall'Antico Regime al 1848. Le origini costituzionali dell'Italia moderna.* Bari: Laterza, 1974.

Ghisalberti, Carlo. *Storia costituzionale d'Italia 1848/1948.* 17th ed. Bari: Laterza, 1998.

Ghisalberti, Carlo. *Istituzioni e società civile nell'età del Risorgimento.* Bari: Laterza, 2005.

Godechot, Jacques. *Les institutions de la France sous la Révolution et l'Empire.* 2nd ed. Paris: Presses Universitaires de France, 1968.

Godechot, Jacques, ed. *Les Constitutions de la France depuis 1789.* Paris: Garnier-Flammarion, 1970.

Goldschmidt, Paul. "Die oktroyierte preußische Verfassung." *Preußische Jahrbücher* 125 (1906): 197–216.

Gollwitzer, Heinz. *Die Standesherren. Die politische und gesellschaftliche Stellung der Mediatisierten 1815–1918. Ein Beitrag zur deutschen Sozialgeschichte,* 2nd ed. Göttingen: Vandenhoeck & Ruprecht, 1964.

Gollwitzer, Heinz. *Ludwig I. von Bayern. Königtum im Vormärz. Eine politische Biographie.* Munich: Süddeutscher Verlag, 1986.

Greer, Donald M.. *L'Angleterre, la France et la Révolution de 1848. Le troisième ministère de Lord Palmerston au Foreign Office (1846–1851).* Paris: Rieder, 1925.

Griewank, Karl. *Der Wiener Kongress und die europäische Restauration 1814/15,* 2nd ed. Leipzig: Koehler & Amelang, 1954.

Grimsted, Patricia Kennedy. *The Foreign Ministers of Alexander I. Political Attitudes and the Conduct of Russian Diplomacy, 1801–1825.* University of California Press: Berkeley/Los Angeles 1969.

Grünthal, Günther. *Parlamentarismus in Preußen 1848/49–1857/58. Preußischer Konstitutionalismus – Parlament und Regierung in der Reaktionsära.* Düsseldorf: Droste, 1982.

Grünthal, Günther. "Zwischen König, Kabinett und Kamarilla. Der Verfassungsoktroi in Preußen vom 5.12.1848." *Jahrbuch für die Geschichte Mittel- und Ostdeutschlands* 32 (1983): 119–74.

Gurko, Vladimir Iosifovič. *Features and Figures of the Past: Government and Opinion in the Reign of Nicholas II.* Stanford: Stanford University Press, 1939.

Haan, Heiner, ed. *Hauptstaat – Nebenstaat. Briefe und Akten zum Anschluß der Pfalz an Bayern 1815/17.* Koblenz: Selbstverlag der Landesarchivverwaltung Rheinland-Pfalz, 1977.

Härter, Karl. *Reichstag und Revolution 1789–1806. Die Auseinandersetzung des Immerwährenden Reichstags zu Regensburg mit den Auswirkungen der Französischen Revolution auf das Alte Reich.* Göttingen: Vandenhoeck & Ruprecht, 1991.

Halicz, Emanuel. "La question polonaise à Tilsitt." *Acta Poloniae Historica* 12 (1965): 44–65.

Handelsman, Marcel. *Napoléon et la Pologne 1806–1807.* Paris: Alcan, 1909.

Handelsman, Marceli, ed. *Konstytucje Polskie, 1791–1921,* 4th ed. Warsaw: Nakladem S-ki akc. Polska skladnica pomocy szkolnych, 1926.

Harcave, Sidney. *The Russian Revolution of 1905.* London: Collier-Macmillan, 1964.

Harcave, Sidney, ed. *The Memoirs of Count Witte.* Armonk, N. Y., and London: M E. Sharpe, 1990.

Harcave, Sidney. *Count Sergei Witte and the Twilight of Imperial Russia: A Biography.* Armonk, N. Y., and London: M.E. Sharpe, 2004.

Hartley, Janet M. *Alexander I.* London and New York: Longman, 1994.

Hartley, Janet M. "The "Constitutions" of Finland and Poland in the Reign of Alexander I: Blueprints for Reform in Russia?" In *Finland and Poland in the Russian Empire.* Edited by Michael Branch, Janet Hartley, and Antoni Mączak. London: London School of Slavonic and East European Studies, 1995, 41–59.

Hartley, Janet M. *Russia, 1762–1825. Military Power, the State, and the People.* Westport: Praeger, 2008.

Hecker, Michael. *Napoleonischer Konstitutionalismus in Deutschland.* Berlin: Duncker & Humblot, 2005.

Heydemann, Günther. *Konstitution gegen Revolution. Die britische Deutschland- und Italienpolitik 1815–1848.* Göttingen: Vandenhoeck & Ruprecht, 1995.

Hildermeier, Manfred. *Die Russische Revolution 1905–1921.* Frankfort: Suhrkamp, 1989.

Hintze, Otto. *Staat und Verfassung. Gesammelte Abhandlungen zur allgemeinen Verfassungsgeschichte.* Edited by Gerhard Oestreich, 3rd ed. Göttingen: Vandenhoeck & Ruprecht, 1970.

Hömig, Klaus Dieter. *Der Reichsdeputationshauptschluß vom 25. Februar 1803 und seine Bedeutung für Staat und Kirche.* Tübingen: Mohr, 1969.

Hoff, Johann Friedrich. *Die Mediatisiertenfrage in den Jahren 1813–1815.* Berlin und Leipzig: Walther Rothschild, 1913.

Huber, Ernst Rudolf. *Deutsche Verfassungsgeschichte seit 1789,* vols. 1–3. Stuttgart: Kohlhammer, 1957–1963.

Huber, Ernst Rudolf. *Dokumente zur deutschen Verfassungsgeschichte*, vols. 1–2, 3rd ed. Stuttgart: Kohlhammer, 1978–1986.

Izdebski, Hubert. "Litewskie projekty konstytucyjne z lat 1811–1812 i ich wpływ na Konstytucję Królestwa Polskiego." *Czasopismo Prawno-Historyczne* 24/1 (1972): 93–136.

Izdebski, Hubert, "Ustawa konstytucyjna Królestwa polskiego z 1815 r." In *Konstytucje polski. Studia monograficzne z dziejów polskiego konstytucjonalizmu*. Edited by Marian Kallas, 185–232. Warsaw: Pań. Wydawnictwo Naukowe, 1990.

Jarrett, Mark. *The Congress of Vienna and its Legacy. War and Great Power Diplomacy after Napoleon*. London: I. B. Tauris, 2013.

Jedruch, Jacek. *Constitutions, Elections and Legislatures of Poland, 1493–1977. A Guide to Their History*. Washington: University Press of America, 1982.

Kallas, Marian. *Konstytucja Księstwa Warszawskiego. Jej powstanie, systematyka i główne instytucje w związku z normami szczegółowymi i praktyka*. Torun: Zakłady Graficzne w Toruniu, 1970.

Kallas, Marian, ed. *Konstytucje polski. Studia monograficzne z dziejów polskiego konstytucjonalizmu*, 2 vols. Warsaw: Pań. Wydawnictwo Naukowe, 1990.

Kann, Robert A. *The Problem of Restoration. A Study in Comparative Political History*. Berkeley and Los Angeles: University of California Press, 1968.

Kirsch, Martin. *Monarch und Parlament im 19. Jahrhundert. Der monarchische Konstitutionalismus als europäischer Verfassungstyp. Frankreich im Vergleich*. Göttingen: Vandenhoeck & Ruprecht, 1999.

Klinkowström, Clemens von, ed. *Aus der alten Registratur der Staatskanzlei. Briefe politischen Inhalts von und an Friedrich von Gentz aus den Jahren 1799–1827*. Vienna: Braumüller, 1870.

Knecht, Ingo. *Der Reichsdeputationshauptschluß vom 25. Februar 1803. Rechtmäßigkeit, Rechtswirksamkeit und verfassungsgeschichtliche Bedeutung*. Berlin: Duncker & Humblot, 2007.

Körner, Hans-Michael. *Geschichte des Königreichs Bayern*. Munich: Beck, 2006.

Kondylis, Panajotis. "Reaktion, Restauration." In *Geschichtliche Grundbegriffe. Historisches Lexikon zur politisch-sozialen Sprache in Deutschland*. Edited by Otto Brunner, Werner Conze, and Reinhart Koselleck, vol. 5. Stuttgart: Klett-Cotta, 1984, 179–230.

Korostowetz, Wladimir von, ed. *Der letzte Zar. Briefwechsel Nikolaus' II. mit seiner Mutter*. Berlin: Metzner, 1938.

Kraus, Andreas. *Geschichte Bayerns. Von den Anfängen bis zur Gegenwart*, 3rd ed. Munich: Beck, 2004.

Kukiel, Marian. *Czartoryski and European Unity 1770–1861*. Princeton: Princeton University Press, 1955.

Kusber, Jan. *Krieg und Revolution in Rußland 1904–1906. Das Militär im Verhältnis zu Wirtschaft, Autokratie und Gesellschaft*. Stuttgart: Steiner, 1997.

Kusber, Jan, ed. *Das Zarenreich, das Jahr 1905 und seine Wirkungen. Bestandsaufnahmen*. Münster: LIT-Verlag, 2007.

Laband, Paul. *Deutsches Reichsstaatsrecht*. 6th ed. Tübingen: Mohr, 1912.

Langewiesche, Dieter, ed. *Demokratiebewegung und Revolution 1847 bis 1849. Internationale Aspekte und europäische Verbindungen*. Karlsruhe: Braun, 1998.

Langewiesche, Dieter. *Nation, Nationalismus, Nationalstaat in Deutschland und Europa*. Munich: Beck, 2000.

Langewiesche, Dieter. *Reich, Nation, Föderation. Deutschland und Europa.* Munich: Beck, 2008.

Langewiesche, Dieter. *Die Monarchie im Jahrhundert Europas. Selbstbehauptung durch Wandel im 19. Jahrhundert.* Heidelberg: Winter, 2013.

Lasa Iraola, Ignacio. "El primer proceso de los liberales (1814–1815)." *Hispanica* 30 (1970): 327–83.

Laue, Theodor H. von. "Count Witte and the Russian Revolution of 1905." *American Slavic and East European Review* 17 (1958): 25–46.

Le Moniteur universel, Paris.

Le riforme del 1847 negli Stati italiani. Atti del Convegno di studi. Firenze, 20–21 marzo 1998. *Rassegna storica toscana* 45, 2 (1999).

Leeb, Josef. *Wahlrecht und Wahlen zur Zweiten Kammer der bayerischen Ständeversammlung im Vormärz (1818–1845),* 2 vols. Göttingen: Vandenhoeck & Ruprecht, 1996.

Lentz, Thierry, ed. *Napoléon et l'Europe. Regards sur une politique. Actes du colloque organisé par la direction des Archives du Ministère des Affaires étrangères et la Fondation Napoléon, 18 e 19 novembre 2004.* Paris: Fayard, 2005.

Lentz, Thierry. "Quelle place pour la Pologne dans le système napoléonien ?" In *La Pologne et l'Europe du partage à l'élargissement (XVIIIe–XXIe siècles),* edited by Isabelle Davion et al., 29–39. Paris: Presses de l'Université de Paris-Sorbonne, 2007.

Léon, Paul L., ed. *Lettres de Nicolas II et de sa mère, l'Impératrice douairière de Russie.* Paris: Les Documentaires, 1928.

Lerchenfeld, Gustav von. *Geschichte Bayerns unter König Maximilian Joseph I. mit besonderer Beziehung auf die Entstehung der Verfassungs-Urkunde.* Berlin: Veit, 1854.

Levra, Umberto, ed. *Il Piemonte alle soglie del 1848.* Turin: Carocci, 1999.

Lodolini Tupputi, Carla. "Sulla tacita soppressione dello statuto di Pio IX." *Rassegna storica del Risorgimento* 94 (2007): 323–44.

Lord, Robert Howard. *The Second Partition of Poland. A Study in Diplomatic History.* Cambridge, Mass., and London: Harvard University Press, 1915.

Lotti, Luigi. "Leopoldo II e le riforme in Toscana." *Rassegna storica toscana* 45 (1999): 241–51.

Lovett, Gabriel H. *Napoleon and the Birth of Modern Spain,* vol. 1: *The Challenge to the Old Order;* vol. 2: *The Struggle, without and within.* New York: University Press, 1965.

Lukowski, Jerzy. *Liberty's Folly. The Polish-Lithuanian Commonwealth in the Eighteenth Century, 1697–1795.* New York: Routledge, 1991.

Luzio, Alessandro. "Dalle riforme allo Statuto di Carlo Alberto." *Archivio storico italiano* 84 (1926): 89–127.

Mager, Wolfgang. "Das Problem der landständischen Verfassungen auf dem Wiener Kongreß 1814/15." *Historische Zeitschrift* 217 (1974): 296–346.

Manifest 17 oktjabrja 1905 g. *Krasnyj Archiv* 11–12 (1925): 46–51.

Mannori, Luca. "Le consulte die Stato." *Rassegna storica toscana* 45 (1999): 347–79.

Mansel, Philip. *Louis XVIII.* London: Blond & Briggs, 1981.

Manteuffel, Otto Freiherr von. *Unter Friedrich Wilhelm IV. Denkwürdigkeiten.* Edited by Heinrich von Poschinger, vol. 1: 1848–1851. Berlin: Mittler, 1901.

Martens, Georg Friedrich von, ed. *Nouveau recueil de traités,* vol. 1 (*1808–1814*). Göttingen: Dieterich, 1817.

Martina, Giacomo. "Nuovi studi sulle riforme e sullo statuto di Pio IX." *Rivista di storia della chiesa in Italia* 21 (1967), 131–46.

Martina, Giacomo. *Pio IX*, vol. 1 (*1846–1850*). Rome: Ed. Pontificia Università Gregoriana, 1974.

Martinez de la Rosa, Francisco. *Obras*. Edited by Carlos Seco Serrano, 8 vols. Madrid: Real Academia Española, 1962.

Mazohl-Wallnig, Brigitte. *Österreichischer Verwaltungsstaat und administrative Eliten im Königreich Lombardo-Venetien 1815–1859*. Mainz: Zabern, 1993.

Mazzonis, Filippo. "La monarchia sabauda." In *Il Piemonte alle soglie del 1848*, edited by Umberto Levra, 149–80. Turin: Carocci, 1999.

Mehlinger, Howard D., and John M. Thompson. *Count Witte and the Tsarist Government in the 1905 Revolution*. Bloomington: Indiana University Press, 1972.

Meriggi, Marco. *Amministrazione e classi sociali nel Lombardo-Veneto (1814–1848)*. Bologna: Il Mulino, 1983.

Meriggi, Marco. *Il Regno Lombardo-Veneto*. Turin: UTET, 1987.

Mesonero Romanos, Ramón de. *Memorias de un setentón*. Madrid: Renacimiento, 1975.

[Metternich, Wenzel Clemens]. *Aus Metternich's nachgelassenen Papieren*. Edited by Richard Metternich-Winneburg, 8 vols. Vienna: Braumüller, 1880–1884.

Michajlovič, Velikij Knjas' Nikolaj. *Imperator Aleksandr I*. St. Petersburg, 1999.

Mironenko, S. V. *Samoderžavie i reformy. Političeskaja bor'ba v Rossii v načale XIX v.* Moscow: Nauka, 1989.

Mohl, Robert von. *Politische Schriften*. Edited by *Klaus von Beyme*, Cologne and Opladen: Westdeutscher Verlag, 1966.

Monsagrati, Giuseppe. "Pio IX, lo Stato della Chiesa e l'avvio delle riforme." *Rassegna storica toscana* 45 (1999): 215–38.

Montgelas, Maximilian Joseph von. *Denkwürdigkeiten über die innere Staatsverwaltung Bayerns (1799–1817)*. Edited by G. Laubmann and M. Doeberl. Munich: Beck, 1908.

Montholon, Charles-Tristan, comte de. *Mémoires pour servir à l'histoire de France sous Napoléon. Notes et Mélanges*, vol. 2. Paris: Didot, 1823.

Morley, Charles. "Alexander I and Czartoryski. The Polish Question from 1801 to 1813." *The Slavonic (and East European) Review* 25 (1946/47): 405–26.

Moscati, Ruggero, ed. *Il Regno delle Due Sicilie e l'Austria. Documenti dal marzo 1821 al novembre 1830*, 2 vols. Naples: Presso la R. Deputazione, 1937.

Moscati, Ruggero. "Un duro antagonista della rivoluzione del '48: Ferdinando II." *Archivio storico per le province napoletane* 70 (1947–1949): 1–27.

Nada, Narciso. *Dallo Stato assoluto allo Stato costituzionale. Storia del Regno di Carlo Alberto dal 1831 al 1848*. Turin: Istituto per la storia del Risorgimento italiano, Comitato di Torino, 1980.

Nada, Narciso, ed. *Le relazioni diplomatiche fra l'Austria e il Regno di Sardegna*, IIª serie, *1830–1848*, vol. 4 (4.1.1847–24.3.1848). Rome: Istituto Storico Italiano per l'Età Moderna e Contemporanea, 1997.

Nada, Narciso. "Le riforme carlo-albertine del 1847." *Rassegna storica toscana* 45 (1999) : 253–68.

Napoléon Iᵉʳ. *Correspondance*, 32 vols. Paris: Imprimerie Impériale, 1858–1870.

Navas-Sierra, J. Alberto. "El tratado de Valençay o el fracaso del pacto imperial napoleónico. El caso de la España peninsular." *Jahrbuch für Geschichte von Staat, Wirtschaft und Gesellschaft Lateinamerikas* 27 (1990): 259–304.

Negri, Paolo. "Genesi ed elementi fondamentali dello Statuto carlo albertino." *Il Risorgimento italiano, nuova serie,* 17 (1924): 781–822.

Nesselrode, A. de, ed. *Lettres et papiers du chancelier comte de Nesselrode 1760–1850. Extraits de ses archives*, vol. 4: *1812*. Paris: Lahure, 1905.

Nieuwazny, Andrzej. "Le dilemme polonais de Napoléon: des légionnaires aux "Varsoviens." In *Napoléon et l'Europe*. Edited by Thierry Lentz, 84–102. Paris: Fayard, 2005.

Notario, Paola, and Narciso Nada. *Il Piemonte sabaudo. Dal periodo napoleonico al Risorgimento*. Turin: UTET, 1993.

Ogiński, Michał. *Denkwürdigkeiten über Polen, das Land und seine Bewohner*, part 3. Constance: Belle-Vue, Verlags- und Sortimentsbuchhandlung, 1845.

Oncken, Wilhelm. *Das Zeitalter der Revolution, des Kaiserreiches und der Befreiungskriege*, vol. 2. Berlin: Grote, 1886.

Ostadal, Hubert. *Die Kammer der Reichsräte in Bayern von 1819 bis 1848 (Ein Beitrag zur Geschichte des Frühparlamentarismus)*. Munich: Stadtarchiv, 1968.

Ostrovskij, A. V., and M. M. Safonov. "Neizvestnyj proekt manifesta 17 oktjabrja 1905 goda." *Sovetskie Archivy* 2 (1979): 63–65.

Palme, Anton. *Die Russische Verfassung*. Berlin: Reimer, 1910.

Pando Fernández de Pinedo, Manuel, Marqués de Miraflores. *Apuntes histórico-críticos para escribir la historia sobre la revolucion de España, desde el año 1820 hasta 1823*, vol. 1. London: En la oficina de Ricardo Taylor, 1834.

Pando Fernández de Pinedo, Manuel, Marqués de Miraflores. *Memorias del Reinado de Isabel II*, 3 vols. Madrid: Edición Atlas, 1964.

Parente, Luigi. "Francesco Paolo Bozzelli e il dibattito sulla costituzione." *Archivio storico per le province napoletane* 117 (1999): 75–101.

Pares, Bernard. "The Peterhof Conference of 1905." *The Russian Review* 2/4 (1913): 87–120.

Pene Vidari, Gian Savino. "Lo Statuto albertino dalla vita costituzionale subalpina a quella italiana." *Studi piemontesi* 27 (1998): 303–14.

Pesendorfer, Franz, ed. *Il governo di famiglia in Toscana. Le memorie del granduca Leopoldo II di Lorena (1824–1859)*. Florence: Sansoni, 1987.

Pesendorfer, Franz. *Zwischen Trikolore und Doppeladler. Leopold II. Großherzog von Toskana 1824–1859*. Vienna: Österreichischer Bundesverlag, 1987.

Pienkos, Angela T. *The Imperfect Autocrat. Grand Duke Constantine Pavlovich and the Polish Congress Kingdom*. New York: Columbia University Press, 1987.

Pingaud, Léonce. "L'empereur Alexandre Ier, Roi de Pologne – La "Kongressovka" (1801–1825)." *Revue d'Histoire Diplomatique* 31 (1917): 513–40.

Pokrovskij, M. N. "Perepiska Nikolaja II i Marii Fedorovny (1905–1906 gg.)." *Krasnyj Archiv* 22 (1927): 153–209.

Polovtsoff, A., ed. *Correspondance diplomatique des ambassadeurs et ministres de Russie en France et de France en Russie avec leurs gouvernements de 1814 à 1830*, vol. 1. St. Petersburg, 1902.

Predtečenskij, A. V. *Očerki obščestvenno-političeskoj istorii Rossii v pervoj četverti XIX veka*. Moscow-Leningrad: Izdatel'stvo Akademii Nauk SSSR, 1957.

Prutsch, Markus J. *Making Sense of Constitutional Monarchism in Post-Napoleonic France and Germany*. Houndmills: Palgrave Macmillan, 2013.

Radowitz, Josef von. *Nachgelassene Briefe und Aufzeichnungen zur Geschichte der Jahre 1848–1853*. Edited by Walter Möring. Stuttgart and Berlin: Deutsche Verlagsanstalt, 1922.

Raeff, Marc. *Michael Speransky. Statesman of Imperial Russia, 1772–1839*. The Hague: Nijhoff, 1957.

Raeff, Marc. *Plans for Political Reform in Imperial Russia, 1730–1905*. Englewood Cliffs: Prentice Hall, 1966.

Recueil des traités, conventions et actes diplomatiques concernant l'Autriche et l'Italie. Paris: Amyot, 1859.

Rimscha, Wolfgang von. *Die Grundrechte im Süddeutschen Konstitutionalismus. Zur Entstehung und Bedeutung der Grundrechtsartikel in den ersten Verfassungsurkunden von Bayern, Baden und Württemberg*. Cologne: Heymann, 1973.

Röhl, John C. G., ed. *Der Ort Kaiser Wilhelms II. in der deutschen Geschichte*. Munich: Oldenbourg, 1991.

Romanelli, Raffaele. "Nazione e costituzione nell'opinione liberale avanti il '48." In *La rivoluzione liberale e le nazioni divise*, edited by Pier Luigi Ballini. Venice: Istituto Veneto di Scienze, Lettere ed Arti, 2000, 271–304.

Romeo, Rosario. *Il Risorgimento in Sicilia*. Bari: Laterza, 1970.

Romeo, Rosario. *Cavour e il suo tempo*, 3 vols. Bari: Laterza, 1971–1984.

Romeo, Rosario. *Vita di Cavour*. Bari: Laterza, 1984.

Sabbatucci, Giovanni, and Vittorio Vidotto, eds. *Storia d'Italia*, vol. 1: *Le premesse dell'unità dalla fine del Settecento al 1861*. Bari: Laterza, 1994.

Sánchez Agesta, Luis. *Historia del constitucionalismo español*, 3rd ed. Madrid: Centro de Estudios Constitucionales, 1974.

Sánchez Almeida, Angélica. *Fernando VII. El deseado*. Madrid: Alderabán, 1999.

Sánchez Mantero, Rafael. *Fernando VII. Un reinado polémico*. Madrid: Información e Historia, 1996.

Sarrailh, Jean. *Un homme d'état espagnol: Martínez de la Rosa (1787–1862)*. Poitiers: Éd. Féret, 1930.

Šacillo, Kornelij Fedorovič, ed. *Dnevniki Imperatora Nikolaja II*, Moscow: Orbita, 1991.

Schieder, Theodor. *Das Deutsche Kaiserreich von 1871 als Nationalstaat*. Cologne/Opladen: Westdeutscher Verlag, 1961.

Schiemann, Theodor. *Geschichte Rußlands unter Kaiser Nikolaus I.*, vol. 1: *Kaiser Alexander I. und die Ergebnisse seiner Lebensarbeit*. Berlin: Reimer, 1904.

Schnabel, Franz. *Deutsche Geschichte im 19. Jahrhundert*, vol. 3: *Monarchie und Volkssouveränität*. Freiburg, Basle, and Vienna: Herder, 1964.

Scirocco, Alfonso. *L'Italia del Risorgimento 1800–1871*, 2nd ed. Bologna: Il Mulino, 1993.

Scirocco, Alfonso. "I sovrani e le riforme." In *L'Italia tra rivoluzioni e riforme 1831–1846. Atti del congresso di storia del Risorgimento italiano (Piacenza, 15–18 ottobre 1992)*. Rome: Istituto per la storia del Risorgimento italiano, 1994, 53–107.

Scirocco, Alfonso. "Il 1847 a Napoli: Ferdinando II e il movimento italiano per le riforme." *Archivio storico per le province napoletane* 115 (1997): 431–56; idem in *Rassegna storica toscana* 45 (1999): 271–302.

Scirocco, Alfonso. "Ferdinando II Re delle Due Sicilie: La gestione del potere." *Archivio storico per le province napoletane* 117 (1999): 3–42; idem in: *Rassegna storica del Risorgimento* 86 (1999): 483–518.

Seitz, Johannes. *Entstehung und Entwicklung der preußischen Verfassungsurkunde im Jahre 1848 (mit dem bisher ungedruckten Urentwurf)*. Diss. Greifswald 1909.

Sellin, Volker. "Regierung, Regime, Obrigkeit." In *Geschichtliche Grundbegriffe. Historisches Lexikon zur politisch-sozialen Sprache in Deutschland*. Edited by Otto Brunner, Werner Conze, and Reinhart Koselleck, vol. 5. Stuttgart: Klett-Cotta, 1984, 361–421.

Sellin, Volker. "'Heute ist die Revolution monarchisch'. Legitimität und Legitimierungspolitik im Zeitalter des Wiener Kongresses." In *Quellen und Forschungen aus italienischen Archiven und Bibliotheken* 76 (1996): 335–61.

Sellin, Volker. *Die geraubte Revolution. Der Sturz Napoleons und die Restauration in Europa.* Göttingen: Vandenhoeck & Ruprecht, 2001.

Sellin, Volker. "Die Erfindung des monarchischen Prinzips. Jacques-Claude Beugnots Präambel zur Charte constitutionnelle." In *Tour de France. Eine historische Rundreise.* Festschrift for Rainer Hudemann. Edited by Armin Heinen and Dietmar Hüser, 489–97. Stuttgart: Steiner, 2008.

Sellin, Volker. "Die Restauration in Italien." In *Vergeben und Vergessen? Vergangenheitsdiskurse nach Besatzung, Bürgerkrieg und Revolution.* Edited by Reiner Marcowitz and Werner Paravicini, 125–40. Munich: Oldenbourg, 2009.

Sellin, Volker. *Gewalt und Legitimität. Die europäische Monarchie im Zeitalter der Revolutionen.* Munich: Oldenbourg, 2011.

Šil'der, Nikolaj Karlovič. *Imperator Aleksandr Pervyj. Ego žizn' i carstvovanie,* 4 vols. St. Petersburg: Suvorin, 1897/98.

Simon, Pierre. *L'élaboration de la Charte constitutionnelle de 1814 (1er avril – 4 juin 1814).* Paris: É. Cornely, 1906.

Singer, Kerstin. *Konstitutionalismus auf Italienisch. Italiens politische und soziale Führungsschichten und die oktroyierten Verfassungen von 1848.* Tübingen: Niemeyer, 2008.

Skowronek, Jerzy. *Antynapoleońskie koncepcje Czartoryskiego.* Warsaw: Państw. Wydawnictwo Naukowe, 1969.

Smith, Nathan. *The Constitutional-Democratic Movement in Russia, 1902–1906.* PhD Thesis. University of Illinois, Urbana 1958.

Späth, Jens. *Revolution in Europa 1820–23. Verfassung und Verfassungskultur in den Königreichen Spanien, beider Sizilien und Sardinien-Piemont.* Cologne: SH-Verlag, 2012.

Spagnoletti, Angelantonio. *Storia del Regno delle Due Sicilie.* Bologna: Il Mulino, 1997.

Spindler, Max. *Handbuch der Bayerischen Geschichte,* vol. 4: *Das neue Bayern. Von 1800 bis zur Gegenwart.* Re-edited by Alois Schmid. Munich: Beck, 2003.

Stahl, Friedrich Julius. *Das monarchische Prinzip. Eine staatsrechtlich-politische Abhandlung.* Heidelberg: Mohr, 1845.

Stein, Karl, Freiherr vom. *Briefe und amtliche Schriften,* vol. 4. Re-edited by Walther Hubatsch. Stuttgart: Kohlhammer, 1963; vol. 5. Re-edited by Manfred Botzenhart. Stuttgart: Kohlhammer, 1964.

Straus, Hannah Alice. *The Attitude of the Congress of Vienna Toward Nationalism in Germany, Italy, and Poland.* New York: Columbia University Press, 1949.

Szeftel, Marc. "The Form of Government of the Russian Empire Prior to the Constitutional Reforms of 1905–06." In *Essays in Russian and Soviet History in Honor of Geroid Tanquary Robinson.* Edited by John Shelton Curtiss, 105–19. Leiden: Brill, 1965.

Szeftel, Marc. "Nicholas II's Constitutional Decisions of Oct. 17–19, 1905, and Sergius Witte's Role." In *Album J. Balon.* Namur: Les Anciens Etablissements Godenne, 1968, 461–93.

Szeftel, Marc. *The Russian Constitution of April 23, 1906. Political Institutions of the Duma Monarchy.* Brussels: Éd. de la Librairie Encyclopédique, 1976.

[Talleyrand-Périgord, Charles Maurice de, duc de Bénévent]. "Correspondance du prince de Talleyrand avec la duchesse de Courlande." In *L'Amateur d'Autographes. Revue historique et biographique* 1 (1862/63): 28–46.

Talleyrand-Périgord, Charles Maurice de, duc de Bénévent. *Mémoires*. Edited by the duc de Broglie, 3 vols. Paris: Lévy, 1891/92.

Tatarov, I., ed., "Manifest 17 oktjabrja." *Krasnyj Archiv* 11–12 (1925): 39–106.

Thackeray, Frank W. *Antecedents of Revolution: Alexander I and the Polish Kingdom, 1815–1825*. New York: Columbia University Press, 1980.

Thaden, Edward C. *Russia's Western Borderlands, 1710–1870*. Princeton: Princeton University Press, 1984.

Timmermann, Andreas. *Die "gemäßigte Monarchie" in der Verfassung von Cadiz (1812) und das frühe liberale Verfassungsdenken in Spanien*. Münster: Aschendorff, 2007.

Tomás Villarroya, Joaquín. *El sistema politico del Estatuto Real (1834–1836)*. Madrid: Instituto de Estudios Politicos, 1968.

Tomás Villarroya, Joaquín et al. *La era isabelina y el sexenio democrático (1834–1874)*, 3rd ed. Madrid: Espasa-Calpe, 1991 (Historia de España. Edited by Ramón Menendez Pidal. 34)

Trifone, Romualdo. "La costituzione del Regno delle Due Sicilie dell'11 febbraio 1848." *Archivio storico per le province napoletane* 70 (1947–1949): 28–39.

Turgenev, Nikolaj. *Rossija i russkie* (translated from the French by S. V. Žitomirskij), Moscow: OGI, 2001.

Ullmann, Hans-Peter. *Staatsschulden und Reformpolitik. Die Entstehung moderner öffentlicher Schulden in Bayern und Baden 1780–1820*. Göttingen: Vandenhoeck & Ruprecht, 1986.

Ullmann, Hans-Peter. "Die öffentlichen Schulden in Bayern und Baden 1780–1820." *Historische Zeitschrift* 242 (1986): 31–67.

Ullmann, Hans-Peter. "Baden 1800 bis 1830." In *Handbuch der baden-württembergischen Geschichte*. Edited by Hansmartin Schwarzmaier, vol. 3: *Vom Ende des Alten Reiches bis zum Ende der Monarchien*. Stuttgart: Klett-Cotta, 1992, 25–77.

Varnhagen von Ense, Karl August. *Tagebücher*, vol. 5. Leipzig: Brockhaus, 1862.

Verhandlungen der constituirenden Versammlung für Preußen, vol. 6. Leipzig: Thomas, 1848.

Verner, Andrew M. *The Crisis of Russian Autocracy. Nicholas II and the 1905 Revolution*. Princeton: Princeton University Press, 1990.

Viarengo, Adriano. *Cavour*. Rome: Salerno Editrice, 2010.

[Vitte, Sergej Jul'evič]. "Zapiska Vitte ot 9 oktjabrja." *Krasnyj Archiv* 11–12 (1925): 51–61.

[Vitte, Sergej Jul'evič]. "Černovik vsepoddanejšego doklada Vitte." *Krasnyj Archiv* 11–12 (1925): 62–66.

Vitte, Sergej Jul'evič. *Vospominanija*, 3 vols. Moscow: Izd. Social'no-ekonomičeskoj Literatury, 1960.

Vodovosov, V., ed., "Carskosel'skija soveščanija, part I: Protokoly sekretnago soveščanija pod predsedatel'stvom byvšago imperatora po voprosu o rasširenija izbiratel'nago prava." *Byloe. Žurnal posvjaščennyj istorii osvoboditel'nago dviženija*, no. 3 (25), September 1917, 217–65; part II: "Protokoly sekretnago soveščanija v aprele 1906 goda pod predsedatel'stvom byvšago imperatora po peresmotru osnovnych zakonov." *Byloe* no. 5–6 (27–28), November-December 1917, 183–245; part III: "Protokoly sekretnago soveščanija v fevrale 1906 goda pod predsedatel'stvom byvšago imperatora po vyrabotke Učreždenij Gosudarstvennoj Dumy i Gosudarstvennago Soveta." *Byloe* no. 4 (26), October 1917, 289–318.

Volz, Günther, ed. "Briefe Andreas Georg Friedrich Rebmanns an Johann Peter Job Hermes aus den Jahren 1815 und 1816." *Mitteilungen des Historischen Vereins der Pfalz* 57 (1959): 173–203.

[Vuič, Nikolaj I.] "Zapiska Vuiča." *Krasnyj Archiv* 11–12 (1925): 66–69.

Wandycz, Piotr S. *The Lands of Partitioned Poland, 1795–1918*. Seattle/London: University of Washington Press, 1974.

Weber, Max. "Rußlands Übergang zum Scheinkonstitutionalismus." (1906), in *idem. Zur Russischen Revolution von 1905. Schriften und Reden 1905–1912*. Edited by Wolfgang J. Mommsen in cooperation with Dittmar Dahlmann, Tübingen: Mohr, 1989, 281–684 (Max Weber Gesamtausgabe, part I, vol. 10).

Webster, Charles K., ed. *British Diplomacy 1813–1815. Select Documents Dealing with the Reconstruction of Europe*. London: Bell, 1921.

Weech, Friedrich von. *Geschichte der badischen Verfassung*. Karlsruhe: Bielefeld, 1868.

Wegelin, Peter. "Die Bayerische Konstitution von 1808." *Schweizer Beiträge zur Allgemeinen Geschichte* 16 (1958): 142–206.

Weis, Eberhard. "Zur Entstehungsgeschichte der bayerischen Verfassung von 1818. Die Debatten in der Verfassungskommission von 1814/15." *Zeitschrift für bayerische Landesgeschichte* 39 (1976): 413–44.

Weis, Eberhard, ed., *Reformen im rheinbündischen Deutschland*. Munich: Oldenbourg, 1984.

Weis, Eberhard. "Die Begründung des modernen bayerischen Staates unter König Max I. (1799–1825)," in *Handbuch der bayerischen Geschichte*. Edited by Max Spindler and Alois Schmid, vol. 4: Das neue Bayern. Von 1800 bis zur Gegenwart, part 1: Staat und Politik. Edited by Alois Schmid, 2nd ed. Munich: Beck, 2003, 1–126.

Weis, Eberhard. *Montgelas. Eine Biographie 1759–1838*. Munich: Beck, 2008.

Witte, Graf [Sergej Jul'evič]. *Erinnerungen*, with an introduction by Otto Hoetzsch. Berlin: Ullstein, 1923.

Witte, Count [Sergej Jul'evič]. *The Memoirs of Count Witte*. Edited by Sidney Harcave. Armonk, N. Y.: M. E. Sharpe, 1990.

Würtenberger, Thomas. "Legitimität, Legalität." In *Geschichtliche Grundbegriffe. Historisches Lexikon zur politisch-sozialen Sprache in Deutschland*. Edited by Otto Brunner, Werner Conze, and Reinhart Koselleck, vol. 3. Stuttgart: Klett-Cotta, 1982, 677–740.

Wunder, Bernd. "Landstände und Rechtsstaat. Zur Entstehung und Verwirklichung des Art. 13 DBA." *Zeitschrift für historische Forschung* 5 (1978): 139–85.

Zakonodatel'nye akty perechodnago vremeni 1904–1906 gg. St. Petersburg: Pravo, 1906.

Zanichelli, Domenico, ed. *Lo Statuto di Carlo Alberto secondo i processi verbali del Consiglio di Conferenza dal 3 febbraio al 4 marzo 1848*. Rome: Dante Alighieri, 1898.

Zawadzki, W. H. *A Man of Honour. Adam Czartoryski as a Statesman of Russia and Poland 1795–1831*. Oxford: Clarendon, 1993.

Zernack, Klaus. *Preußen – Deutschland – Polen. Aufsätze zur Geschichte der deutsch-polnischen Beziehungen*. Edited by Wolfram Fischer and Michael G. Müller. Berlin: Duncker & Humblot, 1991.

Index

www.ingramcontent.com/pod-product-compliance
Lightning Source LLC
Chambersburg PA
CBHW020202090426
42734CB00008B/915